Mr. Philip Thiel
4720 7th Ave. NE
Seattle, WA 98105

In the quiet nights sometimes, there was a trembling of the earth, and all the windows rattled from the depth charges on the prowling submarines stalking the blacked out merchant ships along the coast.

Kitty Robertson:
Measuring Time....by an hourglass

As I drove down Argilla Road toward the beach, a view of the marshes opened up at a certain turn of the road like a view from space of an alien but not hostile new planet, with blue veins and green drumlins and a distant white edge of sand dunes.

John Updike:
Due Consideration

No Ordinary Summer

David T. Lindgren

authorHOUSE®

AuthorHouse™
1663 Liberty Drive
Bloomington, IN 47403
www.authorhouse.com
Phone: 1-800-839-8640

First published by AuthorHouse 10/27/2010

ISBN: 978-1-4520-7451-1 (sc)
ISBN: 978-1-4520-7452-8 (hc)
ISBN: 978-1-4520-7453-5 (e)

Library of Congress Control Number: 2010913196

Printed in the United States of America

This book is printed on acid-free paper.

Also by David Lindgren

Trust but Verify

In All Good Conscience

Atahualpa's Gold

Chapter One

June 1942

The U-boat emerged silently from the cold, dark waters of the Atlantic like some predatory sea creature. It had departed the Kriegsmarine submarine base at Lorient, France, a week earlier and was now about two hundred miles due east of Boston. During its trans-Atlantic crossing the U-boat had traveled submerged during the day, employing its battery-powered engines to crawl along at little more than six or seven knots. But, at night the sub would surface and engage its diesel engines with the result it could cruise at nearly twenty knots while simultaneously recharging its batteries. The crewmen also enjoyed the nights because it was the only time the hatches could be thrown open to allow the cool marine air to ventilate the sub's hot stuffy interior.

While there had been little chance of being spotted by aircraft patrols in mid ocean, that situation had now changed. For the first time since crossing the Bay of Biscay, there was the very real possibility of being detected. Accordingly, the U-boat had spent much of the day submerged, lying quietly on the bottom. Because the U-boat's captain, *Oberleutnant* Werner Frisch, had been briefed to the effect that America's anti-submarine defenses were still relatively primitive, the number of patrolling aircraft had come as a great surprise him. And since he suspected that at least some of them were radar-equipped, he had to be doubly cautious; the last thing he needed in such shallow waters was to be the object of a depth-charge attack, especially after Admiral Doenitz, the head of Germany's submarine service, had made

1

it abundantly clear to him that under no circumstances was his presence in these waters to become known.

Werner Frisch was a U-boat ace, a holder of the prestigious Knight's Cross of the Iron Cross with Oak Leaves, and commander of what military experts considered the most advanced submarine of its kind, the 800-ton Mark IX. This particular vessel, U-128, had been built in the Krupp Germaniawerft shipyard in Kiel and was less than two years old, though it was already showing the effects of almost continuous action. The Mark IX was the largest of the German attack submarines, measuring over two hundred-fifty feet, yet it was an extremely nimble craft. It could dive quickly, possessed a shorter turning radius than any comparable Allied submarine, and was difficult to spot because of its low profile. These qualities, in combination with its load of wake-less, electric torpedoes, made the Mark IX an extremely efficient killer and for this reason a number of them had been deployed to the western Atlantic where in the early months of 1942, as part of Operation Drumbeat, these U-boats had sunk scores of heavily laden tankers and freighters plying East Coast and Gulf ports.

But for the present, the hunt for Allied merchant vessels was not U-128's primary mission. In fact, Frisch had pursued a course across the Atlantic that took his U-boat well to the south of the principal shipping lanes. Even in mid-voyage, when a Greek merchant ship was spotted heading eastward, alone and unescorted, Frisch chose not to attack but instead altered course so as not to be seen. The reason for such extreme caution was the U-boat's cargo. In addition to its regular crew of fifty, U-128 carried two special passengers. Little was known about them since they had slipped aboard unseen and had kept largely to themselves ever since. Needless to say on such a small ship it was almost impossible to remain completely out of view and when at length someone had spotted them wearing Kriegsmarine uniforms with no indication of rank the rumors began to fly. Finally, when one of the torpedo mechanics claimed to overhear the two speaking fluent English, though he knew little himself, that was sufficient for a consensus to be reached--the two men were Abwehr agents, a conclusion that would be confirmed later in the trip when the captain announced the U-boat would be making a brief stop along the Massachusetts coast before proceeding to its ultimate destination, the Caribbean.

Below deck in a tiny galley ordinarily reserved for the U-boat's captain and executive officers, Karl Stoner sat quietly staring into an empty coffee cup. Even sitting down it was obvious that he possessed the rugged build of an athlete. His hair, normally worn close-cropped in Prussian military fashion but allowed to grow out for this mission, was brown and his eyes, now hidden behind closed lids, were almond-colored with just the faintest slant to them, suggesting perhaps some distant Asian ancestry. At the moment his face was expressionless, but even so there was still a hint of arrogance about it. And, then, there were his hands. They were enormous in size with thick powerful fingers. In sum, he presented the appearance of a man with whom it would be best not to trifle.

Stoner had been sitting in the galley for quite some time and to anyone watching, it would have been difficult to determine whether he was deep in thought or actually asleep. In fact, he was neither. He had clearly felt the U-boat surface and the power being shifted from the battery-powered electric engines to the main diesel engines. He had detected the first sweet smell of salt air as the hatches were opened to rid the ship of the carbon monoxide and other noxious gases that had built up while it lay submerged. And he was now perfectly conscious of the fact that someone was approaching him from behind.

"*Guten Abend*, Herr Stoner," said the U-boat's captain before switching to English. "I hope I'm not intruding on your thoughts."

"Not at all, Captain," Karl replied, calmly, looking up at him. "What can I do for you?"

Frisch was wearing a reefer jacket with the breast emblem of the German Navy over the pocket and a peaked cap with a white cover. In keeping with U-boat tradition both the jacket and cap appeared battered and worn. Karl guessed that he and the captain were about the same age, yet Frisch already had the gaunt, hollow-eyed look that was characteristic of so many submarine commanders. His cheeks were sunken, his red Viking beard heavily flecked with gray, and his clothes hung loosely on his slight frame. Too much stress, Karl concluded. Commanding a U-boat was an extremely hazardous occupation and America's entry into the war was making it even more so. Not only had the Americans assigned greater numbers of aircraft and ships to anti-submarine duty, they had also introduced more effective techniques for detecting and destroying enemy submarines. As a result, the North Atlantic, which had long been a graveyard for Allied merchant vessels, was now becoming a similar graveyard for German U-boats. Frisch, like Karl, was only too aware that the odds of his ship and crew surviving the war were getting less with each passing day.

"Your colleague, *Herr* Mueller, is he about?" Frisch inquired smiling.

"Sleeping," Karl replied. "He took advantage of an empty bunk."

"Wise man," Frisch nodded, "since as you're probably aware, we are approaching the drop-off point. Our estimated time of arrival is about twenty-four hours from now, that is, assuming all goes as planned. So, I hope you've enjoyed our hospitality, Spartan though it may have been."

"We have, indeed, Captain, and thank you," replied Karl, wondering what life would be like aboard the U-boat after a month or two at sea. Fortunately, he would not be around to find out.

"Good, so let me just briefly go over how I plan to get you ashore," continued Frisch, all business now. "We are presently pushing ahead at full speed and will continue to do so until daybreak. At that point we should be very close to our destination. We'll then submerge and wait quietly on the bottom. Shortly before midnight we'll surface and run you in as close as we dare."

"And how close will that be," asked Karl, with more than idle curiosity.

"Probably about a mile, maybe a little less," answered the captain. "Our charts show the bay we're to enter as very shallow and filled with sandbars. We'll have to proceed with great care in order not to run aground. That's why I can't get you in as close as I'd like. But, it shouldn't be a major problem. I'll have two of my crewmen take you and your equipment ashore by lifeboat. And, yes, they'll be heavily armed. My orders are to make certain no one interferes with your landing. Anyone who attempts to do so will be killed and his body brought back to the ship for disposal far out to sea."

For all the time Karl had spent thinking about his mission until this moment he hadn't actually given a great deal of thought to the issue of getting ashore. He had simply taken it for granted they would be landed safely. Suddenly, he wasn't so sure; what was that old saying, "Whatever could go wrong, would go wrong." A slight chill rippled up his spine. Fortunately, Frisch interrupted him before he had a chance to think about it further.

"You should get some rest; you're going to need it. We'll have plenty of time to talk again later." He turned and headed back in the direction of the control room. A good man, thought Karl. He hoped the captain would make it through the war. Germany would need such men. But for now it would be wise if he could find a free bunk and get some sleep, though with only twenty bunks to service fifty crewmembers the odds were not exactly in his favor.

Chapter Two

Hardly, it seemed, had he fallen asleep than Karl felt himself being gently shaken and became dimly aware of someone leaning over him. Gradually, Thomas's face came into focus.

"I honestly don't know how you can sleep like that. It's so damp and close in here. I feel claustrophobic and have trouble even breathing. I can't wait until we get ashore and I can finally get a good nights sleep."

Thomas Mueller was slight of build, quiet, and the possessor of almost boyish good looks. Many, including Karl, had wondered why he had even been selected for this mission. He seemed so young and immature though, in fact, he met the two most important criteria for selection—he had been born in the United States and spoke English fluently. But, there was this rumor, never confirmed, that Thomas was a homosexual and had been shipped out to avoid further embarrassing a high-ranking Nazi officer with whom he had been caught in *flagrante delicto*. Whether or not there was any truth to this rumor, it was reason enough for others on the mission to refuse having him as a partner; they were clearly uncomfortable having *ein Schwule* around and they made no secret about it. But, early on Karl had come to realize that Thomas was so much brighter than the rest of the group it was actually embarrassing and so he had agreed to take him on as his partner in spite of all the rumors swirling about.

But now that it was approaching time to go ashore, Karl was beginning to wonder if he'd made the right decision. Although Thomas had admittedly held up well during the training they had just completed, the stress placed upon them simply wasn't very intense. Karl couldn't help worrying about what would happen if they found themselves in an extremely tense and dangerous situation. Would he be able to depend upon Thomas to back him up or would Thomas instead turn out to be a liability?

"Anyway, sorry to wake you," Thomas was saying, "but Frisch would like to see us in the galley."

"All right," mumbled Karl, running his fingers through his hair. "Just let me get my shoes on and I'll meet you there."

When Karl arrived he found Frisch talking to Thomas. Frisch was holding a bottle of cognac in his hand and three small tumblers spread before him on the table.

"It'll be another three hours before you start ashore but those three hours will be busy ones for all of us. I thought it best if we had our final toast now," he announced pouring a healthy shot of cognac into each glass.

Putting the bottle down, he raised his glass and said simply, "To Germany."

"To Germany," Karl and Thomas responded in unison.

Karl was not surprised by the absence of any "Heil Hitlers." It was well known that within the submarine service, as within the Abwehr, little enthusiasm existed for either Hitler or the Nazi Party. Karl suspected there were few, if any, members of the Party aboard U-128.

The final three hours were very busy and they passed quickly. Karl and Thomas said little to one another. Most of the time they spent going over the details of their new identities and checking and rechecking their personal documents to make certain everything was in order--birth certificates, drivers' licenses, social security cards, and draft deferment papers. Then, they checked their equipment. Finally, they put on what in essence were Kriegsmarine work clothes--khaki shirt and trousers, high black boots and a navy cap decorated with a swastika and wings. The hope was that if they were captured going ashore in these clothes they would be treated as prisoners-of-war and not spies for which the punishment in wartime was execution. As they were making their final preparations a medley of Glenn Miller songs suddenly blared from the ship's loudspeaker system. The U-boat's radio operator had obviously picked up the broadcast of a nearby American radio station.

Finally, the word came; it was time to go. Climbing topside, they both breathed deeply of the fresh, salty air. It felt so good to be free of the diesel smell that permeated everything on the U-boat including, Karl realized, the clothes they had just put on. He quickly spotted Captain Frisch, dressed in his usual battered cap along with a heavy lambskin coat to ward off the evening chill. He was giving orders to several crewmen who were helping make ready their departure. The rubber dinghy that would take them ashore was bobbing rhythmically in the water. One crewman was already sitting in it while another was standing on the U-boat's hull doing his best to hold it steady. On the deck were two heavy wooden chests. In addition, there was what appeared to be a suitcase and two small military shovels or entrenching tools. Karl and Thomas were each carrying a waterproof kit bag with extra clothes, money and their identity papers.

When all the gear had been stowed on the dinghy, Thomas clambered aboard. Karl hesitated a moment looking out across the dark water. He could see the outline of the shore against the faint glow of lights from over the horizon. It was at least a good mile away, he concluded.

"Welcome to America, Herr Stoner," Frisch announced with a smile. "And good hunting."

"Thank you for your good wishes and your hospitality," replied Karl with a faint smile of his own. "And, oh yes, Capitan, I hope you won't take it personally if when my mission ends I return to Germany on something larger than a U-boat."

Without waiting for a reply Karl slid easily into the dinghy.

As the crewmen made ready to push off from the U-boat, Frisch yelled down to them, "Remember, if you're not back within two hours I may have no choice but to leave without you. I must make deeper water and submerge before daybreak or we'll almost certainly be spotted. A U-boat won't stand much of a chance in these waters."

The crewmen nodded and began paddling the dinghy in the direction of shore. There was little need to worry about the noise since the roar of the surf crashing on the beach would drown out any sound they made.

The trip proceeded without conversation. After several days spent in the stuffy confines of a U-boat, the clean smell of the ocean had an almost intoxicating effect on the dinghy's occupants. For just a brief moment time seemed to stand still. No one wanted to think about what lay ahead. But, soon they were in close enough that the crewmen no longer needed to paddle; the rising tide was propelling them forward.

As they neared shore Karl slipped over the side gasping as he hit the cold water. He heard one of the crewmen snicker and mumble something about it being a "ball shrinker." No argument there, Karl thought, dragging the dinghy onto the beach. The other three had followed, the two crewmen by this time having swapped their paddles for Bergmann submachine guns.

"You two stay here to guard the dinghy and provide cover for us," ordered Karl. "It will probably take us three trips to get all these supplies up into the dunes. After you've gone we'll bury them; our uniforms will be going back with you. Be alert now; there's always the chance this beach could be patrolled."

Karl was well aware that this was the moment when they were most vulnerable, unloading the dingy and transporting their supplies across the sand. If they were to be detected it was most apt to be now. A sense of foreboding crept over Karl, though he was not certain why. So far everything had gone as planned. Just a few minutes more, he thought to himself, just a few minutes more.

Grabbing hold of the first chest, Karl and Thomas started lugging it inland away from the water. At first the going was easy for though they were walking up a fairly steep incline, the sand was damp and firm. When they reached the top, however, the sand quickly became dry and soft; their feet constantly slipped and their progress slowed dramatically. After a few minutes of struggling they came to a ridge about a foot high, marking the ocean's furthest advance. Dragging the chest up and onto the ridge, they found themselves standing in an ocean of beach grass, which was serving to hold the sand in place here.

The sand had become firm again beneath their feet and they were able to move rapidly across the flat expanse of grass before suddenly coming upon a small grove of pitch pine. It was the perfect location for burying the chests. Not only was the sand moist, permitting easy digging, but the pine grove itself would be a relatively easy place to find at a later time when they needed to gain access to the chests' contents. Just to be on the safe side though, he cut a small notch in one of the nearby trees with his shovel,

"Let's get out of these uniforms and into our civilian clothes," Karl advised. "We'll put the uniforms in one of the kit bags and those guys can take them back to the U-boat."

As soon as they had finished changing, Karl whispered, "Let's go back and get the other chest. I won't be able to relax until that dinghy clears the beach."

Without another word they started back towards the beach. Even without a heavy load, walking through the dunes was slow business. It was also pitch dark and they dared not use their flashlights.

Still, everything appeared to be going smoothly. The heavy surf was muffling whatever noise they were making while an on-shore breeze was covering their tracks almost as quickly as they made them.

After carrying the second chest into the dunes, Karl said to Thomas, "I'll stay here and begin burying these things; you go back and get the remaining supplies. I think there's only the suitcase."

"All right, I'll get whatever's there and send the crewmen on their way," Thomas replied. "I'll also try to cover any tracks the wind hasn't already taken care of."

Thomas quietly melted away into the June night.

Karl stood motionless in the darkness for several seconds, the earlier sense of foreboding returning. He took note of its existence but other than being careful there was nothing else he could do about it. If something happened he would just have to deal with it in the way he'd been trained. But for the moment his highest priority was to protect his supplies, which meant burying them. Picking up one of the shovels he began digging vigorously in the damp sand.

Chapter Three

The spot where Karl and Thomas had come ashore was a lovely strip of white sand known as Crane's Beach. Stretching nearly four miles along Ipswich Bay on Boston's North Shore, Crane's Beach owed its existence to the great continental ice sheets that scoured New England for their final time about 30,000 years ago. The ice sheets had moved southeastward and as they had inched their way towards the sea they pushed massive quantities of rock and soil before them like gigantic bulldozers. Later, these materials were redistributed across the landscape by the melt waters from the retreating glaciers while along the ocean's edge they were reworked by tidal forces and prevailing winds to create a fascinating mix of geomorphologic features including sandy spits, bars and beaches. Crane's Beach was one of the most spectacular of these features.

The beach, however, had not been selected as a drop-off point either for its beauty or its fascinating geological history, but rather because it possessed attributes deemed critical to Berlin. Chief among these was the beach's location at the approximate center of a string of shipyards that stretched from Bath, Maine, in the north to New London, Connecticut, in the south. But, then, there was also the nature of the beach itself. Unlike most such sites along the East Coast, there were no summer homes lining the beachfront here. With the exception of the summer residence of the Crane family for which the beach was named, the only other dwelling belonged to the lighthouse keeper. The Crane residence, situated on a high bluff, possessed a commanding view of the beach, so commanding, in fact, it was once used by local Indian tribes as a lookout to guard against a surprise attack by their enemies. But, as the planners of the mission had been informed, the Crane family never arrived there before July Fourth, America's Independence Day. As for the lighthouse keeper's residence, it had been vacant ever since the lighthouse had been moved to Martha's Vineyard two years earlier.

The information about the landing site at Crane's Beach that had been transmitted to Berlin by a Nazi sympathizer in Boston was essentially correct save for one small detail. The former lighthouse keeper's residence was no longer vacant. Since early May it had become the property of the U.S. Coast Guard. This seemingly minor oversight would not be without consequence for the men attempting to slip ashore that night.

Leaving Karl to bury the chests they had brought ashore, Thomas had headed back in the direction of the dinghy. After his confinement aboard the stuffy U-boat he was relishing the taste of the fresh, salty air now filling his lungs. But, suddenly, he was snapped out of his reverie by a strange sound just to his left. Before he could determine what it was he was struck and knocked to the sand by a snarling apparition that quickly proved only too real by clamping its powerful jaws over his forearm. Screaming for help Thomas tried desperately to protect himself from the animal's vicious teeth but he found it impossible. Occupied as he was, neither did he notice a US Coastguardsman racing towards him with his Enfield rifle at ready. Fortunately for Thomas the crewman from the dinghy did spot him. A burst of gunfire from their submachine guns caught the surprised Coastguardsman in the chest and stomach causing him to pitch over backwards; he never saw the men who killed him. Strangely, his helmet, which had flown off on impact, continued to spin crazily for several seconds before it too finally to rest.

As one crewman cautiously approached the now lifeless body of Coastguardsman, prodding him with his gun just to make certain, the other rushed towards Thomas, who was still wrestling with the attacking animal. There really wasn't much the crewman could do. Waiting for just the right moment so as not to hit Thomas, he fired a short burst at the dog, striking him several times, in the head, the body and shattering one of his front legs. To the crewman's amazement, the animal, a handsome German shepherd, not only refused to die quietly it struggled gamely to get to its feet in an effort to continue the fight. In spite of his admiration for the animal's fighting spirit he had no choice but to deliver the coup de grace.

Before either of the crewmen had even a chance to examine the clearly injured and bleeding Thomas, Karl came rushing up.

"What in hell is going on around here," he snapped. "You were to quietly drop us off and instead you've turned the beach into a battlefield."

"Sorry, sir," answered one of the crewmen, though without the slightest hint of apology in his voice.

"Thomas here was surprised by a patrol and we handled it as we were ordered--kill anybody and everybody."

Karl knelt down to examine his wounds.

"How badly are you hurt?" he asked.

"I'll live," Thomas replied weakly. "But, it sure hurts; it burns like fire where that dog tore into me"

"We've got to get you back to the sub for medical treatment," ordered Karl. "And anyway, with the kind of facial injuries you have you'll have everyone staring at you. I'm sorry but I can't afford the risk to our operation."

Thomas was in no position to argue however he may have felt.

Getting to his feet Karl turned to the two crewmen.

"You'll have a full load going back to the U-boat, Thomas here as well as the dead seaman and dog. And you'll be bucking a pretty strong on-shore breeze. Just don't try to lighten your load by dumping the dead seaman or his dog in the waters around here or I'll never get off the beach."

"Understood," replied one of the crewmen.

"OK, let's load up and get you out of here before someone comes looking for these two. Hopefully no one heard the gunfire."

Within a few minutes the dinghy was loaded and the two crewmen pushed off.

"*Auf Wiedersehen*," said one, as the dinghy disappeared into the gloom.

Karl was already cleaning up the beach, picking up what spent cartridges he could find and covering the bloodstains with sand. When he was done he turned and quickly headed in the direction of the pine grove.

Further down the beach Fred Storey and his nephew, Bob, lay sprawled in the sand behind a half-buried lobster pot, the only cover they could find when the shooting started. They had slipped across the Essex River earlier that evening to try their luck at landing a few striped bass. Since the war had begun the price of fish had skyrocketed and so fishing off the beach was almost worth the risk of getting caught. Or so it seemed to Fred until he had heard the gunfire. Now he was not so sure.

"We've got to get back to our boat," Fred whispered.

"I know, I know," Bob responded, clearly in no hurry to leave his hiding place behind the lobster pot. "Let's just wait a few minutes more."

They waited for nearly half an hour before Fred finally said, "I think whoever it was has gone. Let's get outta here."

Crouching low, Fred and his nephew set off down the beach in the direction of the Essex River.

"We'd better keep quiet about what went on here tonight, not that we actually know what went on," warned Fred. "Nevertheless I could possibly lose my job at the shipyard if it was to get out we were down here fishing."

"You don't have to worry about me," gasped Bob, whose main concern at the moment was getting off the beach safely, not whether Fred might lose his job.

Chapter Four

Karl did not have the luxury of watching the raft disappear into the night, he had to move quickly and get off the beach. Any moment now other Coast Guardsmen might appear. Admittedly it was easier to move about alone though the operation had been planned around teams of two agents. But for some strange reason he was feeling a sense of relief. As much as he had come to accept Thomas as his partner, he could never quite escape the concern that he might not prove tough enough for the mission, that he had been selected only to get him as far away from Berlin as possible. Of course, it would mean he'd have no choice but to scale down the scope of any operation he undertook.

Returning to the task at hand, Karl checked the area to make certain there were no visible indications of the recent skirmish. Hopefully, whatever he might have missed in the dark the wind and the tide would quickly obliterate. Satisfied there was nothing more he could do, he headed back to the pine grove. He still needed to finish burying the equipment he was leaving behind which for the moment included all of the explosives, most of the money as well as the Pistolen-08 handgun he had brought with him. From this moment on he was an itinerant laborer looking for work. He could only hope the clothes he'd been issued were appropriate and would not draw any unnecessary attention to him; that could prove fatal.

They had repeatedly been told that Berlin had spared no expense in mounting this operation, that all the clothes, for example, had been purchased in the U.S. and bore recognizable labels. A cotton shirt, khaki pants, and a pair of rugged work shoes made in Massachusetts would be common enough attire. The clothes had all been pre-washed so as not to appear brand new while the shoes had been properly scuffed. They had been briefed to the effect that shoes more than any other item of clothing could immediately identify an individual as coming from Europe. On the other hand they had all lived in the US for at least some period of time so they were hardly unaware of such things. And, if they did slip up there were no shortage of Germans living in the United States who could help them. These were the same people supposedly providing Berlin with a continuous flow of up-to-date intelligence. Of course, Karl mused, the failure of this intelligence to warn of Coast Guard patrols on the beach only showed how little you could depend on others in this business.

For the moment Karl decided it best to travel lightly—a jacket, a few extra items of clothing, a small sum of money, and a cloth map of the area. The map, prepared specifically for this mission by Abwehr cartographers, was extremely detailed but as he reminded himself he'd have to dispose of it soon. It was exactly the kind of thing, in fact, that would assure his execution.

Time to go. The guy would be missed before long, perhaps already, though without any indication of what actually happened they might just delay mounting a full-scale search until morning. By then he hoped to be a considerable distance away. Unfortunately, his only route off Castle Neck when the tide was high appeared to be a narrow causeway that ran through the marshes for about a quarter mile. There was a small guard post at the entrance to the causeway, though there was no way of telling from the map whether it was manned twenty-four hours a day. Karl could only hope it wasn't since he had no choice but to pass directly by it. He had to get away from the beach and he had to get away immediately.

With the aid of a small compass Karl headed out over the dunes in the direction of the causeway. It was deathly still and he was certain that even the soft rustle his feet made as he walked through the sand could be heard all the way over at the Coast Guard station. The silence actually served to unnerve him. It was nearly three in the morning local time and the Coast Guardsman should have been missed by now, though Karl could detect no unusual sign of activity. Just keep going, he reminded himself, and stay calm.

After about twenty minutes he slid down a steep sand dune and found himself in a thicket of poplar and chokecherry. The vegetation provided good cover but it also made it impossible to move without making noise. Suddenly, there came a loud crashing sound to Karl's right and the sound of two or three bodies racing through the shrubs. Karl automatically dropped to the ground expecting to hear the sound of gunfire. Instead, the sound quickly faded away. Animals of some kind he concluded slowly getting to his feet, his heart pounding wildly.

As it turned out, Karl was standing only a short distance from the causeway, although in the dark he did not at first realize it. Cautiously, he emerged from the thicket and looked out across the causeway. He couldn't see a thing; it was pitch black. There were no lights visible of any kind—no street lights, no lights from any houses, nothing; he would have to pick his way along carefully. It was also incredibly quiet, which did give him the advantage of being able to hear any vehicle coming long before it reached him. Of course, even if he didn't hear a vehicle approaching, he'd see it. No one would dare negotiate this narrow, twisting road without the use of lights, wartime or not. Still, the sooner he crossed the causeway the better for it appeared there were few bushes to provide cover if an automobile did suddenly appear. It was too dark to run so he had to settle for walking as quickly as he dared. Even so it took him several minutes to reach the guard post. To his relief it was dark and unoccupied.

Crouching up against the guardhouse, he turned on his flashlight for just a few seconds to consult his map. He was able to determine that if he kept walking along the road for another five miles he would come to the small town of Ipswich, but he would have to cover that distance quickly for it would be daylight within two hours. Though there appeared to be few houses directly adjacent to the road, there were numerous houses set back several hundred feet or so from it. And, since the area was quite rural, it was almost certain at least some of the owners would have dogs, which always posed a potential danger. The last thing he needed was to be chased by a dog or even to have a dog suddenly begin barking at him. If an owner of one of these houses even suspected there was someone walking along this road at four in the morning, he'd call the police without a moment's hesitation.

Karl had been walking less than twenty minutes when he heard the sound of an automobile heading his way at considerable speed; within seconds a set of headlights came bobbing down the road. Karl found cover in a clump of bushes. He didn't need to see the vehicle to guess its destination was the Coast Guard station. Whatever grace period he had enjoyed up to now, while the Coast Guardsman's mates attempted to figure out what had happened to him, had now ended. The authorities had been alerted and a major search effort would unquestionably be undertaken at the first light of dawn, if it had not begun already.

The sound of the automobile gradually receded in the distance and silence returned. With the exception of a raccoon that momentarily spooked him as it raced across the road and the distant barking of a dog, he was able to proceed with little interruption. After perhaps a half-hour he once again heard the sound of an approaching automobile. This one, however, was not moving especially fast. Karl had plenty of time to once again find cover along side of the road. Even before the first auto passed by his hiding place he heard another. Within the next several minutes several autos and pickup trucks sped by carrying two and in some cases three people. They appeared to be on their way to work. Karl had no choice but to remain in hiding.

Soon traffic began coming from the direction of the beach. They, too, seemed to be workers. His map showed a small shipyard and he concluded the night shift was being replaced. It made sense that wartime facilities like shipyards would be operating twenty-four hours a day. He was going to have to be a lot more careful.

Karl was suddenly startled to hear the sound of voices drawing nearer. As he peered through the bushes he could see two men approaching on bicycles. They apparently were also part of the night shift on its way home. The sight of the two men served to relax Karl somewhat. It was possible that even if he were seen he'd probably be mistaken for one of the shipyard workers. Waiting until most of the workers had gone past, he slipped out of his hiding place and began walking directly into town.

Within about twenty minutes the road had become relatively quiet again. The sun was up by now and it gave every indication of being a beautiful summer day. For the first time Karl could begin to see something of his surroundings. The landscape was an irregular blend of marshland and hayfields, interspersed with occasional wooded tracts of maple, oak and pine. And there were stonewalls everywhere, a constant reminder of the continental glaciers that had deposited so much rock and gravel throughout the region. The scene reminded him a little of home, though the architecture of the buildings and the general irregularity of the fields and woodlands were quite unlike Northern Germany's more orderly landscape.

At that moment Karl picked up the sound of an automobile approaching him from behind. By its slow speed he guessed it was not a military vehicle. Still he dared not turn for fear of appearing apprehensive. Karl held his breath as the vehicle drew abreast of him and slowed.

"Give you a lift into town," a voice called from within the car.

Karl would have preferred to turn down the request but to do so would have seemed strange since he was still some distance from town.

"Yes, thank you, I'd appreciate it," Karl answered, opening the door of a Chevrolet sedan and climbing in.

"I'm Bob Wallace," said the driver by way of introduction. He was a short, slightly overweight young man with thinning hair and a ready smile. To ward off the morning chill he had turned on the car's heater; Karl found the temperature almost suffocating.

"I'm Karl Stoner." They shook hands quickly.

"You're not from around here, are you," Bob noted. "I can tell by your accent."

Well, thought Karl, I'm glad my cover story has me coming from Chicago. What they taught us was undoubtedly true, the closer your cover story comes to the truth, the less apt you are to make a mistake.

"No, I'm not from around here, I'm from Chicago. Came out this way looking for work."

"Out here, at this hour of the morning," Bob asked. He had meant it more as a joke but when he saw Karl stiffen he realized he had taken him seriously. "Sorry, I didn't mean to sound inquisitive. I guess it's this damn war. Everybody's become suspicious of strangers. The newspapers are really to blame for it, always writing stories about German spies or enemy planes coming to bomb East Coast cities. Puts people on edge, you know what I mean?"

"Yah, it's like that everywhere," Karl replied. "In fact, it's probably

21

worse in the Midwest, where they've never trusted outsiders. Anyway, to answer your question, even if you were just joking, I'd taken the train from New York up to Boston, then, managed to hitch a couple of rides in this direction. My last ride was a guy, whom I think said he was going to work at a shipyard. He let me off back up the road."

"Robinson's shipyard. They make sub-chasers cause there's so many German submarines operating in the waters around here. They're incredibly brazen; they'll actually surface in broad daylight and attack oil tankers within sight of shore. It's amazing the nerve they have but I guess it's because they don't have much to worry about. The anti-submarine patrols we have around here are pretty ineffective—a few planes and civilian pleasure boats. "

Karl nodded, not wanting to show any undue interest in the topic. As for Bob, he said nothing more until they passed a sign announcing they were entering the town of Ipswich, established in 1634.

"Any place special I can drop you," Bob asked in a friendly tone. Karl would have liked to ask more about the shipyard but decided it could wait.

"Some place where I can get something to eat," Karl replied, thankful that nothing further had occurred to make Bob suspicious. He certainly didn't need him to report anything to the police, not after what had happened when they were coming ashore.

"The Atlas Lunch is the best place and it's on my way," Bob answered. "In fact, there it is right on the corner there. I assume you've never been here before?"

"My first time," Karl responded.

"Well, welcome to Ipswich, then. It's a great town---small, friendly. I think you'll like it here, if you decide to stick around."

"Thanks for the ride," said Karl, opening the door and sliding out.

As he started off, Bob leaned over and yelled out the open window, "You won't have any trouble getting work around here. The shipyard that guy works at who gave you a ride is looking to hire a lot more workers; so is Sylvania Electronics. Good luck."

Well, well, well, I didn't even have to ask; so, the shipyard is hiring. I've got to do something and that sounds like an interesting place to start, but first things first; I'm starving.

As Karl stood on the street corner he became aware of a larger than life wooden figure of Uncle Sam staring at him from across the street. Uncle Sam was asking the town's residents to donate whatever worn-out aluminum pots and pans they could spare since aluminum was badly needed for the aircraft construction industry. Viewing the odd assortment of old coffee pots, toasters, teakettles and radio parts that had been dumped into the small fenced area at Uncle Sam's feet he suspected it would be exactly the kind of thing Nazi leaders would love to see. It would confirm everything they believed about America, that it was weak and completely unprepared for war. And while it was probably true that America was unprepared for war, it was only a matter of time before it built up its military capability and became a formidable adversary. Once that happened the odds of Germany emerging victorious from the conflict would inevitably shrink.

Karl suddenly felt tired. After the relative boredom and inactivity of the previous couple of weeks, the past few hours had been especially tense and hectic. Though he needed sleep he needed food even more. It was breakfast time after all; at least, here in America it was. With a final glance at Uncle Sam he turned and entered the Atlas Lunch.

Chapter Five

Eddie Sawaski was also hungry, famished, in fact. He had been on duty now for three hours and in that time he had eaten barely a thing. For that matter, if you didn't count the two cups of disgusting coffee and the stale cinnamon donut he had found in a box next to the hot plate, he hadn't really eaten anything.

'I've got to get some breakfast," he announced, pushing his chair back from his desk and getting to his feet. "I'm going over to the Atlas Lunch; you can reach me there if anything important comes up but it's got to be important."

Mike Bradford nodded without even bothering to raise his head. Mike could best be described as ordinary looking. He was medium in height with the slightly overweight body of someone who shunned unnecessary physical activity. His face was an almost pasty white and devoid of any distinguishable features: a small mouth with thin lips, a straight nose, brown eyes, nearly invisible eyebrows, and light brown hair worn short in an attempt to hide the fact he was rapidly losing it. At the moment he was slumped over his desk with the morning edition of the Boston *Post* spread before him; a cigarette hung precariously from the corner of his mouth.

"What are you reading so intently, Mike, the comics?" asked Eddie, grinning.

"Nah, but I might just as well be, I'm reading the sports section. The Braves lost again yesterday." The cigarette bobbed up and down as he spoke.

"That's why you should be cheering for a real team like the Red Sox?" Eddie chided. It was a long-standing joke between them.

"The Red Sox, the Boston Red Sox? They lost even worse; Cleveland walloped them 14 to 1," Mike replied with an obvious note of satisfaction in his voice.

"Well, you can't expect Williams to have the kind of season he had last year. Didn't he hit over 400 or something?"

"He hit 406 to be exact, but you don't really keep up with the Sox very much, do you?"

"No, I don't, to be honest" Eddie responded. "But why do you say that?"

"Well, if you did, you'd know that Ted Williams was not only leading the American League in batting so far this season but in home runs and runs-batted-in as well"

"You want to know something in all honesty, Mike? I've attended only one major league baseball game in my whole life and that was to see the Braves play the Phillies at Braves Field. I've never seen the Red Sox play; never even seen the outside of Fenway Park much less the inside."

Just then the telephone rang. At its sound Eddie headed for the door.

"If it's for me, tell whoever it is I'm not here. If I don't get some food I won't be any good for anything anyway."

Mike motioned for him to get out and picked up the receiver; the cigarette, Eddie noticed, was still dangling from his mouth. It was amazing how it just hung there without falling; Eddie actually found the habit annoying and more than once had to remind Mike to take the damn cigarette out of his mouth when he spoke to people who had come into the office.

"Ipswich Police Department, Sergeant Bradford here."

Mike listened for a moment, then got up and went quickly to the door through which Eddie had just disappeared. Yanking it open he spotted Eddie limping quickly up the street. He had to be hungry to walk that fast, thought Mike.

"Eddie," he hollered, "telephone call for you. Sounds important." He added the latter because he knew Eddie was going to be annoyed having to postpone his breakfast even further.

He saw Eddie turn and head quickly back towards him, his limp even more noticeable now.

"Sorry, Eddie," said Mike apologetically. "It's a Commander Evans from the Coast Guard station over in Salem."

"It's O.K., Mike," said Eddie picking up the phone.

"Good morning, Commander, this is Chief Sawaski. What can I do for you?"

Eddie stood perfectly still as Commander Evans described for him how one of his men stationed at Crane's Beach, a "sand pounder" as they jokingly were referred to by other Coast Guardsmen, had gone out on patrol with his dog the previous evening and had not returned. A preliminary search of the beach and surrounding waters had turned up no sign of either the Coast Guardsman or his dog.

"So what do you think may have happened," asked Eddie with a mixture of concern and curiosity.

"At this moment I have no good explanation," replied the Commander. "The missing man seems to have gotten along well enough with the other men stationed at the beach and they weren't aware of any personal problems he might have had. On the other hand, there are also no obvious signs of foul play though, as you know, the beach is a mess. Those Camp Agawam guys use it as a firing range for rifles, tanks, artillery, just about everything and there are spent shell casings and debris all over the place. So, at this moment I honestly have no idea what may have happened to him."

Almost as an afterthought, the Commander added, "Apparently, he did have a girlfriend, however, and she lives right there in Ipswich. Perhaps she might be able to shed some light on his disappearance."

"What's the girlfriend's name," inquired Eddie, "perhaps I know her?"

"Just a minute, I've got it written down here someplace. Yeah, here it is. Her name is Elaine Sucharski. You know her?"

"Elaine? Sure, I know her well," said Eddie. "She works right here in town at the local Five and Dime store. I suspect if she's not there at the moment, she soon will be."

"Great," responded the Commander. "We'll want to talk to her, maybe as early as this afternoon. Just don't you say anything to her until we can get someone over there. Don't worry, I'll have whoever it is check in with you first."

"I'd appreciate that. So is there anything my department can do to help your investigation in the meantime," asked Eddie. His concern over the missing Coastguardsman had only increased with the knowledge he had been dating Elaine Sucharski. It also brought the case even closer to home.

"As a matter-of-fact there is," answered the Commander, more than happy to have Eddie's cooperation. "Would you be willing to check around, very discretely of course, to see if anyone living or traveling along that beach road may have seen or heard anything out of the ordinary last night. You know, a prowler or maybe evidence that someone tried to break into a house or barn, even something as trivial as a dog barking in the middle of the night. If you could do that it would be an incredible help to me."

"No problem, I'll see what I can turn up," replied Eddie.

"And listen, we really do want to keep a tight lid on this investigation, at least until we have something more concrete to go on. At a time like this rumors spread rapidly and we don't want to worry people unnecessarily."

"Of course, but is there something you're not telling me?" Eddie inquired, his curiosity aroused even further now.

"Not in terms of facts. We've told you everything. Its more a suspicion," added the Commander.

"And what might that suspicion be?" Eddie continued.

"This is off-the-record, mind you, but we've been receiving warnings from the FBI that the Germans may try to smuggle spies into the country by U-boat. And there have been sightings of U-boats in places where you wouldn't ordinarily expect to find them. It could just be that his disappearance is in some way related, though we have absolutely no evidence to support that theory. That's also the reason we want to keep this investigation under wraps as much as possible. On the slight chance there are German spies in the area we don't need to alert them to what we know, or maybe I should say, how little we do know."

At the mention of U-boats Eddie had felt a chill ricochet up and down his spine. He was reminded of the gold star hanging in his mother's window. The star was for his younger brother, Walter, who had been killed earlier in the year when the oil tanker he was serving on was sunk by a German U-boat off the coast of Ireland. His mother had taken Walter's death very hard; she took no pride in being a "Gold Star Mother," in fact, she had become very bitter about it and refused to even mention his name. For that matter had it not been for Eddie she would never have placed the gold star in her window.

The Commander's voice jarred Eddie from his thoughts.

"Listen, I have to go but there is one other thing I'd like to ask of you if you wouldn't mind."

"Name it," said Eddie, the thought of his brother still fresh in his mind.

"Ipswich is a pretty small town so I was wondering if you might take note of any strangers that had recently been seen in your town. Now, I don't want you to follow them or anything like that, just find out what you can about them."

"That's not going to be easy as it sounds," replied Eddie. "There are over two hundred enlisted men alone at Camp Agawam, not to mention the dozens of out-of-towners who've come here to work at Sylvania and Robinson's Shipyard. A year ago a stranger in Ipswich would have stood out like a sore thumb but unfortunately that's not the case anymore."

"OK. I understand, just do whatever you can," said the Commander, clearly disappointed. "But if by chance you do find something, no matter how insignificant it seems, let me know. I guess I should also inform you that the FBI will probably take over the case if it turns out to be something more than a simple case of desertion or suicide."

"So, if I understand you correctly, the appearance of the FBI will mean the government suspects the Germans may well be involved in the Coastguardsman's disappearance," Eddie declared.

"Yeah, something like that. Well, look, I gotta go; for the moment I'm still in charge, but I'll keep you posted one way or another." And with that Evans hung up.

For a moment Eddie just stood there with the phone in his hand. German spies here in Ipswich? Ridiculous! There's got to be another explanation, he thought to himself, though if there is I can't come up with it. So until someone does, I'd better start doing my job.

Although he had only recently turned thirty-five, Eddie Sawaski had been the police chief in Ipswich for nearly six years. It was a testament to

29

his dedication and honesty that the town's residents had entrusted him with the job at such a young age. Most women would have described Eddie as good looking with his blond hair and piercing blue eyes. He also possessed the kind of fair complexion they would have envied were it not for the fact that in summer the sun turned his face a blotchy red giving him the appearance of being perpetually embarrassed. At 5' 9" Eddie was not especially tall, but he was broad-shouldered and when he dressed up in his blue police uniform with his captain's hat, gently crushed in the style popular with fighter pilots, he looked really quite impressive. In spite of all this, Eddie had never married, had no prospects of doing so, and continued to live at home with his widowed mother, who in spite of having emigrated from Poland three years before he had even been born could speak barely a word of English.

When the U.S. officially entered the war Eddie's brother had quickly joined the merchant marine, but for Eddie military service was never an option. A fractured ankle, incurred when the bike he was riding skidded in some loose sand and sent him crashing into a water hydrant, failed to heal properly leaving him with a permanent limp. He was classified 4-F by the local draft board but, as it turned out, that didn't mean there wasn't plenty to do on the home front even for a small-town police chief.

Ipswich was one of the nation's oldest communities having been settled in 1634 by settlers sent out from Boston. The early residents of the town were overwhelmingly farmers, fishermen, shipbuilders and traders, but by the early 1900s Ipswich had become the home for both an expanding textile as well as electronics industry. Not surprisingly this growth had spurred a demand for labor that could not be satisfied locally. It was met instead by an influx of immigrants from Ireland, Nova Scotia, Greece, Poland, and Italy. And to this increasingly diverse permanent population could be added the hundreds of seasonal residents, who had begun coming to Ipswich each summer to enjoy the local beaches and small-town atmosphere.

Like most communities in America, however, Ipswich was changed dramatically by the coming of war and the impact of these changes was to generate a whole new set of security problems for the local police department. For example, the Sylvania Electronics plant, located directly in the center of town, was taken over by the U.S. Navy for the duration of the war. The work it was now required to do was heavily classified and the plant had to engage its own security force. The force's jurisdiction, however, was strictly limited to Sylvania's property so all other security problems were the responsibility of the local police force. The same was also true for Robinson's shipyard located at the mouth of the Ipswich River near Crane's Beach. Before the war this shipyard had specialized in building yachts for the wealthy; it was only when the German U-boat offensive had begun along the East Coast that the U.S. Navy had contracted with the shipyard to build crucially needed minesweepers, sub-chasers and landing craft. Unfortunately, its extremely isolated location made the shipyard unusually vulnerable to sabotage and so it, too, had to hire a private security force to guard its property. Once again, everything outside the shipyard's security fence, including the roads leading to the shipyard and the beach, became the local police department's responsibility.

But, when it came to problems for Eddie and his fellow officers, there was nothing quite like the problems generated by Camp Agawam. The U.S. Army had decided to establish a boot camp in Ipswich and a vacant tract of land on the edge of the town was leased for this purpose. Unfortunately, the barracks for the recruits could not be completed before they began arriving in town and as a result they had to be temporarily housed in an empty three-story building directly across from the railroad station. Worse still for the Ipswich police was the fact that most of these recruits were Southerners, who'd never spent a day away from home. To suddenly plunk them down in the middle of a small town in "Yankee country" was only asking for trouble; it was like starting the Civil War all over again. The town hadn't experienced anything quite like it in its three hundred year-history. Fortunately, the bulk of the fighting ended up being between the recruits themselves and Eddie was generally successful in keeping them isolated from the local residents.

Eddie could find no reports of any unusual behavior along the beach road for the previous evening, though he would continue to pursue this part of the investigation. But, now, it was almost noon and he had yet to have his breakfast. So, for a second time that morning he started downtown for something to eat. Rather than going to the Atlas, he decided instead to just grab a quick sandwich at the soda fountain of Quint's Drug Store. The store was on the other side of the square and, as he crossed over, his gaze was drawn instinctively to the huge red-and-white banner hanging over North Main Street. The banner displayed two stars--one blue, the other gold. The blue stood for the Ipswich residents presently serving with the armed forces; there was the number 208 appearing below it. The gold stood for those residents who had died in action. At the moment that number was eight and one of those eight was Eddie's brother. Every time Eddie crossed the square he looked up at that banner and every time he was overcome with a mixture of pride, sorrow, and anger, especially anger. Anger that the military had taken Walter but not him; anger that Walter had been killed at such a young age; but most of all anger at the Nazis for starting a war that had already consumed so many innocent lives with no end in sight.

Chapter Six

Karl was relishing every bite of his breakfast. After two weeks of U-boat fare, the fried eggs, bacon, home fries, toast and coffee tasted like manna from heaven. And, everything was so fresh—the strawberry jam, the butter, the cream. He had to literally force himself to eat slowly. Though there were only a couple of other customers in the restaurant, he had no desire to draw any unnecessary attention to himself by wolfing down his food.

Unfortunately, just when he concluded he had pulled it off, the counterman startled him by saying, "You must have been hungry. Been a long time since I've seen anyone clean his plate like that in this restaurant."

Johnny Pantekis was the owner of the Atlas restaurant, but on this day he was also the counterman and cashier. It had become difficult to hire even part-time help with so many young men rushing off to the service.

"Just as well," Johnny continued. "I've just about run out of sugar and bacon; coffee will be next. And the government hasn't even begun to ration yet, still those things are becoming nearly impossible for me to get. I suppose I shouldn't complain though. It's the least I can put up with to make sure Mussolini's thugs get what's coming to them. Can you imagine them attacking Greece like that? Those bastards, if you'll excuse my French, are lucky the Nazis came and bailed them out or Rome would be in the hands of the Greeks by now."

Karl guessed the guy was Greek judging by the way he was getting worked up so he decided it was probably a good time to leave. But, he was certainly right about one thing; Hitler had made a pretty poor choice of allies.

"Well, it was good, and I was hungry," admitted Karl, getting up from the counter. He retrieved his duffel and walked over to the cash register.

"How much do I owe you?" Karl inquired.

"Fifty cents should do it," replied Johnny, wondering if he just might have offended a paying customer.

But it was Karl who suddenly realized he faced a potential problem. All the money he had was either in twenties or fifties. The Abwehr had been unable to obtain small denomination bills in any quantity. So, while the money was real, Karl worried that a large denomination bill might appear unusual coming from someone who had just claimed to be out of work.

"All I have is this twenty; I've been trying to see how long I could go without breaking it but I guess this is it."

The twenty-dollar bill he handed over was a new one, though not so crisp one would automatically think counterfeit coming from a stranger.

"Do you have enough change for it," Karl asked, noticing the owner hesitated as he glanced in the drawer of the cash register.

"I think I have enough," Johnny replied. "Probably wouldn't have yesterday at this time. The place was dead. I mean, almost no one came in all morning; it was strange. Thank God it's been a little better today."

Taking his change, Karl pushed the two quarters towards Johnny as a tip.

Sliding them back to Karl he said, "Thanks, but you can leave a tip the next time you're in. You're going to need every cent of that money before you get through."

"I really appreciate that," Karl replied, taken aback by the owner's generosity. "But I insist."

"Thanks," Johnny replied, "I can use it. I suspect it's going to be a long war."

"I suspect so, too," said Karl getting up from the counter.

"So, where are you from," Johnny asked. "I used to know everyone who came in here, but not anymore. What with the war on there are so many strangers in town I can't keep track of everybody."

"I'm from Chicago; came out here hoping to find work."

"Chicago, huh, never been out there," he said clearing away Karl's dirty dishes. "I could just tell from your accent that you weren't from around here, well, that you weren't from the North Shore, anyway."

Even after living five years in the States Karl was well aware he spoke accented English; there was nothing he could do about it for the moment. Fortunately, most people in America seemed to speak with some kind of accent. He had just been hoping that Ipswich was the kind of place where no one would notice. So much for that, he sighed.

Heading for the door Karl turned and asked, "By the way, is there a place in town where I might get a room?"

"Sure, try up the street at the Hayes Hotel; it's your best bet. They always seem to have rooms available though with all the new recruits in town it's possible they could be filled up."

"Recruits?" responded Karl with surprise. "What recruits?"

"Army recruits," Johnny replied. "The military is building a boot camp just outside of town. Unfortunately, for those of us who have to live here it's not yet finished so in the meantime they've stuck the recruits in the building next to the hotel. And, it's just possible they may be using some of the hotel rooms for the recruits, as well."

"Well, thanks, I'll go check."

Walking out the door all Karl could think about was that no matter how carefully you plan an operation, you always had to be prepared for the unexpected. Who would ever have suspected there would be an army training camp in a town as small as Ipswich? Of course, that's why you had to have good intelligence and once again none of the agents working in this area had learned of the camp, or if they had they'd failed to pass that information along. From now on he wasn't going to depend on any intelligence provided by Berlin, it had already proven too unreliable.

Once outside, Karl turned to his left and set out in the direction of the Hayes Hotel. Passing a newspaper store he felt a sudden urge to go in and purchase a pack of cigarettes; he hadn't had one since he left Germany. Karl bought himself a pack of Lucky Strikes. Quickly lighting one up he inhaled deeply. There was nothing in the world quite like an American cigarette, he concluded. His years living in Chicago had spoiled him; there were unquestionably many things he liked about America. Still, he was here to do a job and he had to remember that. America had to recognize that Germany was a powerful nation that was owed the right to be treated with respect.

Continuing his walk up the street, Karl was surprised how few people were on the street even for mid-morning and the stores too appeared nearly empty. The one exception was the local meat market that was doing an unusually good business. Customers were clearly stocking up on either scarce food items or those about to be rationed. As he passed the store, he had to laugh because taped to the window was a poster with Hitler's picture on it and the caption under it read "Hoarding Helps Hitler." In fact, as he looked around he noticed similar posters on other store windows. But what really caught his eye were posters exhorting Americans to provide relief for China. These posters surprised him because there had never been any mention of American aid to China during his training and now here were posters everywhere declaring that China's resistance was vital to America's security. He made a mental note to pass this information along.

Approaching Depot Square, Karl noticed the large three-story building on the corner that Johnny had said housed the recruits. There was little sign of activity at the moment, which meant they were probably out training somewhere. Turning the corner he spotted the Hayes Hotel, another three-storied building with a large porch in front. While its faded red clapboards looked like they could use a coat of paint, the well-worn appearance of the structure gave it a sort of rustic charm. A sign near the door announced Board by Day or Week, while another proclaimed Meals at All Hours. Exactly what I'm looking for, thought Karl, now if only there's a vacant room.

Karl need not have worried. There was no shortage of vacant rooms. The war had greatly reduced the flow of salesmen and vacationers through town and the hotel was feeling the pinch. The desk clerk seemed especially pleased when Karl, who not only expressed an interest in staying several days, appeared more than willing paying in advance. For that Karl was given his choice of rooms. He opted for one on the second floor in the back, as far away as possible from the street. He was certain the noise level out front would increase dramatically whenever the recruits were around. He also wanted to minimize his contact with them as much as he could.

The clerk gave Karl his key and pointed him up the stairs. The interior of the hotel was much like the outside—worn but comfortable. Passing an empty dining room to his left, Karl ascended the carpeted stairs and walked down a dim hallway. His room was at the very end. As he opened the door and entered he detected a slightly musty smell; the room had apparently not been used for some time. He wandered over to the window, and after struggling for several minutes to open it, was finally rewarded with some fresh air. A glance around the room afforded an uninspiring scene—a lumpy bed with a well-worn covering, a small scratched dresser, a bare wooden table, a chair, and a floor lamp that had clearly seen better days. As for the walls, they were covered with a green and beige colored wallpaper that was peeling in several places. There were also two doors. One was closed and was probably a small closet; the other, partially ajar, led to the bathroom. The latter contained a sink, toilet and a bathtub that was so badly stained he wondered if he could ever summon up the courage to use it. All in all, though, the room would meet his immediate needs; he did not plan on staying there very long.

After carefully placing his few items of clothing in the dresser, Karl sat down on the edge of the bed and removed his shoes. He considered taking a hot bath, but quickly dismissed the idea. Maybe later, he mused, lying back on the bed. Within seconds he was sound asleep; he didn't leave the room the rest of the day.

The following morning, after a quick bath and shave, Karl locked his door and headed downstairs for breakfast and some information. His immediate concern was what to do with the several thousand dollars he had in his possession. He would have preferred to leave the money somewhere in the room but the flimsy lock on the door provided no real security. Other than that, however, he had nothing else on him or in the room that should arouse suspicion if discovered. He had brought no weapon with him from the beach and had even disposed of the map he had originally been carrying. His papers, though forgeries, should pass any cursory examination.

The man at the front desk was not the one from the day before but he greeted Karl in a friendly manner. In response to Karl's question about breakfast, he suggested either the dining room or Russell's Lunch in the hotel annex. Karl decided to try Russell's. The man was also quick to provide the other information Karl asked about.

"Plenty of jobs," he reported. "There are so few men around they're having to fill in with housewives and high school kids. You can just about have your pick—Robinson's Shipyard, Sylvania, and even many of the smaller, local businesses, you name it."

"The shipyard sounds interesting, what exactly do they do there?" Karl asked.

"Not exactly sure, but from what I understand they make small boats of some kind; I think they use them for hunting submarines. There are a lot of German subs around, or at least that's what I've heard. You know, if you're interested, there's an employment office for the shipyard right up on Central Street. It's only about a five-minute walk from here."

For obvious reasons the shipyard intrigued him and he instantly made up his mind to do his best to get a job there. There were, he thought to himself, a number of good reasons for working at such a place. For one thing, security was probably less tight than at an electronics factory. Then, too, if the shipyard were small enough, he could probably conduct the operation entirely by himself. If the briefings he had received were correct, there would be no significant German population around this area. And, anyway, developing a network of agents to carry out such an operation would take time and involve risks. The important thing, they had all been reminded, was to bring the war to the United States. The Americans must be made to understand there would be costs even at home to waging war against Germany and that Hitler could reach even across the Atlantic to attack them. So, if he could destroy the shipyard, it would send just such a message. And, if as a result of the damage the shipyard were put out of commission even for a few weeks, it would reduce the number of sub-chasers operating out there. That thought reminded him of Captain Frisch. Anything he could do to improve the chances of Frisch surviving the war made the whole thing worth it Karl decided.

After another huge breakfast, Karl headed up the street to the shipyard's employment office. He was a little early, though he noticed there were already several people waiting for the office to open. They were all men and clearly too old for military service. They eyed him curiously, but made no attempt to engage him in conversation; so much for it being a friendly town. He concluded they probably thought him a draft dodger or something; the employment officer would probably think the same thing. It made him a little uneasy. Unquestionably, his deferment papers and medical records would be scrutinized with unusual care.

At nine the office opened, by which time there were nearly a dozen people waiting in line. As each person entered the office he was handed an application form to complete. One by one the applicants were then invited to a table where an older man went over the completed forms. When it was his turn Karl took a seat, handing the man his application.

"Hmm, looks good," murmured the man, after carefully going over it. "Don't get many men here your age, all in the service."

Karl nodded silently. His birth certificate showed him as having been born in Chicago of an American father and a mother who had immigrated to the United States from the Austro-Hungarian city of Graz. And had he been asked why he spoke English with just a hint of an accent, he would have explained that his father had abandoned them shortly after his birth and that his mother, whose English was never very good, had raised him by herself. The issue, however, never came up.

"It says here you've had tuberculosis."

Karl couldn't tell if it was a question or just a statement of fact but he answered anyway.

"Yeah, many years ago. I don't have it now, though. Unfortunately, I suffered some permanent lung damage so the military won't take me. I've tried a couple times but the result was the same—sorry." Karl said all this with a audible dose of disappointment in his voice. "But, I can still do a full-day's work, no problem. I'll even work the nightshift if you want. I just want to do my part in defeating the Nazis."

Karl had made certain that everyone in the office had heard his comments. He wanted to allay any suspicions that others might harbor about him. He suspected that in a small town like Ipswich, gossip spread very quickly.

"You may have to work one of the night shifts," said the man, relieved to find someone so willing to do it. "I suspect you'll be hearing from us in the next day or so. There's a lot of work available right now. We just have to do some routine checking on your application, but you appear to be exactly the kind of guy we're looking for."

"Great," said Karl. "I can be reached at the Hayes Hotel."

Getting up from his chair Karl realized he had poured it on pretty thick but he just wasn't that certain how good his papers were, not after all the problems he had already encountered. He had to hope the individuals responsible for his identification papers back in Berlin had done a thorough job.

Chapter Seven

Eddie was working on the weekly duty roster when the door to the police department swung open and a tall, rugged-looking man, with slicked back hair and a big grin on his face, stepped into the office.

"Special Agent Bill McCarthy, FBI," he announced, with just a touch of an Irish brogue audible in his voice. "You Chief Sawaski?"

"Yes, I am," replied Eddie, quickly getting up from his desk. "But everybody calls me Eddie."

"All right, Eddie," said the Agent, offering Eddie his hand. "Call me Mack."

Eddie calculated that Mack was probably in his early forties, though he obviously kept himself in good shape. His dark suit fit him perfectly and he stood ramrod straight, as if he had been in the military. He was the perfect image of what a G-man should look like, Eddie thought to himself, though that image had been shaped by Hollywood movies.

"Have a seat," Eddie proposed, motioning to a chair. "I was just talking to a Commander Evans from over in Salem; he said the FBI might be entering the case. Does this mean that you think the Germans may somehow be involved with the missing Coastguardsman?"

"Not at all," answered Mack. "In fact, I'm not even absolutely certain we have a case yet. There's no body, no clues, and no motive. All I actually have is a report stating that a Coast Guardsman and his dog went missing after going out on a night patrol at Crane's Beach."

"What about the reports of U-boats being sighted off-shore," asked Eddie.

"U-boats have been operating off the coast here for months,"

41

Mack acknowledged. "For the moment, at least, we have no evidence connecting their presence to our missing Coast Guardsman. For that matter we have no evidence period."

"So, who is this Coast Guardsman, anyway?"

"His name is Frank, or Frankie, Destino. He comes from Boston, the North End."

"Have you spoken to anyone in his family," Eddie asked.

"This morning, I spoke to one of his sisters. The parents are both from Italy and although they've lived in this country for many years they speak very little English. Unfortunately I learned little from them that had any bearing on his disappearance but at least now I'm able to draw a better picture of Frankie himself. I don't know how much you know about the North End but it's a very close-knit Italian community and everybody there seems to know him; he's actually something of a local hero. Frankie's an only son and his father made sure he stayed in school; he actually graduated from high school, which is highly unusual in that neighborhood. Turns out he's quite an athlete. At East Boston High School he was All-Scholastic in both football and baseball. And get this, he just signed a contract with the Boston Braves as a catcher. I haven't actually had time to check this out with the Braves organization yet, but since so many people I met on the street mentioned it, I have no reason to doubt it."

"So, he doesn't sound like the kind of guy who'd go AWOL, then, does he," Eddie concluded.

"Definitely not. In fact, from what I understand he was one of the first young men in his neighborhood to sign up for the service."

"But why would he join the Coast Guard?" Eddie asked. "It would never occur to me, for instance. I thought most guys were just naturally drawn to the army or the navy, maybe even the marines, but the Coast Guard?"

"Couple of reasons, I suspect," explained Mack. "For one thing the Coast Guard has a good reputation among the fishermen in and around the Boston waterfront. There's probably not a fisherman there who hasn't had to call them for help at least once in his lifetime. I'm certain that's one reason the Coast Guard has opened a recruiting office right there in the North End. But, there's another, maybe even more important reason why Frankie may have joined the Coast Guard. You know, within the military there's this concern that the first allegiance of many Italian-Americans may still be to Italy. It's not an unimportant concern since these guys may end up having to fight in Italy against their former countrymen. So, the Coast Guard would avoid all that. Of course, from my perspective it shouldn't even be an issue. I've worked with plenty of Italian guys in the Bureau and they're just as patriotic as the next guy, maybe more since they feel they have something to prove."

"But how did he end up here at Crane's Beach?"

"Well, the Coast Guard's been under heavy pressure to bolster its anti-submarine defenses along the New England coast so they sent him to boot camp at Gallups Island right in Boston Harbor and then posted him at the new station they opened up here; coincidence really. Anyway, that's about all I've been able to discover so far. What about you, have you turned up anything yet?"

"Nothing yet, I'm afraid," Eddie responded, "although I'm having one of my officers check with everyone living along Argilla Road, that's the road leading to the beach, to see if anyone remembers anything unusual about that night."

"OK, good," said Mack, conducting his own appraisal of Eddie. "Now the main reason I'm here is, not only to fill you in on what we had learned, but to interview this Elaine Sucharski, the missing guy's girlfriend. Evans said you knew her, so I thought it might be a good idea if you came along. Among other things you could show me how to get to her house."

"Be glad to," replied Eddie ignoring Mack's last comment. "Anything would be better than just sitting still."

Eddie grabbed his hat and followed the agent out the door.

As Eddie settled into Mack's black sedan he asked, "How long have you been with the Feds, Mack?"

"Nearly twenty years now," Mack responded. "I joined right after I graduated from college."

"I would have liked to have been a G-man," said Eddie a little wistfully. "But when my father died that ended right there whatever small chance I probably had of going to college."

"You seem to have done all right for yourself. I wouldn't mind being a police chief in a nice small town like this."

"I'm not complaining," Eddie quickly replied, "though picking up high school kids for drinking too much on Saturday night or for getting into a fight at a local basketball game can get a little boring. So, what kinds of exciting things have you been involved in?"

"Since Pearl Harbor most of us have become involved in wartime security in one way or another; before that I worked in the organized crime division. You know, Mafia, bootlegging, gunrunning, tax evasion, that kind of stuff. I did a tour in Kansas City, another in Washington, before being assigned to Boston. It's great to be back home."

"Oh, so you're originally from Boston," Eddie asked.

"Cambridge actually. Born there, went to school there, and would have probably stayed there working in the post office with my father if the war hadn't come along. I spent two years in Germany and when I got back I decided I wanted to go to college. I started part-time at Northeastern but then transferred to Holy Cross. That's where I graduated from."

"So, two years in Germany, did you see much combat?" Eddie was always fascinated talking to men who had actually been in the trenches. He decided it had something to do with the fact he couldn't serve.

"A few months. I took part in the Meuse-Argonne offensive; that was like the last big battle of the World War I. I consider myself very lucky because so many Americans were killed in the fighting there. After that I spent about a year in occupation, actually living with a German family in the city of Koblenz. They were really nice people; they treated me more like one of the family than as an occupying soldier. I kept in touch with them for a while but now it's been years since I've heard from them. I hope they're all right. Unfortunately, their only son must be in his late twenties so he's probably in Hitler's army somewhere, if he's still alive."

Mack remained silent for a few minutes while Eddie examined his own feelings about the Germans. Unlike Mack, he didn't have much good to say about them.

"So, how did you get from Holy Cross to the FBI," Eddie asked, changing the subject.

"A friend of my father's from the post office. His brother worked for the FBI and he was always pestering my father to have me contact the local FBI office in Boston. During my senior year in college I finally did it, as much for my father's sake as mine. I just wanted the guy to leave my father alone."

"So you went into the local office and they made you an offer?"

"Well, it wasn't quite as simple as that because all the hiring is done from Washington but in time, yeah, they offered me a job. And, as you probably well remember, jobs weren't easy to come by at that time since it was the middle of the Depression so I wasn't in any position to turn the Feds down. As it turned out I've really enjoyed the job; not that it hasn't had its moments mind you. Looking back though I wouldn't trade it for anything; unless, of course, it was for your job."

They both laughed, though probably for very different reasons.

"That's the house right over there," Eddie announced. "The one on the corner to the right."

The Sucharski's lived on Topsfield Road, not far from the Sacred Heart Church. Their house was a two-story white colonial with a screened-in porch on each level. The Sucharski's lived on the second floor of the house; Elaine's maternal grandparents lived on the first.

Elaine, along with everyone else in the house judging from the number of faces at the windows, had been expecting them. Eddie introduced Elaine to Mack and then the two of them followed her upstairs and into a rather formal living room. At Elaine's invitation they both took seats but politely refused her offer of something to drink. Though neither Eddie nor Mack ever actually saw her, they sensed the mother listening from out in the kitchen.

"You know, your mother may join us," explained Mack.

"No," replied Elaine, taking a seat opposite them. "My mother's English is not very good, and anyway, she's really a very shy person. She'd rather stay in the other room if that's all right with you."

"No, that's fine," said Mack. "So let me begin by repeating how truly sorry we are to be here under such circumstances, but the fact remains we have to find out what happened to Frankie. Maybe you could begin by telling us how well you knew him."

It was clearly not an easy situation for a sixteen-year old to be answering questions about a boyfriend who might be dead though she handled it surprisingly well; she was clearly a very mature young woman.

45

"We dated a few times, that's all. We had made plans to go out this Friday night."

For the first time it appeared she was fighting back tears.

Mack hesitated for a moment before continuing.

"What can you tell us about him?"

"Very little really. I know he was from Boston, the North End, I think. He said everybody in his neighborhood was Italian; his parents were from Italy, I know that. He's been wanting me to meet them, though he warned me they didn't speak much English. I'm afraid that's about all I know."

"So, there were no family problems you were aware of?"

"Oh, I'm positive there weren't. Frankie loved his family and talked about them all the time."

"He never mentioned anything about going anywhere," Mack asked.

"Definitely not. Boston was his whole world. Well, I take it back, he did say something about Florida."

"Florida?" said Mack. "What did he say about Florida?"

"The Braves had invited him to spring training next February," replied Elaine sadly. "They were going to give him a tryout. He's a really good catcher and all he's ever wanted to do is play for either the Braves or the Red Sox."

"Interesting," responded Mack thoughtfully. "You know, the parents never said anything about his being a baseball player. I had to learn about it from his friends. I wonder why they never even mentioned it?"

"That's easy, they didn't approve of his playing professional baseball," Elaine replied. "His father wanted him to do something more respectable like being a teacher or owning a business."

"What a shame," said Mack shaking his head. "Obviously his old man has never heard of Joe DiMaggio or Phil Rizzuto."

By now it had become clear that Elaine knew absolutely nothing relevant to Frankie's whereabouts and, other than further upsetting her, there was little to be gained by continuing the questioning.

"Well, thank you for your time, Miss Sucharski," said Mack, getting to his feet. "If anything occurs to you that might appear to be related in any way to Frankie's disappearance, anything, no matter how minor it may seem, contact Chief Sawaski here. He'll pass whatever you have to say along to me."

"I'm really sorry I couldn't help you more." She walked them downstairs to the front door where they said their good-byes.

Walking to the car Mack said, "No wonder this Frankie fell for her; she's one beautiful young woman. Did you happen to notice her eyes? They're this incredible blue, well, almost like yours come to mention it, but she has a much nicer body than you. And, by the way, with that blonde hair of hers and those blue eyes, she honestly has movie star looks. I really feel badly for Frankie, and her, too, of course. I only wish she could've helped us more."

"Perhaps she did at least confirm some things, like he probably didn't walk away by himself. And if he didn't that makes it sound more like a kidnapping, or worse, like a homicide."

"Now you're sounding like a cop, Eddie, and that's good," Mack responded with the big grin back on his face. "I've got a feeling there is a case here, but unless we begin to find some solid evidence, conjecture alone is not going to solve it. We definitely need a break and we need it now."

Chapter Eight

On the third day following his visit to the employment office on Central Street, Karl found a message waiting for him at the front desk when he returned to the hotel after lunch. A Mr. Riley had called to inform him that his application for employment at Robinson's Shipyard had been approved. He need only stop by the employment office to sign a couple of papers and he could begin work immediately.

Karl was greatly relieved by the message. Among other things it meant that his papers had passed their first real test. Now he could begin to look for more suitable housing; he was far too exposed living in the hotel. Whenever there was trouble, it seemed, the hotel was inevitably one of the first places checked by the authorities. But in the case of the Hayes Hotel, it was further complicated by the presence of the army recruits temporarily living next door. In spite of his best efforts to avoid them, he had still come dangerously close on a couple of occasions to having physical confrontations with drunken recruits. He had to get out of there before something truly serious happened.

While waiting to hear about his job application, he had taken the opportunity to check the classified section of the Ipswich *Chronicle*, the local weekly newspaper, to see if there were any rooms or apartments available for rent. Surprisingly, there were. Clearly, a number of people had decided to augment their incomes by renting out space made vacant by family members serving in the armed forces. Karl was immediately struck by the irony of his possibly occupying the room of someone who might very well be fighting in Europe against his own countrymen.

Of the several notices appearing in the latest edition of the *Chronicle*, one in particular caught his eye. An apartment was being advertised as rent-free on the condition that the person occupying it would be willing to do general maintenance work around the owner's house and grounds. And what made the arrangement even more attractive to Karl was the apartment's location--Argilla Road, the road that led both to Robinson's Shipyard and to Crane's Beach, where his supplies were buried. The notice even emphasized the fact the apartment was convenient to the shipyard.

Karl had jotted down the telephone number to call about the apartment, waiting only for confirmation that he had a job before doing so. Now that he had one, he concluded he'd better move fast before someone else took the apartment; it seemed almost too good to be true.

"Mind if I use your phone for a moment," he asked the desk manager.

"Not as long as it's a local call," he replied, pushing the telephone over to him.

Karl picked up the receiver and waited for the operator. When she came on the line he gave her the number he had taken down from the newspaper ad. After a few seconds he heard the phone on the other end of the line begin to ring. It rang several times and he was just about to hang up when he heard a breathless "hello?"

"Hello," he responded. "My name is Karl Stoner and I was calling about the apartment you had advertised in the local newspaper?"

"Oh, yes, the apartment," replied the voice. "I guess I'm just a little surprised to have gotten a response so soon."

"You did say it was near the shipyard and I've just taken a job there and need a place to live. May I assume from your comment you haven't found anyone to rent it yet?"

"Yes, or no, I haven't rented it yet. To be honest you're the first person to call about the place. I wasn't really sure anyone would even be interested. Anyway, I imagine you'd like to see the place. Do you know how to get here?"

Karl explained that he didn't have a car.

"That's no problem," she explained. "I can easily come in and pick you up. Would this afternoon about three be convenient?"

"That would be great; the sooner I could move in the better," Karl replied. "Where should I meet you?"

"How about the corner where Quint's Drug Store is located? Do you know where I mean?"

"I can find it."

"So, how will I recognize you, then," she asked

"No problem, I'll be wearing a light blue shirt and, let's see, I'll be holding a copy of the local newspaper."

"It sounds like I'm making contact with a spy," she chuckled, her voice displaying animation for the first time. "I said that only because our local newspaper has been running excerpts from a book entitled *She Loved a Spy*; I've really been enjoying it. I never knew anything about spying or the FBI before I started reading these excerpts. I'm sorry, I'm just rambling on and I haven't even told you my name yet; it's Anne Westbrook, by the way."

"Well, Mrs. Westbrook, I'll see you at three. And, I guess we'll see just how much you learned from that spy story," he chuckled, suddenly realizing it was the closest he had come to laughing since he'd landed on American soil.

"Anne," she said quickly, "please call me Anne. Mrs. Westbrook seems too formal, especially during wartime when we're all in this together."

"All right then, Anne, I'll see you at three."

Putting the receiver down, he pushed the telephone back to the desk manager, who hadn't missed a word that was said.

"So, you're gonna rent an apartment from Anne Westbrook."

"No, I'm going to see about renting an apartment from her," Karl snapped. It made him wonder if he was making a mistake settling in such a small town. Clearly keeping anything a secret in this place was not going to be easy, another reason for moving out of the hotel.

"She's quite a looker, you know," the desk manager continued, undismayed by Karl's obvious sarcasm. "And eligible too since her husband died. But I wouldn't get my hopes up too high if I were you; you're not her type. She's part of that Argilla Road crowd. They're mostly from Boston; only spend their summers here. They have lots of money and generally only hang out with their own kind, which you don't appear to be. They don't think much of us townies unless, of course, they want their lawns mowed or their houses painted. The women are worse than the men; they can be real bitches."

"Thanks," Karl replied, eager to get away from the guy. "I'll keep all that in mind."

Chapter Nine

Anne Westbrook had reluctantly concluded she was not going to be able to maintain her home on Argilla Road by herself unless she could find someone to help around the place. If she were not able to find such a person then her only other alternative was to move back to Boston with her parents for the duration of the war, not a thought that particularly excited her though she knew her parents would love having her at home. But, finding help was not going to be easy what with every able-bodied man either in the service or otherwise involved in the war effort. Even the usual teenagers who spent their summers hanging out at the beach were notable by their absence. Most had no choice but to remain in Boston with their parents. The Office of Price Administration had just announced that gasoline rationing was going to be instituted along the East Coast, so pleasure driving for most people would be severely restricted.

Her only chance of finding someone, she decided, was to offer free accommodation in the apartment above the garage in exchange for general carpentry and landscaping work. She was hoping she might interest one of the single men at the shipyard since her home was only about a mile away. Still, it was with considerable trepidation that she had placed an ad to that effect in the local Ipswich newspaper.

Anne Spencer Westbrook came from an old distinguished Boston family. Her father, Frederick Spencer, had recently retired after a successful career in finance, the last twenty years of which were spent as president as one of Boston's largest banks. He had graduated from Harvard, class of '94, and gone on to serve with Teddy Roosevelt in

Cuba during the Spanish-American War. While there he had contracted a serious case of malaria, so serious, in fact, his doctors gave up all hope of recovery. However, the same stubbornness that would later prove so useful to him as a banker would enable him to pull through his illness, and forty years later he was still alive and well.

Anne's mother, Elizabeth, was also still alive and although younger than her husband, she had not enjoyed the same good health in recent years. For some time now she had been under the doctors' care and only infrequently left her house in Back Bay. She had met her future husband through mutual friends; he had just graduated from Harvard as she was completing her first year at Smith. When two years later Frederick Spencer asked her to marry him, she agreed and dropped out of school to do so. Almost immediately she began questioning whether marrying him had been such a good idea, especially after he informed her he was joining the army along with several of his Harvard classmates. And when he later came home suffering from malaria, it was Elizabeth who had to care for him. How ironic, she often said to Anne, that Frederick now had to spend so much time caring for her.

Most people who knew the family agreed that Anne took after her mother both in looks and personality. And a good thing, too, they generally added. Whereas her father had a tendency to be somewhat brusque and business-like, Anne's mother was an attractive, warm and gracious woman. Because, as it turned out, she could not have any more children after Anne was born, Elizabeth and her daughter became very close, even to the point of attending her mother's college, although unlike her mother she stayed around to graduate.

That she, too, didn't drop out to get married, Anne owed entirely to her mother. On a skiing weekend at Killington, Vermont, during her junior year, Anne had taken a nasty fall while trying to navigate one of the expert slopes. No bones were broken but she had to be helped down the hill by a young ski patrolman. Over a cup of hot chocolate at the lodge's first aid station Anne found out that the solicitous young man's name was Alan Westbrook. He came from Concord, Massachusetts, and was presently a senior at Middlebury College. It was love at first sight and when Allan graduated that following June he began pressuring Anne to marry him. It was Anne's mother who insisted she receive her diploma first.

"I made a big mistake giving up college to marry your father," she told Anne. "I always felt so dependent upon him knowing I wasn't equipped to get a real job. Don't you make the same mistake I made. Believe me, you'll end up regretting it if you do."

So Anne waited to be married until the summer after her graduation from Smith. Still, the wedding didn't proceed without its fair share of complications. The most serious for Anne was the fact her father did not approve of Alan, and he did everything he could to talk her out of the marriage. For, unlike her father, Alan didn't trace his ancestry back to the Mayflower, nor was he from what in Boston was often referred to as "old money." His greatest sin, however, was that he had not attended Harvard, and to make matters worse, he had been accepted there. How, her father had asked quite seriously, could any sane person pass up going to Harvard for Middlebury? But, in time he relented, with a great deal of prodding from Anne's mother, and "gave his daughter away." Before settling into a very comfortable apartment on Beacon Hill, the two newlyweds enjoyed a delightful honeymoon in Europe, another concession by Anne's father.

As it turned out Anne barely had a chance to adjust to married life before she discovered she was pregnant. When a few months later Anne gave birth to a healthy son, Robert, she and Alan decided they should find a larger place to live and preferably one in a more rural environment. That place turned out to be Wayland, a small town a few miles west of Boston.

The town of Wayland proved a wonderful spot to raise their young son. Bob, as he was now called, and his friends could ride their bicycles all over town there was so little traffic; there weren't even any traffic lights. And, not far from the Westbrook home was a large open field where the neighborhood kids gathered for pickup baseball and football games. There were also acres of marshes and woods to explore and ponds for skating in winter and swimming in summer. If there were a downside to living in Wayland, it was the educational system. There was only a single school that housed both the elementary grades as well as the high school. And so while Anne was not overly concerned about Bob attending elementary school in the town, she balked at sending him to high school there. With great reluctance Anne sent Bob off to Exeter Academy in New Hampshire.

By the spring of his senior year Bob found himself having to decide where to attend college. He had been accepted at several, including Middlebury, his father's alma mater, Bates and Dartmouth: he decided upon Dartmouth. His father jokingly teased him about not wanting to follow in his illustrious footsteps but, then, only a few days before Robert was to leave for school, Alan had a heart attack; it was completely unexpected as heart attacks so often are. After a couple of weeks in the hospital, Alan was allowed to go home, though only on the condition he would not return to work for at least a month. Two weeks later, however, he suffered another attack; this one proved fatal. Anne and Bob were devastated. Nevertheless, Anne insisted that he begin his freshman year at Dartmouth.

It had been about the time Bob left home to attend Exeter that Anne began to experience bouts of loneliness. At first she thought it was simply Bob's absence and that it would disappear in time. When it did not she began to realize it had to do with her marriage, not Bob. Her marriage, she reluctantly concluded, had grown stale. Alan no longer showed her the warmth and affection she had grown accustomed to. He frequently complained of being tired. In an effort to give her life at least some new direction, she had pushed Alan into spending more time in Ipswich. He made no objection claiming he could commute to Boston just as easily from there. Later, she came to wonder if he suspected he had a serious heart problem.

It was her parents who convinced her to buy the place. It had become impossible for them to ever get there and they loved the idea of Anne owning it. They sold it to her for one dollar. Money, of course, would not have been an issue for Anne because she was become a very wealthy woman. Her father had established a generous trust fund for her years before and she now had the proceeds from the sale of the house in Wayland, not to mention Alan's life insurance. Much of this money she used to remodel the house. It had been built as a summer place with only a large fireplace to provide heat on those occasional damp, chilly days. But, if she were going to live there all year round, the fireplace would not provide heat enough. She'd have to put in a furnace and have the entire house insulated.

The house was fairly large; a modified colonial in style with naturally weathered hardwood shingles. On the second floor there were four rather plain bedrooms with two full baths, but it was the ground floor that gave the house its charm. There was a spacious living room with a huge fieldstone fireplace and large over-stuffed furniture, and a formal dining room, or at least formal by summer home standards, where she and Alan had entertained frequently but for which she had little use now. And, then, there was her favorite room--the kitchen. It was the coziest room in the house. It had a large iron stove and a huge picture window, which gave a stunning view of the Castle Neck estuary with its vast marshes and Hog Island, on whose grassy slopes sheep could be seen grazing during the summer months. Adjacent to the kitchen was a screened porch, a very useful retreat on those hot summer days when the greenheads and deer flies made being outside simply impossible.

The house was located about an eighth of a mile off Argilla Road, linked by a dirt driveway that wound upward through a grove of mixed hardwoods and conifers. The house itself was situated at the top of a hill from which lawns radiated in all directions, some literally extending down to the marshes themselves. To the left as one approached the house was another large structure that doubled as a stable and a garage. The stable could hold four horses, though Anne kept only a single horse there now; hay was stored in the loft above. Over that part of the barn used as a garage there was a relatively spacious apartment complete with its own kitchen facilities and full bath. It had been built to house additional guests when the four bedrooms in the main house were occupied.

The remodeling of the house had been just about completed and when it finally was, the house would be in good shape. The outside of the house was an entirely different matter. That's what Anne was most concerned about. The flower gardens were already overgrown, with the exception of a couple adjacent to the house that she worked on herself. And then there was the vegetable garden, or victory garden, as they had become known since the war began. She had planted some lettuce and put out a dozen or so tomato plants but what the deer didn't devour the woodchucks and raccoons did. In addition to the lawns that required mowing, there were several trees that had blown down during the winter. They now needed to be cut up and the wood stacked in the barn for use in the fireplace.

More and more these days Anne found herself frustrated by her inability to look after the place by herself. She was convinced that there really was more work to be done than any one person could accomplish. At the same time she realized there were many women who were raising families by themselves as well as working in defense plants, while their husbands were away doing their military service. Why am I so helpless, Anne lamented? At the very least I should be doing something to help the war effort. But I'm doing absolutely nothing. And to make matters worse, I can't even take care of my own house!

Anne concluded sadly that for all her warnings, she had become just like her mother. Her father had never let her mother be independent and have a life of her own; Alan had done the same thing with her. Both men had been overprotective to the point of almost suffocating their wives. That's why it was so important for her to learn how to take care of her house while at the same time doing some kind of volunteer work either at the local rationing board or the Red Cross.

Anne had been working outside when the phone rang and she had barely reached it in time. The last thing she been expecting was that it would be someone inquiring about the apartment. And when the caller did ask about it, Anne found herself momentarily at a loss for words. The idea of renting the apartment to a total stranger had literally never occurred to her. She had been assuming all along that the person living there would be someone she knew, or at least knew of, but now the reality dawned on her that the kind of people she was thinking about would not be in need of an apartment. Maybe I'm being too hasty, she thought to herself. Perhaps I should just tell this Karl Stone or Stoner or whatever his name is that I've changed my mind and I don't want to rent the apartment. I know it's unfair because I did run the ad and he clearly needed a place to live. But, only now did it dawn on her how it would look to the townspeople for a single woman to have a strange man living in her apartment over the barn. She could hear the gossip already. The whole thing was insane! How could she ever have come up with such an idea?

By the time she left to meet Karl, her mind was made up.

Chapter Ten

Anne recognized him immediately. Even had he not been the only person standing in front of Quints' Drugstore, his blue shirt and newspaper would have identified him; he was smoking a cigarette. Beyond the shirt and newspaper, though, everything else about him was unexpected. He was much younger than he had sounded over the phone; he couldn't be much more than thirty, she decided. And she hadn't anticipated he would be quite so good-looking, or at least he appeared good-looking from a distance.

Pulling up to the curb directly across the street from him she called over, "Hi, I'm Anne Westbrook. By any chance are you Karl Stoner?"

"Yes, I am," answered Karl, quickly flipping his cigarette into the gutter and starting across the street.

The desk clerk at the hotel had not been kidding when he said Anne was a "real looker." When he had made the comment Karl had not paid much attention assuming the old codger would have found any woman attractive who still had some teeth. In point of fact, the clerk had not done Anne justice; she was an extremely attractive woman. Karl guessed she must be a few years older than he was, but she obviously kept herself in great shape. From what he could see she had a slender build though the white blouse she was wearing seemed meant to downplay the fact she was amply endowed. Anne's golden-brown hair, disheveled by the ride, hung down loosely over her shoulders, and as he drew closer he could tell that her lightly tanned face was devoid of makeup. As Karl walked up to the car, she took off her sunglasses and smiled, displaying a pair of the most bewitching green eyes he had ever seen.

She motioned for him to get into the passenger side of the car. It had been her intention to apologize and then go on to explain she had decided not to rent the apartment. But there was something about this man now slipping into the car next to her; was it his rugged good looks, his sense of self-confidence bordering on arrogance? She felt a little flustered and unable to say what she had intended. Instead she found herself asking him if he was serious about wanting to see the apartment. And, when he nodded that he was, she decided it might be best to tell him later over the telephone that she had decided not to rent the apartment. Yet, deep down she was already beginning to wonder if that would actually happen.

As she shifted the car into gear and pulled away from the curb Anne was so lost in thought it took her a moment to realize that Karl was speaking to her.

"I'm sorry, my mind was elsewhere," she said, feeling even more embarrassed now. She was just glad he couldn't read her mind, though the curious smile he directed her way made her wonder.

"I was just remarking, I don't know how long it's been since I've ridden in a convertible with the top down."

"I probably shouldn't have put it down. I'm sure many people in town would look upon it as a sacrilege what with the war on. It is being rather frivolous, I suppose. But it was just such a beautiful day I couldn't resist."

"I don't think I'd worry about it if I were you," Karl replied. "Even with all the visible reminders of the war, people still have to go on with their everyday lives."

Anne did not reply to his comment though she appreciated it nonetheless. Several minutes passed without either speaking before Anne finally asked, "So, Mr. Stoner, where are you from? You mentioned on the phone you had just arrived in town."

"Please call me Karl. I thought we had already agreed to do that on the phone."

Anne smiled; she liked his no-nonsense manner. "Your right. So, Karl, where are you from?"

"Chicago. I came out here to find work."

"You mean there wasn't any work in Chicago? I'm rather surprised to hear that what with a war on," Anne chided. "But, to be honest, I'm more surprised that you're not in the service."

"No, you're right, there was no shortage of jobs there. I just needed to get away and start a new life; I've had some personal problems that I'm trying to put behind me. As for why I'm not in the service, it's not for lack of trying. Unfortunately I had tuberculosis when I was young, though I feel perfectly fine now; it's only the military that seems to think I'm unfit for duty."

"I'm sorry," she said. "But, you're right, you certainly look fit to me."

The way he looked over made her blush. It had sounded like a line from a Mae West movie. But it had been a long time since she'd been alone with a man.

"I didn't mean to pry," she continued, "I just thought if I were going to rent you the apartment, I should know at least a little something about you."

Another ill-advised comment, she reminded herself. By this time he had to have concluded she'd already made up her mind to rent him the apartment when, in fact, she hadn't, or at least she didn't think she had although it was possible she was simply too scared to admit it.

Several minutes had passed without further comment when Anne slowed the car and made a right turn onto a gravel driveway that twisted its way up a steep hill. Along its entire length, the driveway was roofed over by a dense canopy of white pines, through whose branches danced muted shafts of sunlight. And, when they finally broke out into the front yard of Anne's house, Karl found himself momentarily blinded by the sun's intense glare. As his eyes gradually accustomed themselves to the bright light, he saw materializing before him a broad expanse of emerald-green marshland veined with numerous saltwater creeks and dotted here and there with posts from some long ago haymaking operation. Far in the distance a line of low, wooded hills marked the horizon. It was a breathtaking panorama.

"So what do you think?" asked Anne, climbing out of the car and walking over to a spot where they could get a better view of the marshes. "And, take a deep breath, can you just smell that salt air?"

"I can, and as for the view it really is quite spectacular," Karl replied, shading his eyes with his hand in order to see the marsh more clearly. "I can see why you like living here."

"I love everything about this place and always have. My earliest and fondest memories are of the summers I spent here with my parents. Actually, my father only came down here on weekends since he worked in Boston, but my mother and I spent hours together—walking the beach, horseback riding, playing tennis. And when my father did get here, we'd go sailing or have big cookouts for all the neighbors. Of course, the highlight of our summer was always the garden party we'd attend up at Crane castle. It was always such an incredibly lavish affair with famous and interesting people to meet. Do you know, I once played a game of croquet with President Woodrow Wilson?"

Anne suddenly caught herself. "I'm sorry. I do get carried away once I start talking about this place."

"It's all right," Karl assured her, smiling wanly. "It's reassuring to know there are people in this world who had a happy childhood. But who are the Cranes that the President of the United States would attend one of their parties?"

"Well, Mr. Crane is one of the wealthiest men in the country. His family owns a huge company that sells plumbing supplies, or something like that, all over the world. The Cranes live most of the year in Chicago, that's where the company headquarters is. I'm really surprised you've never heard of them."

"My family doesn't move in those circles," Karl answered wryly.

Anne apparently missed the sarcasm in his response for she went right on talking.

"So the Crane family owns this gorgeous estate right up there on Castle Hill. They spend all summer there. It really is an amazing place. There are literally acres of terraced gardens, a massive lawn that stretches from the Great House all the way to the ocean, and an outdoor swimming pool large enough to accommodate half the town of Ipswich. Well, I'm exaggerating a little there. I'll have to take you up and show you the place sometime."

There I go again, she thought to herself. Why do I keep doing that? I'm sure by this time he's certain I'm going to rent the apartment to him.

It was Karl himself who let her off the hook by changing the subject.

"So, you live here all alone?" he asked.

She couldn't believe she was telling a complete stranger that she lived alone in such an isolated location, but it was after all the reason she was even talking to him.

"Yes, I do live alone, or at least I do at the moment. Unfortunately, I'm just not sure I'll be able to stay here unless I can find someone to help me around the place. And with the war on, finding such a person is just about impossible."

"But you do have family, don't you?" He didn't let on he knew about the death of her husband.

"My parents are both alive, although they're old and in poor health. They live in Boston. I have a son, but he's away at college, and destined shortly for the navy. As for my husband, he died a couple of years ago so in response to your question, no, there are no family members to help me with the place."

"I'm sorry to hear about your husband," was all Karl could think to say.

Anne did not respond, nor did Karl notice any overt reaction.

When finally she did speak it was as if she hadn't heard his last comment.

"I'm most worried about the winter down here. If we have a heavy snowstorm I could never shovel out the driveway even if the town does keep Argilla Road open so people can get to work at the shipyard. That's the main reason why I placed the ad in the newspaper."

She realized she was selling him on the apartment again. But standing here, she also knew she wouldn't be able to handle the place on her own, and the man next to her, if nothing else, looked capable of doing physical labor. The decision, she realized fully enough, was not that simple. For one thing, she could just imagine what the townspeople would say about her having a young man living at her place and the news of it would spread quickly. And, then, there was her son, what would he think? She highly doubted he'd approve; he'd probably be even more suspicious than the townspeople. As for herself, she wasn't certain of anything, much less her own emotions.

Anne was relieved when Karl roused her from her thoughts by asking to see the apartment.

"Yes, of course. This way," she replied, directing him towards a flight of stairs that ran up the side of the barn. The barn was situated on the north side of the oval-shaped driveway. It had been painted red with black doors and trim but that had clearly been some time ago. In the years since the harsh New England winters had served to mute the barn's colors and give it a worn, deeply weathered appearance. The apartment was located at the east end of the barn above the garage. The doors of the garage were open revealing an old black pick-up truck and an assortment of rakes, pitchforks, and scythes hanging on the back wall. At the other end of the barn were the stables and above them a hayloft. A handsome Morgan horse eyed them curiously from an adjoining paddock.

Anne walked up the stairs ahead of Karl and opened the door. Stepping in she warned, "I'm afraid it's going to be a little hot in here. It's been closed up for some time and I totally forgot to come up here and open any of the windows."

Karl, who had stopped on the landing to take another view of the marshes, reassured her it was no problem.

Entering what appeared to be the kitchen, Karl was surprised by the comfortable and well-maintained feel to the place. The walls had been painted a shade of soft white that contrasted nicely with the hardwood floors and cabinets over the sink. There was a large black stove, with an adjoining hot-water heater that appeared to be fueled by kerosene, and a fairly large icebox. Adjacent to the window, which looked out over the driveway, was a table with a couple chairs drawn up to it. To the right a doorway led into what was obviously the bedroom. It, too, was simply but comfortably furnished. There was a small bureau with a mirror and a substantial bed over which hung an old oil painting entitled Louisburg Square in Winter. The bedroom had its own wooden stove and through an open door Karl could see a bathroom with a toilet and small shower stall. It was clearly not your typical rental unit.

"Unfortunately, you'll have to put some kind of blackout curtains over the windows if you plan to use lights at night, which I assume you would; it's now required, though for the life of me I can't remember if we're worried about German submarines or German airplanes."

"Submarines," Karl replied matter-of-factly. "At the moment the Germans don't have aircraft capable of reaching America."

"Oh," she replied simply, then added, "I'm glad one of us keeps up on the news. So, back to business; what do you think of the apartment?"

"I'm impressed," said Karl, after completing his inspection. "So what would I be expected to do in exchange for such accommodations?"

"Whatever needs doing," she replied. "It might be snow shoveling, cutting wood for the fireplaces, keeping the lawns mowed, general maintenance around the house; whatever comes up."

"I'd have no trouble with that," he answered casually. But, in fact, the set-up was perfect for the plan that was beginning to take shape in his mind. "And since it appears I'll probably be working one of the night shifts, I should have plenty of time during the day to do whatever you need done. So, when can I move in?"

Anne had been anticipating this moment ever since she first met him and had found herself unable to tell him she'd changed her mind about renting the apartment. She was caught; she didn't know what to say. Of course, he had been the first person to call so there was good reason for delaying the decision for a couple more days. Perhaps someone else would contact her. On the other hand, it was also possible that no one would call and in the meantime he might find another place to live. And, she had to honestly admit, he appeared perfect for the job; she just wished he weren't so young and good-looking. What should she do? Dare she take a chance with him?

Sensing her indecision, Karl said, "Look, I really need a place to live and if it's an issue, I'd be happy to pay rent. I have money. I'm not penniless."

After a brief pause during which her instincts warned her to be careful, Anne replied, "No, money won't be necessary, it's the help around the place I need. The apartment is yours. You may move in anytime."

There, she'd made her decision. She could only hope the whole thing would work out. In the meantime she'd have to come up with an explanation for his living here that wouldn't create a scandal. Oh, God, she thought, what had she just done?

Karl, on the other hand, was greatly relieved. He couldn't believe his luck. In less than a week he had not only found a job working at the largest shipyard in the immediate area, but he'd also found a convenient place to live. Even more amazing, his landlord was a single woman living alone; it was the perfect cover.

"I really appreciate it," he said, giving her a reassuring smile.

At that moment Anne needed all the reassurance she could get. She was convinced she had just made the biggest mistake of her life. Unfortunately, it was too late now to do anything about it. She would just have to pray that everything would work out all right.

It was nearly six when Anne finally dropped Karl back in town. They had agreed he would move into the apartment the following day. As he walked up Market Street in the direction of the hotel, Karl spotted a sign for the Ideal Grille diagonally across the street from him. It wasn't an especially impressive-looking place, but as he drew nearer he saw the words "Good food at reasonable prices" printed on the window. For the moment that was enough for him.

On this evening the restaurant was anything but busy. Karl could see only three other diners, all of them sitting at the long counter. Taking one of the empty stools, he grabbed a well-thumbed menu wedged between a napkin dispenser and a pair of salt and peppershakers. The counter-man, a skinny guy wearing a dirty white apron and badly in need of a shave, slid a cup of coffee over to him. His fingers, Karl noticed, were yellowed with nicotine stains, not exactly an encouraging sign. Screwing up his courage, Karl ordered the day's special, a sliced-chicken sandwich, a bag of potato chips and a drink.

As he sipped his coffee, he gradually became aware of the jukebox playing at the far end of the room. Some guy was crooning about losing his heart at the stage-door canteen. For some reason it made him start thinking about his mission and of Thomas, his partner who had been badly bitten by the dog on the beach. He wondered where he was? Probably still on the U-boat, he decided? How he must be dreading that. And what of the other members of the operation, had they all made it safely ashore? They were an unimpressive lot. It was possible they hadn't all made it across the Atlantic; U-boats were being sunk every day even though those carrying Abwehr agents were supposed to stay away from the main convoy routes, where America had concentrated it's anti-submarine forces. If they didn't make it that was one thing; what worried him was if they had been captured coming ashore for they would almost certainly give away the operation, including his possible location.

Just then the waiter came with his sandwich, which looked surprisingly good. He quickly decided that just about anything was going to look good after the kind of food he was forced to eat on the submarine.

It was still light when Karl came out of the restaurant; the streets, however, were nearly deserted. Most stores closed at six and the evening workers at Sylvania were already two hours into their shift. The only people Karl could see appeared to be headed for the Strand Theater where a line was gradually forming at the ticket window. According to the marquee the movie showing that evening was "To the Shores of Tripoli" starring John Payne and Maureen O'Hara. Karl had heard of Maureen O'Hara and just briefly thought about buying a ticket to see the movie. For whatever reason, he decided against it and kept walking towards his hotel. It was a decision he would soon regret.

Approaching Depot Square Karl was suddenly reminded of the enlisted men living in the Damon Building by the noise coming through the windows; they were obviously back from the day's training. Typically, if he were returning to the hotel at this hour he would approach it from the other direction to avoid bumping into any of them. But, since he didn't see any of them on the sidewalk he decided it was probably safe enough to walk past their quarters. And anyway, it was still far too early for them to have been doing any serious drinking.

Unfortunately, just as he was passing the entrance to the hotel, four young men strode down the steps and onto the sidewalk blocking his way. His instincts immediately warned him to be careful. The four were arguing animatedly among themselves and, at least, initially appeared to take no notice of him. But as he moved to step around them, the largest of the four suddenly separated from the group and placed himself directly in Karl's path.

"Going somewhere, Polack," he taunted.

He was about Karl's size and actually lighter in complexion and hair-color. Karl couldn't for the life-of-him figure out why the man might think him Polish except for the fact a number of Polish families lived in that part of town.

Karl said nothing and, in fact, stepped off the curb in an effort to avoid the confrontation he suspected was coming. The man did the same, continuing to taunt him as he did so.

"How about going home and bringing your sister down here. Living in this poor-excuse-of-a-town she would probably enjoy a good time and we're just the kind of guys to give it to her."

His three companions laughed but they did so nervously, seeming to instinctively sense what their friend did not--that Karl was not someone to anger. For whatever reason, possibly boredom or prejudice or simple ignorance, their friend seemed determined to start a fight and they were not about to stop him, especially since the odds favored him.

Had his taunts been only verbal, Karl would have let them go unchallenged. He had already concluded the man possessed more the surface toughness of a barroom brawler than the guile and ruthlessness of one trained in hand-to-hand combat. And, as if to prove him correct, the man clumsily stepped forward and began poking Karl in the chest, not once but several times, hoping all the while to get some kind of reaction out of him. He was still poking him, in fact, when Karl did exactly what the guy was trying to get him to do, except he reacted with such suddenness that Karl himself would have difficulty remembering whether his decision to attack was conscious or entirely reflexive. Later he would decide it was the latter, that he was only doing what he had been trained to do in such circumstances. After all, getting involved in a fight was not in his best interests.

Nevertheless, Karl grasped the outstretched arm and in a single motion twisted it behind the man's back with such violence that the upper arm disconnected from the shoulder joint. Simultaneously, Karl struck the man's neck a vicious blow with the edge of his open hand. The man crumpled to the ground and lay unconscious without ever having uttered a cry of pain.

The suddenness of Karl's response served momentarily to freeze the other three, but only momentarily. One of them now rushed blindly forward, lowering his head as if to tackle Karl. Before he could make contact, however, Karl's right foot lashed out catching the attacker squarely in the face shattering his nose and sending blood flying in all directions. But Karl wasn't finished. Grabbing the front of the bleeding man's shirt, he pulled him forward while driving his knee into the man's groin. The man let out a gasp and fell to the sidewalk, gathering himself into a fetal position while moaning loudly.

Karl glanced quickly at the other two recruits, just to be certain they didn't want a piece of him as well. He needn't have worried. They wanted no part of Karl, at least for the moment. Fortunately, for Karl the entire episode had taken only a minute or so for he quickly realized that reinforcements could start pouring out the door at any moment. Without a word, he turned and headed for the hotel, though he was careful not to go directly in. He had to assume he was being watched so he walked around the corner, then doubled back and entered the hotel by the rear door. He was safe but for how long he couldn't be sure.

Chapter Eleven

Eddie had just stretched out on the couch to listen to the evening news when the kitchen phone rang. Having come off duty only an hour before, he was inclined to ignore it, but too late he heard his mother pick up the receiver. She seldom did that when he was home, preferring to let him answer; she could tell he was tired. Just my luck tonight, he thought, as he heard her call out, "Edjoo, it's for you." There was not another person in the world that still called him Edjoo now that both his father and brother were gone. It was Sergeant Bradford on the phone.

"I'm really sorry to bother you at home, boss, but I just got a call reporting a fight up at Depot Square. Apparently a couple of the Southern boys got themselves beaten up pretty good. Not sure yet who the guy is that did it, though the caller thought he might be staying at the Hayes Hotel."

"So, you're pretty sure it wasn't just a fight among the recruits themselves, right," Eddie responded. It wasn't that he doubted Mike, he only wanted to be absolutely certain before he dragged himself out of the house.

"Afraid not," Mike replied. "The guy who did it appears to have been a civilian though no one seems to know who he is. Anyway, I've sent Smitty up to investigate. I'll let you know what he found out when he gets back. I only called to keep you informed; I know how hard you've worked to keep peace between the townspeople and those recruits up there."

"I'm glad you called, Mike, thanks. However, I think I'd better

71

go down and check things out for myself just in case. I'm curious now about the guy you say may have done this. I suspect more than a few people in town would like to see him get a medal or something. I'll check in with you later."

Karl was certain he had placed the entire operation in jeopardy. By getting into this fight he had broken the first commandment of espionage: Don't do anything to draw unnecessary attention to yourself and especially do nothing that would give the authorities cause to examine your documents. So, here he was, waiting very probably for the police to come and arrest him. How could he be such an idiot to let that guy bait him into a fight?

As he lit a cigarette, a sure sign he reminded himself he was feeling anxious, he wondered what the police might charge him with. He was certain they couldn't tie him to the killing of that Coast Guardsman. If those guys from the U-boat did what they were supposed to do, there wouldn't even be a body yet, if ever. Now, the police might discover his papers were forged, but to do so would require quite a bit of checking and he doubted a local police department would have the means of doing so. They'd probably have to call in the FBI and they'd be very reluctant to do that without good reason. No, the worst they could get him on was assault, he concluded, and even that would require someone to press charges. Maybe his training in the law was about to come in handy, though it hadn't touched on the American legal system except in passing.

His confidence was slowly returning when he was startled by a loud knock on the door. Slipping quietly off the bed, he looked about unsuccessfully for something with which to defend himself. It was entirely possible some of the recruits from next door may have discovered where he was staying. He cursed himself for having left his gun at the beach, though he realized that adding a homicide to his evening's activities, even in self-defense, would hardly strengthen his case.

"Who is it," he barked, hoping that his aggressive tone might give any would-be attackers second thoughts. Thinking back to the stupidity of the guys who attacked him, he doubted it would.

"The police," answered a non-threatening voice. "We'd like to speak with you for just a moment. Open the door, please."

Karl had already rejected the notion of running away. It would be tantamount to terminating the mission. His best hope, he had decided, was to act like the victim and bluff his way through.

Karl opened the door cautiously. A blonde-haired man who looked to be about his own age stood in the doorway; he was dressed casually. Behind him, however, was a uniformed policeman whose hand, Karl noticed, rested comfortably on the handle of his still holstered .38 caliber Smith & Weston.

"Are you Karl Stoner," the blonde guy asked in a manner that was neither friendly nor adversarial.

"That depends on who you are," Karl responded cautiously.

"My name is Eddie Sawaski; I'm the police chief here in town. And, this is Sergeant Smith. We'd like to ask you a couple questions about a fight that took place outside here earlier tonight. May we come in?"

Karl stepped back for them to enter. Until he heard what they had to say he would neither admit to nor deny a thing.

"We got your name, by the way, from Pete down at the front desk. He also told us you've been living here for three days. Is that correct?"

Karl nodded, but remained silent.

"We have good reason to believe that you were one of those involved in that fight. In fact, that looks like dried blood on your shirt and unless you tell me you cut yourself shaving, I'll conclude it probably belongs to one of the guys you did a job on."

Someone had obviously seen him and reported him to the police so, he decided, there was probably nothing to be gained by pretending he wasn't the guy they were looking for.

Eddie stared at him for a moment, then continued, "These Southern boys are always getting into fights. Fortunately, most of them are with each other and when that happens it's the military's problem, not mine. However, when the fight involves a civilian, then it becomes my problem. So that's the only reason why I'm here."

"They started the fight," Karl replied matter-of-factly. "In fact, I did my best to avoid the whole thing but they were obviously looking for trouble from the moment they came out of that hotel. It was the bigger of the two guys who put his hands on me first, and you'll enjoy the irony of this, Chief Sawaski, is it? He called me a Polack and invited me to bring my sister over for a good time."

"Yeah, I can imagine that must have really annoyed the hell out of you," said Eddie sarcastically. But, he also detected the slight accent in Karl's speech, though that didn't mean much these days. What with the war on it seemed that only a minority of Ipswich residents spoke with the flat Boston accent so common to the region.

"So, let's get back to the fight. To be honest, I don't really give a damn that you knocked the crap out of these guys. I'm even prepared to believe they probably deserved it. I also suspect that for a host of reasons, not the least of which is that they'd be too embarrassed to do it, they won't press charges. I'm just here to make certain you have no plans to do so."

"I hadn't really thought about it," answered Karl. In fact, it was the furthest thing from his mind, but he suddenly realized it was a chance to strengthen the impression he had nothing to hide from the authorities.

"My advice to you is don't; just leave well enough alone," replied Eddie sharply. "Oh, and one more thing. Just out of curiosity where did you learn to fight like that? From what I can see you got barely a scratch, while apparently both of them needed medical treatment."

Karl was not surprised by the question; he rather welcomed, in fact. If he answered right, it might even enhance his cover story.

"The streets of Chicago; it's a tough city. Growing up out there was, what should I say, very different from growing up in a small town like this."

Karl was watching Eddie closely and he could tell the police chief was not entirely buying his answer. He decided to give him a little more to think about.

"And, yeah, if you're wondering, I did have some training," Karl continued. "I had TB when I was a kid and the doctors told me if I wanted to lead a normal life I'd better build myself up. I spent a lotta time at the gym--took up boxing, though only as a hobby; I never fought professionally. I probably could have."

Eddie remained silent and outwardly, at least, appeared to accept Karl's explanation. Starting for the door, he stopped and turned back towards Karl.

"Let me give you some advice. Either get out of town, or at least find yourself another place to live. These Southern boys will be laying for you and sooner or later they'll catch you when the odds are on their side."

"The odds were on their side," replied Karl smugly. "There were four of them, remember?"

But his answer was wasted. Eddie and Sergeant Smith had already closed the door behind them and were heading down the hallway.

Eddie and the sergeant had also used the rear door to avoid attracting the attention of the recruits. Glancing cautiously around the corner Eddie could see a large number of them either milling around on the sidewalk or sitting atop a couple of military vehicles that were parked in front of their quarters. Across the street another group could be seen over by the Diner restaurant. Eddie was certain there wasn't one of them who hadn't already heard about the fight.

"You know," said Eddie ruefully, "it might have been a lot better for us if those four Southern boys had actually beaten up that guy upstairs, and not just because I don't like him. But at least they'd be lying low right now. As it is, they're all out here looking for some kind of revenge and what I'm worried about is that they're going to jump the first high school kid who wanders into this part of town. Until tempers cool a bit we'd better cordon off the square each evening and keep the townspeople as far away from this area as possible. God, I can't wait to get these guys out of here and into their barracks over at Camp Agawam. In the meantime, I guess I'd better go and tidy things up with the base commander. See you in the morning."

Chapter Twelve

The next several days passed quickly for Karl. He had moved out of the hotel the morning after the fight, delaying his departure only long enough for the recruits to be trucked out to their training areas. Anne had met him up town, and after giving him a chance to purchase a few food items, had driven him back to her home. By late in the afternoon Karl was settled in and, for the first time in several days, had a chance to simply relax. He thumbed through a couple of old magazines he found in the kitchen, made himself something to eat, had a couple beers, and finally went in and sprawled on the bed.

As he lay there, he could hear the rumble of thunder in the distance. Watching his room darken with the approaching storm Karl found himself thinking about his aunt back in Chicago. For five years she had been like a mother to him, a lot better than his real one. He didn't have to wonder what she would think if she learned of his mission; she'd be crushed and would do everything in her power to dissuade him from going through with it. While she was fiercely proud of being German, she was an American now and in her own way probably even more proud of that. Not for a moment would it occur to her that Karl might feel differently. After all, the Germany she had originally left behind was a defeated, dismembered nation plagued by poverty, hunger and unemployment. That's why she had immigrated to American and later had eagerly taken Karl in for those five years. And, though they had never talked about it, he knew she would never share his view that whatever one might say about some of Hitler's policies, he had restored Germany's pride by rebuilding it into one of the world's most powerful nations. No, his aunt would never understand that; she was an American now and he was pretty sure she shared America's dislike of everything Hitler stood for.

The rumbling of thunder was growing steadily louder while the flashes of lightning illuminating his room had become brighter and more regular. Karl found the storm strangely comforting and he fell into an uneasy sleep just as the first raindrops began to rattle against the windows. Too soon he found himself dreaming that he was walking at night along the water's edge of a deserted beach when all at once the sound of gunfire erupted around him. He couldn't tell whether the person was shooting at him or not, but he decided to run anyway. Suddenly, he literally stumbled upon a body lying directly in his path. Staring down at the ghostly, white face he noticed something strangely familiar about it. And, then, it struck him, he was looking at the same face that greeted him every morning in the mirror; it was his face he was staring at.

He awoke with a start, his shirt soaked with sweat from the now oppressive heat. After what he had experienced on the beach the dream didn't completely surprise him, but the fact that it was his body lying there left him uncertain. Was it a premonition of some kind or should he simply interpret it as a bad dream? He felt a slight shiver ripple down his spine. Closing his eyes he tried to go back to sleep but it proved impossible. All he could picture was that ghostly white face.

The following day Karl began work at the shipyard. He had taken the four to midnight shift since that would enable him to get a good night's sleep and still have most of the day free to complete whatever jobs Anne had in mind for him. An old bicycle that he found hanging up in the barn became his chief means of getting back and forth to the shipyard. And, though, it was only a three-mile round trip, there was no shortage of challenges. For one thing the bicycle wobbled badly because of the way he had been forced to patch one of the tires. Buying a new tire was out of the question; rubber had been one of the very first materials rationed by the government. Then, there was his trip home at midnight when he had to ride in almost total darkness because of the absence of streetlights. A small lamp on his handlebars provided the only light available to him for most of the trip. There was, of course, the illumination from the other workers' autos, but due to wartime restrictions even they had to drive with only parking lights on. As for the road, it was so narrow and covered with such loose gravel that he had to be careful not to skid into the bushes whenever he moved to the side for a passing car. Yet, in spite of all this Karl found the ride home the most relaxing part of his day. Whether it was just the silence that engulfed him or the bracing smell of the salt air, whatever it was, it had the effect of clearing his mind and sharpening his thoughts.

The shipyard proved an unexpected surprise to Karl. For one thing it was much larger than he had expected, though nothing, of course, like the huge shipyards he had visited in Kiel and Bremerhaven. There were nearly five hundred employees at the shipyard and rumor had it that number was expected to increase by another hundred before the end of the year. The owner of the shipyard, William Robinson, had negotiated a number of contracts with the War Department for the construction of several types of vessels including submarine chasers, minesweepers, landing barges, diving tenders, and sea-going tugs. To fulfill these commitments Robinson had assembled the finest collection of ship designers and builders the region had to offer. Without question, then, it provided a tempting target.

The shipyard itself occupied a four-acre tract of marshland on the banks of Fox Creek, a shallow man-made canal connecting the Essex and Ipswich rivers. There were approximately a dozen structures crowded together within the yard's fenced enclosure of which about half were construction sheds. These sheds were fairly large, laid out parallel to one another with slips that stretched down to the water's edge. They were constructed of prefabricated steel and covered with corrugated galvanized metal, which made them like ovens under the blazing July sun. Often, it was not until well into the evening that working in them became bearable.

The construction of ships at the yard was an assembly-line operation. Keels were laid within the large sheds and work continued until the outer structure was complete. At this point the vessel was hauled outside where its construction was completed. In the meantime, a new keel was being laid, usually for the same type of craft, and the process would be repeated. When a vessel was ready for launch, a crew would be sent by the navy to take it out for trials. This was typically done at night so as not to draw the attention of any German U-boat lurking offshore.

Karl was assigned to work on landing craft tanks, or LCTs as they were most commonly known. These were large barges, nearly 120-feet long, and made of iron. They were used for ferrying cargo from naval warships to shore. The Mk5 built at Robinson's shipyard was modeled after a British version of the LCT. It housed a twelve-man crew, plus one officer, and was capable of carrying four 40-ton tanks or 150 tons of cargo ashore. Though powered by three 225-horse-power diesel engines it weighed nearly three hundred tons so it could manage little more than seven knots. It was also lightly armed with only one 20-mm anti-aircraft and two 50-cal. machine guns for protection. Since at the time of the attack on Pearl Harbor the navy had almost no amphibious landing craft, shipyards like Robinson's were under enormous pressure to turn out LCTs as fast as they could.

On his first day of work Karl learned he was to become a welder, though he'd made clear he knew absolutely nothing about it. To handle his education he was apprenticed to a master welder, a gregarious Irishman named Tom O'Malley, to whom he took an instant liking. In short order Karl discovered that Tom was also a heavy smoker and very possibly an alcoholic as well. By his own admission Tom claimed to spend most afternoons drinking at Russell's Tavern and by the time he arrived at work he was often in no shape to operate an acetylene torch whose flame could reach 5500 degrees Fahrenheit. Fortunately for him, Karl had picked up the art of welding effortlessly so was able to cover for him whenever he showed up unable to work. The Friday evening shift inevitably proved too much for Tom. Since it was the last shift before the weekend, a number of workers had taken to smuggling liquor bottles in with their dinner pails. These bottles were passed around freely and typically by the time they were empty, Tom had passed out. Tom's friends appreciated the fact that Karl looked after him. For that reason they would have been shocked and amazed if someone had told then that Karl was planning to use Tom's Friday drinking habits to shut down the shipyard.

With whatever free time he had, Karl roamed about the shipyard gathering every bit of information he could on its layout as well as its various security procedures. The yard, he quickly discovered, was surrounded on all but the waterside by a six-foot chain-link fence crowned by several strands of barbwire. There was only a single entrance to the yard with a gatehouse that was manned twenty-four hours a day. Although anyone entering the shipyard was required to show proper identification, Karl noted the guards were fairly lax in enforcing this regulation. Family members faced little difficulty entering and leaving the yard, as did most regular deliverymen. As for the security guards themselves, they were generally older men, World War I veterans in many cases, he guessed, and lightly armed. While most seemed to favor the .38 caliber police special, he noted there was at least one double-barrel shotgun stored in the guardhouse.

But the looseness of security was not the only thing Karl found surprising--the shipyard was also totally unprepared for a major fire. As far as he could determine, there was only a single hydrant and one very ancient fire truck to handle any contingency. He concluded it was a miracle that there hadn't already been a fire what with so much debris and wood shavings scattered about, not to mention the carelessness of workers like Tom O'Malley. And if a fire did get started Karl suspected it would quickly engulf the tightly concentrated shipbuilding sheds long before firemen from uptown could ever respond. So, that's what he would do, create an explosion and fire; it would not be as spectacular as the explosion and fire that nearly destroyed Halifax in 1917 when an ammunition ship blew up in the harbor, nor would it cripple America's war effort, but it would frighten people and make it clear to them that Germany was a force to be reckoned with. What more could he do? Working alone, there were very definite limits to what he could accomplish, and he had no intention of bringing anyone else into his plans.

As his first week drew to a close Karl found himself caught up in an unusual and highly ironic situation. Picking up his paycheck, he was asked if he would like to have money automatically deducted from his salary towards the purchase of war bonds. Though his immediate reaction had been to decline, he quickly changed his mind when he learned that the owner had set a goal of one hundred percent participation by the shipyard's employees. He worried that if he ended up being the only employee not to purchase war bonds, it might draw unnecessary questions, most obviously, why he had chosen not to buy them. As it turned out, his decision was a wise one since by mid-July one hundred percent participation was achieved. Ruefully, Karl decided he might just be the most patriotic American in the ranks of the Abwehr.

When Karl was not at the shipyard he spent most of his waking hours working around Anne's place, where initially, at least, there was plenty to do. With the exception of a few little things she had managed to accomplish on her own, no serious maintenance had been done since her son had left for college over a year before. Karl began by cutting up a number of large trees that had come down during a hurricane the previous year. A few actually pre-dated the infamous "hurricane of thirty-eight," which local residents still talked about as if it had happened only months rather than several years before.

During his first few weeks living and working there Karl saw little of Anne. Other than asking him to do various tasks, they exchanged few words. She seemed to him to have a fairly active social life. He knew Anne frequently took the train to Boston because she generally informed him whenever she was going to do so. She also had a number of women friends who dropped by fairly often. They usually sat on the screened porch and, judging from the laughter and furtive glances, he was clearly one of their favorite topics of conversation; he even began to wonder if he was one of the reasons they came by so regularly. He had to admit, they were an attractive group of women.

In addition to her social life, there was also a steady procession of tradesmen who had to be dealt with---the Cushman baker, the milkman, and the vegetable man; there was even a man who sold bananas. And, of course, there was the iceman; he came two or three times a week depending on the weather to replenish her icebox as well as the one in Karl's own apartment. The only obviously missing element in her life appeared to be a man and for such an attractive woman Karl found this unusually strange.

When she wasn't in Boston or with friends she would spend most sunny days working in her flower and vegetable gardens and riding her favorite Morgan whom Karl suspected must have recently thrown her. He had noticed Anne limping badly for a few days after her last ride. Karl didn't ask her about it and she volunteered nothing. It remained a very formal relationship. Still, when she was puttering about the place Karl couldn't help occasionally casting a glance her way. Like her friends, she was a very attractive woman and on those hot summer days when she went around in very short shorts, he couldn't help but admire her long, shapely legs and well-rounded hips. He also began to suspect she was aware he was watching her.

Early one afternoon as he was replacing one of the fence posts for the paddock, he saw Anne heading his way. Approaching him, she asked if he'd be willing to go up town with her to pick up several bags of grain for the horse. He realized that he hadn't been in town since the day after the fight so it was probably a good time to once again show his face. There was also the possibility that the recruits had left the hotel and were now restricted to their base just outside of town.

"I'd be glad to. I could use a change of scenery," he responded with a smile.

"We'll need to use the pick-up truck in the barn. I haven't used it for weeks so I'm not even sure whether it will start. If it does, would you be willing to drive? I hate driving it."

"Of course. Just let me run in and wash up before we go."

He had no difficulty getting the truck running, though he did have to clean several months' worth of dust off the seats and dashboard. Within a few minutes they were on their way.

Driving along Argilla Road Karl thought back to the night he had been put ashore on Crane's Beach and how he had traveled this road to get up town. It had been an unsettling experience, in large part because the area had seemed so foreign to him. Now, it almost felt like home.

Anne must have sensed his mind was elsewhere.

"A penny for your thoughts," she said with a smile.

"Oh, I'm sorry," he stammered. "It was nothing."

She blushed slightly. He wondered if just maybe she thought he had been thinking of her.

"I was wondering how you thought the arrangement was working out," she asked.

"Arrangement?" Karl replied, knowing very well what she meant.

"Yes, you know, the apartment and the work I ask you to do for me."

Again she seemed slightly embarrassed.

"Oh, that. It's working out fine. I just hope you're satisfied with it," he added, glancing over at her.

"Oh, I am. Very satisfied. It just seems like it might be rather a lonely existence for you. You almost never get to town, though I can't say if you did there would be much to do there. Ipswich is not a very exciting place under the best of circumstances."

It was the closest she had ever come to asking him anything personal other than the few perfunctory questions she had raised at their initial meeting. She was a curious woman, thought Karl. Until now at least, she had kept an almost public distance from him, yet she appeared to be a very warm and friendly person with just about everyone else, including the deliverymen. Was she afraid of opening up to him? It was possible, of course, someone had told her about the two men he had beaten up. It was, after all, a very small town and news undoubtedly traveled fast.

"No, it's not that lonely," he finally responded. "I get plenty of time to socialize at the shipyard. The fact is I've never been a very social person. I guess I'm really something of a loner."

But, she was right; it did get lonely at times. That was an inevitable aspect of his job. Of course, compared to the fighting on the Eastern Front, his job was easy, so easy in fact it was beginning to make him feel more than a bit guilty. For that reason alone he had to move ahead with his plan. Perhaps once he had done so he could begin to feel he was making some small contribution to the war effort. If there were one thing he had no doubts about it was that Germany could not afford to lose this war as it had the last one.

Neither spoke. He guessed she would have liked to continue the conversation but wasn't really sure what to say. She was still uncomfortable around him and for the moment that was fine with him; it was probably in his best interest to do nothing to change that.

Chapter Thirteen

Mike Bradford was engaged in two of his favorite pastimes when the phone on Eddie Sawaski's desk began ringing—having a cigarette and daydreaming. Annoyed at the interruption, Mike slowly pushed himself out of his chair and made his way over to answer it. Picking up the receiver, he glanced up at the clock on the wall, just in case the call had to be logged; the clock showed the time as one thirty-five. In point of fact, it was actually two thirty-five but no one had ever bothered to reset the clock to Daylight Savings Time. It would have required a stepladder to reset it, and anyway, as Mike constantly reminded Eddie, all a person had to do was add an hour to whatever time was showing on the clock. An idiot could do that.

"Ipswich Police Department, Sergeant Bradford speaking." The usual cigarette was hanging from the corner of his mouth.

"Yes, Sergeant Bradford, this is Mack McCarthy from the FBI office in Boston. Is the chief in?"

At the sound of Mack's voice Mike involuntarily snapped to attention.

"No, he isn't," he replied crisply. "He's somewhere downtown. Can I take a message?"

"Yes, I'd like to pass along some information that just came across my desk. It might, and I emphasize the word might, have some bearing on the case of the young Coast Guardsman who was reported missing up there."

"Let's have it," answered Mike, desperately looking for an ashtray in which to snuff out his cigarette. "As you know we haven't had much luck at this end of things. We've interviewed everyone presently living along Argilla Road but haven't found anything that sounds related to this case."

"Well, this may just have some relevance. It appears that two possible German spies were picked up in the vicinity of Norfolk Naval Base in Virginia. They were carrying forged papers, though damn good ones, and a sizable amount of American money. Hoover himself will be holding a press conference later today to announce the arrests. It will be on the radio so you might want to listen to it. Don't expect many details though. The only thing you'll really learn is that the Nazis are no match for America's G-men," he laughed. "But, then, you already knew that."

"So, how did you guys catch them?" Mike asked eagerly.

"Naturally, I'd like to say it was brilliant investigative work on the part of the Bureau," Mack replied, "but, it was more like dumb luck with the emphasis on the dumb. Someone called the local police to report that two suspicious-looking people were hanging around the entrance to the navy base; the police in turn alerted us. Of course, since the war began we've been getting literally hundreds of these kinds of reports. Most of the time it turns out to be nothing, but in this case the report actually panned out and we now have the two possible spies sitting in the DC jail. To be precise, there's only one there since the other was severely wounded trying to escape and is in the hospital. It's doubtful he's going to make it."

"What do you think will happen to them? I mean, I know they'll go to prison, but will they be executed or something?" Mike couldn't help feeling just a bit excited. To be actually working with the FBI on a case, and not just any case, but one involving German spies, was an entirely new experience for him. For that matter, it was an entirely new experience for everyone on the Ipswich police force. Auto accidents or the occasional house break-in were their usual fare; neither he nor most of his fellow officers had ever drawn their guns with the intent to use them.

"Many of the details have yet to be worked out, but if President Roosevelt gets his way, the trial will be held as soon as possible. The big question right now is whether they should be tried in a civil court or military court."

"Why would they be tried in a military court? They couldn't have been that dumb to be wearing German military uniforms when they were arrested, were they," Mike asked, a little confused.

"No, they were wearing civilian clothes all right, but this wouldn't be the first time civilians have been tried in a military court. The guy who shot Lincoln, what was his name, Booth... John Wilkes Booth, well anyway, he was tried before a military court. Apparently there are some definite advantages from Washington's point-of-view. For one thing prosecutors can almost guarantee the death penalty, something that can't be done in a civil case. And furthermore, they don't have to put up with so much arguing over legal technicalities, which leads to a much quicker trial."

"Makes sense," Mike agreed. "So what about the guy in jail, has he been questioned yet?"

"Yes, he has," Mack replied, "and this is where the story gets even more interesting. Though we haven't had time enough to corroborate his story, he claims to have been brought to the US by submarine."

"Ahh, "exclaimed Mike jumping in, "so you're thinking maybe a German submarine dropped a couple of spies off at Crane's Beach and that in coming ashore these guys may have killed our Coast Guardsman, right?"

"Exactly," Mack responded. "Of course, it's a long shot, but it's the best scenario we've come up with so far for what may have happened to the Coast Guardsman; actually, it's the only scenario we've been able to come up with so far."

"Look, I don't mean to downplay your theory but I've fished the waters off the beach all my life and there's no way a submarine could operate in them. Ipswich Bay is really shallow and it's filled with sandbars that shift with every storm. They'd have to have incredibly detailed and up-to-date hydrographic charts to get in there."

"Believe me, if such charts exist the Germans could get them; they have no shortage of agents working in this country and it's been that way for years. In fact, German agents are responsible for the worst case of wartime sabotage in US history. You're probably too young to remember, but back in July of 1916 agents working for the German government blew up the munitions depot on Black Tom Island in New York harbor. There were several million pounds of ammunition and explosives stored on barges and freight cars awaiting shipment to England and France. That's what they wanted to stop, and they did! Apparently the blast was so powerful it could be felt out in western Massachusetts. I remember it because it got me to thinking for the first time about enlisting, though I was too young at that moment. Perhaps more importantly, it played a big part in the passage of the Federal Espionage Act of 1917, the very act we'll be using to prosecute these guys. But, you know, even without the guys Hitler is sending over, there's no shortage of sympathizers here more than willing to do his bidding."

"Well, you've certainly made your point, Mack. I'll make sure the chief gets this information and thanks. As for us, we'll keep digging to see what we can come up with."

As Mike hung up the phone, Officer Smith came through the door.

"Hey Smitty, you wanna cover the phone for a few minutes," Mike asked. "I gotta go find the chief."

New England was in the midst of its first real heat wave of the summer. Temperatures, which had been hovering in the high seventies to low eighties all week, were now expected to reach the low- to mid-nineties by the up-coming July Fourth weekend. In the past, such temperatures would have delighted the local merchants because they would have drawn thousands of tourists to the region's beaches, but with the war, and especially with gas rationing, the numbers this year were expected to be far smaller. In addition, traditional Fourth of July celebrations were being toned down in many communities and eliminated completely in others.

Eddie had taken his hat off for a moment to wipe his forehead. He was roasting in his heavy, dark uniform. It would be the last time he'd leave the office with his coat on, he decided, regardless of what the regulations were.

Glancing up the street he could see someone changing the number under the gold star on the banner recognizing Ipswich's contribution to the war effort. A voice behind him said, "It's the Sweeney boy from up on Pineswamp Road. He was in the navy; killed somewhere in the Pacific."

Eddie turned and saw old Jim Conley standing right behind him.

Jim was the local gossip in addition to being the possessor of the sharpest tongue and most acerbic wit of anyone in town. And it had nothing to do with his age; he had always been that way. He was probably best known for his artless displays at town meetings, in which he would engage in long harangues against local officials over some minor issue until someone would finally try to quiet him. But, even this did not always work since more often than not he would simply turn his wrath on the offending individual. Eddie seemed to be one of the few people to get along with him, although for the life of him he couldn't figure out why.

"Morning, Jim. For some reason I hadn't heard about Kevin. What a shame! I don't really know his parents very well but I knew him. He was a good kid, a little wild maybe, but a good kid nevertheless. Kevin was a couple of years ahead of my brother in school though I think he dropped out before graduating to go to work at the Shell gas station up on Lord's Square. I often wonder how many more kids like him we're gonna lose before this war is over."

"You know, we wouldn't be in this war if it weren't for Roosevelt and that Churchill character. The two of them had been trying to get us into this war for years. Churchill needs us to keep the British Empire going, but there are plenty of people right here at home that wanted us in, particularly Roosevelt's Jewish friends like Baruch and Morgenthau and that disgusting Ickes fellow. You know what they call Roosevelt's New Deal, don't you? The Jew Deal. If there's money to be made in something they'll be all for it."

"If I remember correctly, it was Japan that attacked us at Pearl Harbor and Hitler who followed it up by declaring war on us," Eddie reminded him, trying his best to tone down Jim's comments.

"For God's sake, Eddie, Roosevelt all but encouraged the Japanese to attack us so he could get us into the war; Congress never would have voted for it otherwise. He cut off the sale of oil to them and later when he learned of what they planned to do at Pearl Harbor, he hushed it up; everybody knows that. And as for Germany, we forced them to accept all the blame for starting World War I when it was really that damned England's fault and then made them pay such heavy reparations their economy collapsed. That's what brought Hitler to power. Now we're about to repeat the same mistake."

Jim was only getting started.

"Any intelligent person will tell you there can't be a stable and prosperous Europe without a strong Germany, but, of course, England doesn't want that. She doesn't want the competition. England wants to continue to run the world when she has neither the military nor the economic power for it, so what does she do? She gets America to provide the muscle and the money she lacks, that's what. We pulled England's chestnuts out of the fire for her in World War I and now unbelievably we're in the process of doing it all over again."

Eddie was reminded once again why it was such a big mistake to get into any kind of political debate with Jim. He had strong views on everything and he didn't need much of an excuse to begin expressing them. Jim Conley's parents had emigrated from Ireland and they brought with them an intense hatred for everything British. Though the parents were suspected of sympathizing with the Nazis, they were careful what they said about the war in public. Not so their son, however, who openly criticized Churchill and Roosevelt at any and every opportunity to the resentment of those who had family members serving overseas.

"And look at your country," he continued. By "your country" he meant Poland, where Eddie's parents had been born. "The Germans and Commies divided it up, killed thousands, and what did the British do? They sat on their fat arses and did nothing. Oh, sure, they declared war on Germany, but that's all they did. If the Germans hadn't overrun France and begun making plans to invade England, they'd still be sitting on their arses. In fact, that's what they're calling it, the Sitzkrieg! I'm telling you, we've got no business getting involved in another European war. And, unfortunately, this one is going to be a helluva lot worse than the last one."

With considerable relief Eddie caught sight of Mike Bradford signaling to him from across the street.

"Sorry, Jim, I've got to rush. Sergeant Bradford over there wants me for something. Always a pleasure talking to you."

The old man was still grumbling about the war as Eddie raced across Market Street.

Eddie caught up with Mike in front of the news store.

"Sorry, to pull you away from your conversation with Jim Conley,"

Mike said, in mock seriousness. He was sure Eddie was so glad to get away from him he'd probably buy him lunch if he asked.

"So, what's up," Eddie asked, eager to discover why Mike had in fact called him over.

"You just got a call from Mack McCarthy. He wanted to pass along some information he'd received from Washington."

Mike went over what the FBI agent had told him.

"Well, it's a pretty good theory Mack has. I just wish we could have found some kind of evidence to support it," Eddie commented wistfully.

As they were talking Harold Brown strode up. Harold was the owner of the local hardware store, located just a few doors away from where they were standing.

"Hey, I've been hoping to run into you guys. This Saturday afternoon I'm having a little get-together over at my house. You know, some clams, lobsters, corn-on-the-cob. How about it, can you guys pull yourselves away from police work long enough to stop by? There'll be plenty of food and plenty of beer. Come on, even you guys must have to eat once in a while."

"Thanks, Harold, but I've got the late shift that day," said Eddie. "Mike should be free though."

"What do you say, Mike, can you stop by? I'm having the Woodmans and the Storeys up from Essex, as well as the usual Ipswich suspects. It'll be a good time."

"Ahh, why not," replied Mike with his usual lack of enthusiasm. "That's assuming, of course, there's nothing better on my social calendar."

"There's never anything on your social calendar," Eddie laughed, "unless you call having lunch at Quints' drugstore a social event."

Mike gave Eddie a dirty look. "I wouldn't talk about anyone's social life if I were you."

"OK, OK, you guys," Harold interrupted. "We'll probably start about four and go on 'til we run out of beer. Seriously, stop by if you can, Eddie, even if it's just for a few minutes."

With that Harold disappeared into the store.

"Well, I'm going to head back to the office," said Mike, turning to go. "Too hot out here for me. Speaking of the heat, what are you doing in that heavy jacket?"

Before Eddie could respond, his attention was suddenly drawn to a passing pickup truck.

"Hey, did you see the truck that just went by," exclaimed Eddie, nodding in the direction of the disappearing vehicle.

"Of course I saw it, what about it?" Mike responded, uncertain as to what Eddie was referring.

"Did you see who was in that truck?"

"Isn't that Anne Westbrook's old clunker?" Mike replied, still without any clue as to what had gotten Eddie so worked up.

"Exactly, but who do you think was driving it."

"For God's sakes, Eddie, I haven't the slightest idea what you're talking about. Enough with the twenty questions, just tell me who was driving the pickup truck? I'm roasting out here," Mike barked impatiently.

"That guy, Stoner, you remember him? He was the guy who beat up those two recruits outside the Hayes Hotel. So, tell me, police officer Bradford, what in hell is he doing chauffeuring Anne Westbrook around town? She was in the truck, too."

"I haven't the slightest idea why he's chauffeuring her around town; just maybe he's working for her, did that ever occur to you? She's got tons of money and she lives alone in the big house down by the beach. So, what's the big deal anyway?"

It was a good question. What was the big deal? To be honest he wasn't completely sure, but the sight of that guy driving by with Anne had unquestionably angered him. Could it be he was just a little jealous?

"You're right, it's probably nothing. Why don't you go ahead back to the office; I'll stick around town for another hour or so and then head back myself."

Eddie stood watching Mike light up a cigarette as he ambled up the street, but his mind was on Anne Westbrook, or more correctly on the guy in the truck with her. It had taken him a few minutes to recognize what was really bothering him; he was jealous, yes, jealous! For as long as he could remember he had harbored this secret crush on Anne. It had begun long before her husband had passed away. In his imagination Anne was everything a man could possibly want in a woman, although he was also realistic enough to understand that the social chasm that existed between the Argilla Road residents and "townies" like him would never be bridged in his lifetime. On the other hand, if this were the case, what was this Stoner character doing driving her around town?

Harold's voice interrupted him before he could come up with any kind of a plausible answer.

"Remember, stop by Saturday, at least for a little while."

"I'll try, really," said Eddie. He had no intention of going; he didn't enjoy sitting around with a bunch of guys drinking beer anymore. He would have said it was age were not for the fact that they were all older than he was. Whatever the real reason, then, he didn't even want to think about it.

Eddie crossed over Market Street and started walking in the direction the pickup truck had disappeared. As much as he hated to admit it, he was curious to find out where they were going. In the back of his mind was this agonizing thought they just might be headed for the Hayes Hotel.

Chapter Fourteen

Driving through the center of town, Karl noticed two policemen standing in front of the newspaper store; they were deep in conversation and it appeared to be a very serious one at that. As he drew abreast of them, he recognized the shorter of the two as the police chief, who had questioned him in his hotel room the night of the fight. He must have done something to catch his attention for as he drove passed, the police chief turned his head and looked directly at him. In that brief span Karl caught the look of surprise on the policeman's face. And, then, he slipped out of view. It was becoming increasingly evident this policeman neither cared much for him nor trusted him. He would have to be extremely careful and avoid trouble at all costs. This guy was unquestionably going to be watching his every move.

As Anne and Karl turned into Depot Square, they drove directly passed the spot where Karl had fought with the recruits. He glanced over to see if Anne would react in some way, but she didn't, or if she did, it wasn't obvious. Of course, even had she heard about the incident, there was no particular reason why she should have known Karl was involved; she hadn't even met him at that point. And, while there was a pretty good chance one of her women friends may have said something to Anne, the fact he was still employed by her suggested otherwise. She just wasn't the type to put up with having someone like that around her place, especially living alone.

Just as he was beginning to feel more relaxed Anne startled him by blurting out, "There, right there." As it turned out, she simply wanted him to turn right onto a narrow dead-end street that led to the grain company.

Straight ahead Karl could see a complex of large gray buildings with corrugated aluminum roofing; the words Horton's Grain Company were painted in huge letters on the exterior wall of the largest building. He turned into a gravel parking lot that was so filled with potholes it almost proved too much for the pick-up truck's aging shock absorbers. Karl pulled up directly in front of the main office and shut off the engine. No sooner had he done so than the door of the office was flung open and a rather corpulent, middle-aged man with a reddish face and wide grin came rushing out to greet Anne as she climbed down from the truck. For a moment Karl couldn't determine whether the display of enthusiasm was because she was such a good friend or just a good customer. It didn't take long to figure out it was the latter.

"Anne, so good to see you again," the man gushed. "I haven't seen you in ages."

"Hello, Tom. You're right, it has been awhile," she answered, coolly. It had appeared as if he had been about to give Anne a hug, but something in her manner made him quickly change his mind. He offered his hand instead. Anne took it only briefly before introducing him to Karl who, thrusting his muscular arm out the window, grasped the man's outstretched hand; it was fleshy and damp with sweat. Karl noted as well that the man found it impossible to make eye contact with him, not even for a moment. No wonder, Karl concluded, that Anne wasn't anxious to have the man touch her; he really was quite a repugnant individual.

Turning back to Anne, the man now dropped any pretense of being friendly and assumed a more business-like manner.

"I have your order ready," he stated flatly. "It's right over there on the loading dock."

Without waiting for directions from Anne, Karl started up the truck and drove over to where the hundred pound bags of horse feed were piled up. As he began tossing them into the back of the truck, he could hear the man explaining to Anne that the price of grain had gone up because of the war. Anne didn't seem overly concerned. Her attitude about money was a complete mystery to Karl. He had never known any women in Germany with the kind of financial independence she had. Most were entirely dependent upon their parents or husbands. He wondered just how wealthy Anne really was.

She strode over to the truck just as he was throwing the final bag in the back.

"We'd better get going," she suggested. "I wouldn't want to be responsible for making you late for work."

Karl couldn't tell if she were just joking or being serious.

"I'm all set," he replied.

"We will have to stop at Mac's service station up the street and fill this truck up with gas, if there is any. Next week the ration books come out and the board has already decided to allot me the minimum, since I don't have a regular job. Whatever I receive I should save for the car which gets better gas mileage."

Fortunately, they were able to fill up. The attendant told them had they been a day earlier there would have been no gas, but this morning the gas truck came in with the station's weekly allotment. Clearly, mused Karl, the war was beginning to have an impact, even on the wealthy, though they certainly weren't complaining. He wondered how long that would last. He couldn't imagine the Americans willingly giving up very much for the defense of Europe. Why should they?

The trip back was similar to the trip uptown--mostly small talk with little attempt at serious conversation. Karl suspected that Anne had something on her mind, but he made no great effort to find out what it was; he knew she'd tell him when she was ready. As they neared the driveway, Anne finally spoke up.

"Karl, tomorrow I'm having several neighbors over for lunch. It's the Fourth of July, you know, and my husband and I always used to celebrate it by having a huge cookout for all the people who were summering along this stretch of Argilla Road. It was a lot of fun, but it would probably be inappropriate to do anything like that with the war on. For that matter, there aren't even that many people around here this summer. Still, I want to do something, so I've invited six friends over for lobster. It's a dollar fifty a pound but I don't know how much longer lobster will be available at whatever price. I was hoping you'd be willing to help me boil the lobsters and, of course, join my friends and me for dinner."

The invitation took Karl totally by surprise. He knew she had been working up the courage to ask him something; he just hadn't expected anything like this.

"Let me think about it," he replied. "The fact is I know nothing about cooking lobsters; I've never even eaten one."

"Oh, it's not difficult, and they're delicious. I'm just a little squeamish about cooking them myself, you know, dropping them alive into boiling water. It was one of those things my husband always took care of. He was a good man," she sighed. "I think you would have liked him."

It was first time she had ever mentioned her late husband to Karl. She wasn't certain why she done it now, but she felt better for having done so. And, while Karl was always very formal around her, she was beginning to feel a little more relaxed with him.

In the meantime Karl had pulled the truck into the barn and had begun unloading the bags of horse-feed. Anne had gotten out of the truck and was standing next to it watching him; the bags were far too heavy for her to even try to lift. She was so thankful he was around to do jobs for her like this.

"What will your friends think about having the gardener dine with them?" Karl asked with more than a hint of sarcasm. He realized she was trying to be nice and deep down he knew he shouldn't have responded in that manner. Unfortunately, he had always been sensitive about his working class origins, especially after his university years when his wealthy classmates had gone out of their way to exclude him from their activities. Worse, they didn't think that a person with his background should even be allowed to enroll in the university. That he was a better student than most of them seemed only to exacerbate their already snobbish behavior towards him. It was one of the things that initially attracted him to the Nazis, their attempt to break down many of the class distinctions. While he didn't always approve of their methods, he couldn't help but sympathize with their objective.

"Please don't think like that," Anne replied, snapping him out of his reverie. "They're really very nice people. You'll like them; I promise you. Tell me you'll join us."

Stacking the last bag Karl turned and faced her. He was perspiring and covered with grain dust.

"OK, I really will think about it. But you do realize that I have to work that night. President Roosevelt, he had almost slipped by saying "your" President Roosevelt, has suggested that the best way a person can show his patriotism on the Fourth is to show up for work, so I was planning to go."

"That won't be a problem," Anne responded, certain now she had convinced him. "The cookout will be over long before then; I promise."

"I really must go," he said, heading for the steps to his apartment. " I'm already late for work as it is."

Anne continued to stand there even as she heard Karl racing up the stairs to his apartment. She couldn't help wondering why his coming to the cookout had suddenly become so important to her. She certainly wasn't attracted to him, she thought to herself. But, the more she thought about it the less certain she was. She decided it was probably best to just put it out of her mind for the moment.

At the beginning Anne felt more than a little inhibited having a strange man working about the place. Before he moved in she had typically gone about the place on hot days wearing shorts or even a bathing suit. She still liked dressing that way only now she had decided it was best to be more discreet about it. Still, there was nothing, in his outward behavior at least, that had ever given her any reason to have second thoughts about hiring him. He was always unfailingly polite and whenever she spoke to him about various work assignments, he always responded with a warm smile, even making suggestions on how best to do it. And so gradually she became more at ease with him to the point where from time to time she would suddenly catch herself watching him. Though she was a little surprised by her actions, feeling a bit like a voyeur, the fact remained she found an unexpected sense of pleasure in doing so. And, now the cookout would provide her the opportunity to observe him in the company of other people, to see how he reacted to them, or better still, how they reacted to him.

Inviting him to the cookout seemed a reasonable enough idea at first, what anyone would do in similar circumstances, especially on the Fourth of July. But, his reluctance to attend had taken her by surprise and it began to worry her. She knew he didn't have much of a social life, but she had attributed that to the war; normal social relationships had become completely disrupted, and anyway, people were working such long hours there wasn't much time for anything else. But, she wondered if it were possible that Karl just didn't much care for people, that he simply preferred being alone; it was not unheard of. Still, she couldn't escape the feeling that deep down she wanted him to be there.

There was also another issue that was starting to occupy her thinking, the fact she had not dated anyone in the two years since Bob's death. She had not even allowed herself to be coupled up at dinner parties. She had always insisted on going by herself and coming home by herself. But she couldn't escape the fact she was becoming very lonely again. Her husband was gone and her only son away at college, soon in fact to be overseas. More than once recently she had found herself staring wistfully at herself in front of the full-length mirror in her bedroom. The image reflected back was of an attractive woman, admittedly a forty year-old woman but an attractive one nevertheless. And, she knew men found her attractive, not just from the way they looked at her, but from comments her friends passed along to her. For that reason she had always been careful not to flirt or do anything that might encourage them. Now, suddenly, she discovered herself fantasizing about what it would be like to be with a man. At first she felt guilty about such thoughts, but after deciding there was absolutely no reason to, she actually began to take pleasure in them.

Not surprisingly, because he was the only man she saw some days, Karl became the object of many of her fantasies. She wished she knew more about him. He was obviously several years younger than she, but exactly what his age was she had no idea. Had he ever been married, she wondered? Could there be a wife with children back in Chicago at this very moment? And what about his education? Had he even graduated from high school? No, there was something about him that made her suspect that he was well educated. Whether it was his extreme self-confidence or his slightly mocking manner, she wasn't sure. But there was also something in the way he carried himself, something faintly military in his bearing. Certainly her female friends, who had seen him working shirtless about the place, had been impressed.

Still, judging from their comments, they saw him as someone with whom to have a weekend fling, not someone you invited into your home when you had friends over. And, there had been that rumor, one of her friends had passed along, that Karl had been in a fight downtown and had sent two men to the hospital. She had good reason to be a little uneasy, she decided. Her friends could definitely be snobs and there was a real question how they would react to him assuming, of course, he made up his mind to come. On the other hand she had to wonder how he would get along with her guests? She couldn't help but detect the hint of sarcasm in his voice when she had extended the invitation. The more she thought of it the more she concluded it might actually be better if he didn't come.

Karl was a few minutes late getting to work though nothing was said. He had thought of asking Anne if he could use the pickup truck but had decided it was a bit presumptuous of him, especially after her comments about gasoline rationing. It never even crossed his mind she might be upset with him because of the way he had responded to her invitation to the cookout. Karl had never learned to read women very well. With the exception of his aunt, women had never played an important part in his life.

Tom O'Malley was not there when he arrived. Then, he remembered, it was a Friday night before the Fourth of July weekend. Tom was in all probability off sharing a bottle with one of his friends, Karl decided, he could smell a liquor bottle the way a bear could smell honey. It was amazing that Tom hadn't been fired. He obviously had friends in the right places. In fact, someone had recently mentioned to him that only a few years ago Tom had been a member of the town's Board of Selectmen, but had lost when he had come up for reelection. The townspeople had decided they didn't want an alcoholic for a selectman.

Lighting his torch and pulling his protective helmet down over his face, Karl picked up where he had left off the night before. As a welder Karl was provided with no shortage of opportunities to damage the craft upon which he was working. A poor quality weld at a critical seam would be all it would take. It would have to be done carefully, however, for there were federal inspectors whose responsibility it was to check for just such things. But, he had decided early on that if he were going to destroy the yard anyway there was no point in getting caught for doing inferior quality work that would only jeopardize the success of the larger operation.

Over the din of the construction activities Karl could make out a couple of men somewhere up near the bow of the LCT arguing about the war. It was not unusual; it had become the most popular pastime among the men and women working at the yard. He generally tried to stay out of such arguments, though from time to time he felt it necessary to interject an opinion, if for no other reason than to avoid suspicion. The last thing he needed was for someone to question whether he supported the war. His co-workers, many of them veterans of World War I, were extremely patriotic and were quick to criticize anyone who did not share their very vocal support for the war.

A sudden lull in the clamor enabled Karl to hear the argument more clearly. They were debating who were more hated, the Japs or the Germans. From their conversation he gathered that Japanese-Americans living on the West Coast had been forcibly moved into some kind of camps in the interior of the country; the government was worried they might engage in espionage or sabotage against the US. He heard someone raise the issue he would have raised had he been a participant in the conversation. Why hadn't they rounded up Italian-Americans or German-Americans? He then heard an unknown speaker declare that a German guy living up on County Road had been forced to move to Boston so he could regularly report in to government authorities. One thing was very clear from the conversation. If these guys were your typical Americans, they had an incredible hatred for the Japs that didn't seem to extend to either the Italians or Germans. Of course, none of these guys had probably ever met anyone from Japan, while there were plenty of people living in the area from Italy and a few from Germany. Karl had long since concluded from his years living in the US that Americans and Germans were really not so different from each other. That's why it was such a shame that the two countries were on opposite sides in this conflict. It was like the First World War all over again, he reflected, sadly.

In time their conversation trailed away and Karl's mind wandered back to Anne's invitation. He imagined everyone there would spend the entire time talking about the war; probably about how the Americans would once again have to save Europe from a Germany bent on world domination. He found conversations like that unbearable in large part because Americans seemed so ignorant of European history. What made it so difficult for him, of course, was that he had to bite his tongue and refrain from countering their ridiculously uninformed arguments. If only he had come ashore a couple of weeks earlier he might now have been in position to destroy the shipyard on the Fourth of July. Now, those would be real fireworks!

He did decide that the weekend would be a perfect time to visit the beach and retrieve some of his supplies. They could very easily be hidden in the barn. The main problem was getting down to the beach and back without being seen; it was not going to be easy. Worse, it was probably going to require several trips to get everything he needed. The advantage was that things should be more relaxed on the weekend; many servicemen would probably be given furloughs and with weather like this there might even be people walking the beach.

After thinking more about it, he also concluded it would be in his own best interest to attend Anne's cookout. By remaining aloof it might only make her friends suspicious and begin asking questions about him. For his own protection, then, it would probably be better if he, not Anne, were the one to answer those questions.

Chapter Fifteen

The Fourth of July dawned sunny and hot with a pale blue sky unmarred by even the hint of a cloud. By mid-morning the temperature had already climbed to eighty degrees and gave no indication of slowing; the humidity was rapidly becoming oppressive. The good news was that a fast-moving cold front was expected to bring some relief by late afternoon, though not before potentially violent thunderstorms were expected to sweep through the area.

Even with his windows wide open, Karl's apartment was becoming more stifling by the moment; there wasn't even the hint of a breeze to provide relief. Unable to sleep, he arose from his sweat-soaked bed and took a long cold shower. He emerged refreshed. After getting dressed he headed down the stairs and ambled across the yard.

He had decided it best to accept Anne's invitation to lunch. He would help her cook the lobsters and whatever else she needed, though he would do his best to stay away from her friends. It took him only a few seconds to reach her door but in that time he found himself already becoming soaked in sweat. He hated this kind of heat and had come to accept the fact he'd never get used to it. How, he wondered, could anybody live in the tropics where it would be like this day after day for weeks at a time. If nothing else it explained why Europeans living there always seemed to end up becoming alcoholics; he'd probably become an alcoholic too if he had to endure this kind of heat for long stretches.

Karl knocked on the screen door and from somewhere within the house he detected a faint "come in." As he crossed the screened porch to the kitchen he suddenly realized he'd never been in the house before. He stepped into the kitchen just as Anne entered from the living room.

"Oh, Karl, it's you," she exclaimed, clearly surprised to see him.

She was barefoot and wearing only navy blue shorts and a white halter that did little to cover her ample breasts. In response to the heat she had put her hair up fastening it behind her head. Karl was again struck by how attractive she could look even when not trying to do so. And for the first time he noticed her tan. It occurred to him he had never seen her out sunbathing and yet somehow she had managed to tan her entire body, or at least that part he could see and that was most of it. Sensing he was appraising her, she blushed slightly and crossed her arms over her chest.

"I didn't mean to interrupt you," Karl said quickly, noticing her discomfort. "I only wanted to say I'd be pleased to accept your invitation to lunch, if it's not too late, that is. And I'll be glad to help you with the lobsters as long as you explain to me what to do."

Anne's surprise quickly gave way to the most delightful smile; she also seemed to relax just a bit. "No, it's not too late at all; I'm delighted you've decided to join us. You'll like my friends," she assured him, "although I'll be the first to admit they can be a little stuffy at times. But they are very nice. They've always been there for me when I've most needed their support."

She hadn't meant to say quite so much for she had already made up her mind that Karl would probably not like any of them. He was a little strange, she decided. Well, maybe not strange, but certainly different from most of the people she knew. He definitely wouldn't have much in common with any of them; even he seemed to be aware of that. Anne couldn't help worrying a little over how he'd react; he didn't say much but she sensed he was a very proud individual who might not put up with the kind of kidding her friends constantly engaged in, nor their political views either about which they could be very outspoken. Anyway, it was too late to do anything now; she could only hope everything would work out for the best.

As Karl was about to head out the door, he stopped. "Oh, there is one thing. I hope your friends won't be offended by the informality of my clothes. Until now I really haven't had much need for new ones so all I have are those I use for work."

"Oh don't worry about that, it's a very casual affair, especially in heat like this. But wait a minute, I have an idea."

Anne turned and disappeared back into the living room. He heard her footsteps as she raced up the stairs. After about five minutes he heard her coming back down and then there she was walking into the kitchen carrying several summer shirts.

"Here, take these," she offered. "They should fit you perfectly. They were meant for my husband; he simply never had a chance to wear any of them. As you can see for yourself they're brand new; a couple of them still have tags on them. I wish I could give you pants to go with them. Unfortunately, any pants he had would be far too baggy for you."

"No, really, I can't take these," Karl protested, embarrassed by her generosity.

"Why not?" she replied. "They've just been sitting upstairs in a drawer. I've been planning to give them away I just haven't gotten around to it. Of course, if you feel uncomfortable wearing them…"

She turned as if to take the shirts back upstairs.

"No wait, I'll take them," Karl announced abruptly. "I mean if you were seriously going to give them away, I'll take them. I have very few clothes and most of the ones I have are in poor condition. I really could use some new shirts."

"I really was going to give them away, I just hadn't decided who to give them to. And, to be honest, I'd rather you have them than just give them to strangers."

He stepped forward and took them from her.

She smiled at him clearly pleased he had changed his mind. It was obvious to her that Karl was unaccustomed to having people do things for him without some ulterior motive involved. But, did she have an ulterior motive, she wondered?

"I appreciate your generosity. For everything," he quickly added, motioning to the apartment. "What time would you like me to come back?"

"How about eleven. My guests should be arriving about noon."

"I'll be here! And, thank you again for the shirts," he said more formally than the situation required.

Karl turned and headed quickly out through the screened porch. He was still feeling slightly embarrassed by her generosity, though not enough to prevent him from picturing her standing there in front of him looking so beautiful in her shorts and halter. It was an image he found strangely exciting.

Returning to his apartment Karl felt it too hot to do much of anything so he grabbed a beer from the icebox and sat down at the kitchen table. The beer was warm since most of the ice had melted and it would be another two days before the iceman came again. He pushed it aside and lit up a cigarette. Inhaling deeply, he looked over at Anne's house on the rare chance he might catch sight of her, but she was nowhere to be seen. Out of sheer boredom he clicked on the radio. It was a small Philco he had found stored in one of the cabinets. Unfortunately, it was so old it could only pick up a few very local radio stations. To improve reception Karl had made an antenna out of a piece of wire that he ran up the side of the window but even that didn't help very much. Twisting the dial, he moved from station to station hoping to find a news program. But, since it was the Fourth of July, most stations were either carrying speeches by political leaders in Washington or they were simply filling the airwaves with patriotic music. After several minutes of "The Battle Hymn of the Republic" and "Coming In On a Wing and a Prayer," he clicked off the radio in disgust. He was feeling restless, not to mention guilty at having accomplished so little. He had to move ahead with his mission.

He wondered if it might not be time to establish communication with his handler in Berlin. He had yet to do so and there were a number of things he could report. For one, he wanted to inform Nazi leaders that Americans were going about their daily lives without any outward sense of fear or concern; their morale was very high. Of course, this news would not be something Berlin would want to hear. Hitler was firmly convinced that Americans had no stomach for this war and it was the main reason why, against the advice of his military staff, he had declared war on them. It was just one more example of how little Hitler understood about American society. His belief that Americans were soft and totally unprepared for a long, bloody war was more a product of his own wishful thinking than any hard evidence. If there were one thing Karl had learned during his years living in Chicago was never to underestimate the toughness and tenacity of the American people. This was exactly what the Nazi leadership appeared to be doing and in the long run Karl was certain it was going to cost Germany dearly.

But, underestimating America's morale was only one of a number of errors the Nazi leadership was making. Karl had already concluded they were doing the same thing with America's industrial capabilities. If only they could see for themselves the speed with which America was turning out ships. Karl was already impressed with the operation at Robinson's relatively small shipyard, but the men he worked with were constantly telling him that the larger shipyards at Bath, Maine, and Quincy, Massachusetts, were cranking out ships at an even faster rate. And the workmanship was superb.

Karl was especially amazed at the quality of the vessels turned out by Robinson's designers and builders. Not only did he marvel at the speed of these sleek wooden minesweepers and sub-chasers but what impressed him even more was the fact that being made of wood they were also immune to the magnetic mines German U-boats were laying up and down the East Coast. Before the war apparently the shipyard had turned out yachts for the wealthy and if the couple of photos he'd seen were any indication, these yachts had been incredible. Some were as large as ninety feet in length. He couldn't help picturing himself sailing one of these yachts along the coast of the Mediterranean or through the islands of the Caribbean with someone like Anne lounging beside him on the deck.

The sound of a bumblebee buzzing against the outside of the window screen snapped him back from his reverie. Returning to the idea of contacting Berlin, he wondered how exactly he should go about it. He actually had several options. He could use the short-wave transmitter contained in one of the wooden chests buried at the beach, which had been designed specifically for the Abwehr by Telefunken, Germany's largest producer of telephones and communications equipment. The transmitter was so compact that it could fit comfortably within a normal suitcase, for example, and it was also very powerful, capable of reaching Berlin under almost any conditions. Unfortunately, even the briefest transmission from this device had the potential of being be detected and would alert the authorities to the presence of an agent in their midst. At this point in the mission it was not a chance worth taking. He decided instead to opt for the more cumbersome but safer method; he would send the information by mail. Buried with the radio was a small watertight tube containing several sheets of a special white paper along with a dozen or so ordinary-looking match sticks. Like the paper the matches were anything but ordinary. They had been impregnated with quinine so when they were used as a pencil, nothing that was written on the special paper was visible until it had been immersed in a chemical solution. If he were to retrieve the paper and matches, then, he could prepare his report and simply post it to a safe house in Portugal, where it would be received and forwarded to Berlin.

Karl glanced at his watch. Damn, it's almost eleven, he said, leaping off the chair and heading for the shower.

Anne's guests arrived within a few minutes of each other. Altogether there were five, three men and two women. They all seemed to Karl as fit and tanned and clearly accustomed to the good things in life. But there was something about their exuberant behavior that bothered him. They acted as if they were totally oblivious to the war going on, or at the least that America had nothing to worry about. It was this attitude of superiority—moral, political, military—that Karl found most annoying about America and Americans.

Suddenly, the sound of sirens could be heard in the distance; strangely, it seemed to be coming from several different directions at once.

"It's noon," Anne announced. "I heard on the radio this morning that every fire station along the East Coast would be sounding its sirens precisely at twelve noon. Since there won't be many parades or fireworks displays this year, I guess the sirens will probably be the limit of our Fourth of July celebration."

Anne took advantage of the interruption to direct everyone onto the porch where they would be eating since it was too hot in the house and there were too many mosquitoes and deer flies to eat outside. Unfortunately for Karl and Anne, most of the cooking was being done on the outdoor fireplace, so until the food was ready the two of them had to endure the insect attacks as they hurried back and forth between the house and the fireplace. To his dismay Karl was only able to hear bits and pieces of various conversations as he moved about helping Anne. It appeared to be mostly small talk and at least initially broke down along gender lines. The men, all of whom seemed to be either bankers or lawyers, talked business with an occasional reference to the war. The women, on the other hand, if they were not discussing their golf or tennis games, largely gossiped about acquaintances, that were not in attendance.

When Karl was finally able to join them for dinner, the conversation quickly and uncomfortably turned to him. Fortunately, the questions were surprisingly innocuous: Where was he from? Why wasn't he in the service? What had brought him to Ipswich? Still, he was glad that it was he answering them rather than Anne since he couldn't be certain what she might say.

Were it not for Anne's cheerful personality, the entire occasion might well have turned into a terrible bore, Karl decided. But Anne was there and though he did his best not to be obvious, he couldn't help but glance over at her from time to time. He suspected she noticed him doing it as she would occasionally return his glance with just the faintest of smiles. He couldn't believe how cool and composed she looked in spite of the heat. For the luncheon she had let her hair down now and was wearing a sleeveless white shirt with a short skirt of a floral design. Karl found it fascinating that Anne was able to look so much more vivacious than her friends when they appeared to have put so much more effort into it.

When the meal ended, the men took their drinks and wandered into the living room, all except for one who wandered outside and lit a cigarette. No one paid him any attention until a few seconds later when a loud bang caused everyone to jump.

"Christ, what was that," someone yelled nervously.

Everyone rushed out onto the porch and looked towards Kit; a wisp of smoke could be seem rising from the far side of the lawn

"Come on, it wouldn't be the Fourth of July without a cherry bomb or two," he laughed. "But, don't worry, it's the only one I brought."

"I hope so," Anne exclaimed. "The last thing I want is for someone to call the police; you know fireworks have been banned!"

"I'd hardly call a single cherry bomb fireworks but on the slight chance one of your neighbors calls them we'll just say Karl did it. We'll explain that Karl is from out-of-town and didn't know about the ban," he responded. "Since they won't know him they'll hardly charge him with anything."

Karl knew he was joking but it still made him uneasy. The police chief was already suspicious of him and there was no telling how he'd react even to something as minor as this. Just the thought of the police coming down here made him more than a little nervous.

By this time the men had drifted back to the living room while the women, along with Anne, gathered in the kitchen. Anne made it clear that Karl's help was no longer needed and with a delightful smile that hid her sense of trepidation had sent him off with the men. Without the women present the conversation reverted to what appeared to be their favorite topic, worrying about what impact the war would have on their personal financial situation if it were to last for several years. It was not something Karl had much to say about so he basically kept quiet and listened. So lost in their discussion did they become that Karl was all but ignored. They seemed to take him for what he was, a shipyard worker who was at the cookout because Anne in a moment of pity had seen fit to invite him. The old guy at the hotel had been right again, Karl thought to himself, and far more perceptive than he had given him credit for. The people who summered down here really did see themselves as a class apart from the locals.

Karl had just decided he'd had enough of Anne's pompous friends when they were all startled by the sound of a car racing up the driveway and skidding to a halt by the backdoor. Almost immediately Anne could be heard excitedly calling out, "It's Bob, everybody, it's Bob."

Karl glanced into the kitchen just as a tall young man wearing the uniform of a Naval Reserve officer came through the door; he gave his mother an enthusiastic hug. There was no question he was Anne's son thought Karl to himself; they shared the same good looks and disarming smile.

"I really can't stay. I had to go into the Boston Navy Yard to sign some documents and now I have to rush back to Dartmouth. I just wanted to stop by and say hi."

"You can at least stay long enough to have something to eat, I hope," begged his mother.

"I'm really sorry, Mom, but I can't; I honestly have to be back on campus, in fact, I should have been there an hour ago."

The disappointment was visible on her face.

"Well, the least you can do is come in and say hello. I think you know everyone here."

By this time Anne's friends had all crowded into the kitchen. The women were all hugging him and the men shaking his hand and slapping him on the back. Backslapping, Karl had long since concluded, was a uniquely American habit. It was just at this moment he heard Anne say, "There is one other person I'd like you to meet."

"Bob," she said, directing her son over to Karl, "This is Karl Stoner. He lives in the apartment over the garage and helps me look after this place now that I'm alone here."

The broad smile that her son had seemingly directed towards everyone in the room was instantly replaced by a puzzled expression. Though he quickly stepped forward and extended his hand it was also clear he was quite unsure what to make of this stranger who was now living at his home. Karl suspected he was trying to figure out whether there was anything more to the relationship.

Turning to his mother, he said, "I've really got to go; as I said, I'm late already."

Anne took his arm as they walked through the kitchen and out into the yard.

At the same time one of the men whispered to his wife, "We should probably be going along, too, dear."

When the others nodded their agreement, Karl decided it was a good time to make his exit as well; it would give them an opportunity to say goodbye to Anne without him being around. Quickly making his own goodbyes to everyone he stepped out onto the screened porch. To his surprise, and embarrassment, he discovered Anne standing next to her son's car arguing with him loudly.

The first words he could make out, though clearly not their first they had uttered, were Anne's.

"You're totally mistaken. It's not like that at all and you're not being fair."

Yet only when the son responded, "For God's sake, Mom, he's even wearing one of the shirts I gave Dad," did Karl realize they were arguing about him. Though he did his best to appear as if he had not heard the son's comment, he knew he hadn't succeeded when he saw the horrified look on Anne's face. Hesitating just long enough for the son to slam the car door and roar out of the driveway, Karl opened the screen door and headed for his apartment. He had no alternative but to walk directly past Anne. As he did so he could see she was clearly hurt and was doing her best not to cry. She looked at him as if she were about to say something; unfortunately, her guests chose just that moment to begin spilling out into the yard. Sensing her indecision, Karl turned away without a word and continued on to his apartment.

The only words that came to him at that moment were "Fuck you all!"

Chapter Sixteen

Mike Bradford was so late arriving at the Brown's cookout that most of the people attending had already left. He had been held up because of a phone call from Mack McCarthy. The FBI man had wanted to pass along the news that the German spy wounded during capture had died without ever having gained consciousness. As for the one being held in jail, he was proving to be less forthcoming than had been initially expected. About the only thing they had gotten out of him was that the two of them were not working alone but were part of a larger Abwehr operation. Beyond that, he had said little, though his interrogation would continue. In the meantime, the FBI was preparing to go ahead and issue an alert to all appropriate authorities along the East Coast to be on the lookout for any suspicious activity that might indicate the presence of Abwehr agents operating in their area.

Harold Brown's home was a large, two-story, white colonial that overlooked the Ipswich River and town wharf. Having been there on numerous occasions Mike strode directly around the side of the house and into the spacious backyard. There beneath a huge elm tree sat four men amid the remains of what had obviously been a much larger gathering. The four looked strangely alike since they were all dressed in shorts and white T-shirts; they also shared other similarities, notably their bulging stomachs and spindly white legs. Each had a beer in his hand and, from the shape they were in, they'd apparently finished off more than a few.

"Hey, Mike, glad you could make it though you missed most of the food," said Harold, gamely trying to get up out of his chair, knocking it over in the process.

"Stay put, Harold, I suspect I'm better able to get myself a beer than you are."

"I'll drink to that," Harold laughed, "and, while you're at could you get me another one?"

Mike grabbed two cans of beer out of the cooler.

"You do know everyone here, don't you, Mike? This is Fred, and Charlie, and Jim over here. Oh, and if you want something to eat you'll have to go into the kitchen and ask Ethel to put together a plate of food for you."

"Nah, a beer is fine for now, thanks. I just want to sit and relax for a bit. And by the looks of you guys you've already been doing some pretty heavy relaxing."

"It's the Fourth of July, for Christ sakes," slurred Jim. "And, what with no fireworks or parades it's about the only thing the government let's us do. So, what are you going to do, arrest us?"

"Only if you try to drive," Mike quipped. Everybody laughed.

It was a beautiful summer evening, soft and warm. A cold front that had swept through the area earlier had pushed out the day's oppressive heat and humidity. In the west the setting sun had turned the sky a brilliant crimson and gold, fading into more muted pastels as the evening wore on.

The men had obviously been talking about fishing when Mike arrived and their conversation gradually drifted back to the topic. Before long a beer-induced argument began to rage over where the best bass fishing was. There was no agreement and after awhile the argument petered out. Mike took the opportunity to get everyone another beer.

He had been there about an hour when Harold said almost off-handedly, "Hey, Fred, why don't you tell Mike about that incident at the beach. You know, the one when you and your nephew were fishing over there."

"For crying-out-loud, Harold, I thought you said you wouldn't say anything; that's the only reason I told you. You know very well no one's supposed to be over there," responded Fred, clearly annoyed. "I'm never going to tell you another thing in secret again, you can be sure of that."

"Fishing off the beach is no big deal, everyone does it, isn't that right Mike? And, anyway, he's hardly going to arrest you?"

"Christ, is that what you guys think of me, that all I do is go around arresting people? The beach is not even our jurisdiction anymore, and you know that," remarked Mike, taking a swig of his beer. "It's Washington's responsibility now. But tell me anyway what happened at the beach? I promise, I won't report you to the FBI."

Mike didn't expect much of a story but he was curious nevertheless.

"Look, it was nothing, really. We just heard some shooting when we were fishing over there one night."

"There's always shooting over there," replied Mike, a little disappointed. "Both the army and navy use it as a firing range."

"Not at midnight they don't." Fred didn't like being put down so summarily. "And what we heard was not just someone having a little target practice; it was an automatic weapon that was being fired, or at least that's what it sounded like from where we were."

"When was this? And, by the way, why in hell didn't you immediately report it. You know very well a Coastguardsman stationed down there is missing along with his dog."

Mike was getting excited now.

"Come on, out with it," said Mike, raising his voice now. "When did you hear this automatic weapon being fired? I want to know the exact date."

"It was two or three weeks ago," Fred answered, feeling as if he had just been reprimanded.

"I want the exact date, the actual day," Mike insisted. "For Christ's sake can't you figure it out?"

"It was like the eighteenth or nineteenth of June, both probably since it was close to midnight."

Mike was on his feet by this time.

"I've got to go, Harold. Thanks for the beer. As for you, Fred, we'll be in touch on this; you can count on it. I've got to go talk to the chief. Now, don't let me catch any of you guys driving for the next couple of hours or so help me, I really will arrest you," Mike growled as he headed for his car.

"I'm not going to get in trouble over this, am I?" Fred shouted nervously.

"I told you, we don't have jurisdiction there anymore. Fact is, you might even become a hero; of course, you might also be arrested by the FBI for withholding evidence," Mike yelled back, hoping to scare the daylights out of Fred. He was out of the yard and on his way back to the station before any of them could even push themselves out of their chairs, not that any one of them seemed inclined to do so.

Karl had been hunched over the kitchen table for the past hour doing his best to listen to a news broadcast through heavy static. Unlike earlier in the day when he had found few news reports, there was no shortage now that it was evening. Although news from the front was heavily censored, Karl had developed the ability to interpret what was broadcast as a result of listening to hours of bulletins prepared by the Ministry of Information and comparing them with the information the Abwehr had acquired through its own means. It was like deciphering a code; the crucial phrases always came at the end of an article. He knew, for example, if German troops had been forced to withdraw "to preserve their fighting strength," they had lost and if the fighting had been fierce and they had "performed heroically in the face of superior numbers," they had lost badly. American news bulletins, on the other hand, were never as difficult to interpret because censorship was not as heavy-handed. At any rate what he was hearing at that moment was giving him reason for at least a little optimism.

The story receiving the greatest coverage was the Navy's increasing success in protecting American merchant shipping along the East Coast from German U-boats. Whereas earlier ships had moved along the coast largely unescorted, almost all ships were now moving in heavily protected convoys. Losses to U-boats, it was now being reported, had declined dramatically. What was clear from the report, though never mentioned directly, was that American shipping losses to German U-boats in the first months of the war had been so heavy that they collectively constituted America's worst-ever defeat at sea. While mention was made of having lost scores of ships to German U-boats in recent months, Karl knew from figures made available to the Abwehr by Admiral Doenitz that Operation Drumbeat had been directly responsible for the sinking of well over three hundred ships and their crews. After all, the mission he was participating in was designed to rival the success of Operation Drumbeat.

What Karl found most interesting, though he was unsure what conclusions to draw from it, was that most of the news items he heard concerned the war in the Pacific where the Americans appeared to be desperately trying to blunt the Japanese drive into Southeast Asia. He was at best marginally interested in the Pacific Theatre of war but by switching from one program to another he was able to get updates on both the Russian and North African campaigns. The news from Russia was especially positive, given the depressing appraisal of the situation by the Americans at Anne's cookout. A massive German operation to clear the enemy from the lower reaches of the Don and Volga appeared to be succeeding. Panzer divisions, backed up by Stuka dive-bombers, had routed the Russian forces there and in the process had taken the port of Sevastopol on the Crimea while encircling the city of Voronezh. Witnesses reported that the German offensive was proceeding with such speed and precision, it recalled the initial blitzkrieg that opened the Russian campaign the year before.

As for the news out of North Africa, it was being reported that the troops of Rommel's Afrika Korps had, at least momentarily, been stopped on the outskirts of El Alemein, a mere sixty-five miles from Suez. In anticipation of attacks by German bombers, the British fleet had evacuated Alexandria, an action that apparently had caused panic among that city's civilian population. Though there were reports that the German forces under Rommel were exhausted and suffering diminished morale, these reports could not be confirmed. In the meantime the British were rushing reinforcements to the region. The announcer pointed out that if Rommel could destroy the British forces now facing him, there would be no remaining obstacle to his capturing Suez, sweeping into the Middle East and possibly linking up with German forces pushing down from the Caucasus.

This was precisely the kind of news Karl needed; it served as an antidote to all the frustrations and uncertainties of the past three weeks. He suddenly felt energized and his sense of purpose seemed to have become restored. It hadn't hurt either that he was forced to put up with the self-righteousness comments of Anne's guests. What was it about

Americans that made them so sure of themselves, he wondered? Of course their geographical location didn't hurt, surrounded as they were by weak nations and vast oceans? It was the complete opposite of his country's situation.

He suddenly tensed at the sound of footsteps climbing the outside stairs. He couldn't remember hearing a car coming in the yard, and anyway, who'd come to visit him; he didn't know anyone. There was a soft knock on his door. Cautiously, he opened it and to his great surprise he found Anne standing there, her eyes red and puffy from crying.

"I'm sorry just showing up like this but I just needed to talk to somebody. May I come in," Anne asked uncertainly. "I noticed your lights were on; I thought you had said you'd be working tonight."

"At the last moment I just decided not to go in; I won't be the only one. Please, come in."

For some reason Anne looked much smaller and more vulnerable that she had earlier in the afternoon. She was still wearing the same skirt but had exchanged her blouse for a long-sleeved cotton sweater. Her hair appeared wet and uncombed as if she had just washed it while her face was devoid of any make-up. She was definitely not the self-assured woman he had been observing for the past three weeks. If anything she appeared confused, lonely, and for the moment, terribly sad.

"I'm really sorry to bother you," she whispered. "Maybe it would be best if I go."

"No, sit down, please," he replied calmly, offering her a chair.

Sitting down, she began to sob but quickly regained control of herself.

"It's my son," she sniffled. "He said the most horrible things to me today. He even called me a whore. Can you imagine a son calling his mother a whore? How could he do that? I've never done anything to hurt him."

Suddenly her shoulders shuddered and began to heave as she burst into tears again, only this time she didn't even try to control herself.

"It's OK, it's OK" Karl responded, not entirely sure how he should react, "I suspect your son simply misinterpreted our relationship. Meeting me for the first time and then seeing me in one of his father's shirts, it's really not surprising he reacted the way he did, but he'll get over it and I'm sure he'll end up apologizing to you."

"But why did he have to be so cruel to me," Anne asked between sniffles. "Yes, he lost a father, I know, but I lost a husband. It's been painful for both of us."

"I don't want to seem to be making excuses for your son because I obviously don't know him. But, the fact is he's probably still angry at losing his father; young boys are like that."

He had almost added I was like that too but he'd caught himself in time.

"Adding to his anger was my wearing one of his father's shirts. It must have hurt to think that another man could be taking his father's place. It's a combination of resentment and jealousy."

"I guess I can understand the resentment, but why jealousy?" Anne seemed to be regaining some of her composure.

"Psychology is not my field, but my guess is that after your husband died, your son became the man in your life and he still sees himself in that way. And even though he's no longer at home, instead of being pleased there's someone to look after you, he resents it."

"But I haven't found anyone to take his father's place. I told him that," she responded.

Karl couldn't believe her naivete.

"But, that's my point," he explained, beginning to suspect he wasn't helping much. "On the basis of what he saw in the few minutes he was here, he assumed wrongly that something was going on between us. Don't worry. You'll get it straightened out."

Anne stood up.

"I really must go but I want to thank you for being so patient listening to me. I hope you don't think I'm always like this, that I'm just one of these neurotic, hysterical women you so often hear about. I shouldn't have come, forgive me."

She really was quite beautiful, Karl thought, even with her tear-streaked cheeks. Taking her gently by the arm he walked her towards the door. As he leaned forward to reach for the knob, Anne turned to face him. Her intention, as she would later try to convince herself, had been to give him a light kiss on the cheek for being so supportive and understanding. But, as she was about to do so Karl pulled her to him and began kissing her roughly on the lips. She stiffened, trying unsuccessfully to push him away. Then, abruptly, she felt her resistance cease and she began to return his kisses with a passion and ferocity that surprised her even more than Karl.

As their efforts became more frenzied, Karl slipped his hands under her sweater only to discover she was wearing no bra. Quickly his fingers sought out her full, round breasts. He was unprepared for such delicate softness. He also became aware of her smell. Was it her shampoo or some mysterious body chemical? Whatever it was, the effect was almost dizzying. He began to massage her nipples, a bit too roughly at first for he felt her react. As he became gentler, he felt her nipples harden. She let out a soft moan and pressed more firmly against him. Guiding her towards his bedroom he was surprised when she slipped out of his arms whispering, "Wait, please." A second later, completely naked, she let Karl take her into his bed.

Chapter Seventeen

It was already daylight when Anne awoke and it took her a second to recognize where she was. Aware suddenly of her nakedness, she pulled the sheet up over her breasts and glanced quickly over at Karl. He was sprawled on his stomach, the sheet covering the lower half of his muscular torso; he was facing away from her and snoring lightly. She was relieved to see he was still asleep because she was in no way prepared to talk about what had happened the previous evening. The only thing she wanted to do at that moment was to get out of there without waking him.

Slipping gingerly out of bed, she retrieved her clothes from the floor, where they had been hurriedly discarded, dressed quickly, and went out the door, closing it quietly behind her. Once back in her house she let out a sign of relief. Slowly climbing the stairs to her bedroom she threw herself on the bed. What had she done? And it was clearly her doing; she couldn't escape that fact. She had gone to his apartment and literally flung herself at him. Worse still, she didn't even feel especially guilty about the whole thing.

On the other hand, that didn't change the fact her relationship with Karl had just become very complicated.

Getting up, she wandered into the bathroom where she proceeded to run herself a steaming bath. As she climbed into the tub she suddenly became aware of several muscles that felt just a little sore. Definitely out of shape, she murmured; she found herself unexpectedly smiling. She leaned back, closing her eyes and letting the hot, soapy water cover all but her head and toes. It felt so relaxing; unfortunately, she wasn't

123

going to be able to stay in the tub for very long. She'd been invited to have brunch in a couple hours with the Raymonds, who lived just up the road, and to play a little tennis afterwards. She was glad for the invitation since she had no idea what she was going to say to Karl when she met him.

Soaking there, she tried to decide if she were any different from her friends, who were continually commenting on how they'd love nothing better than to "jump into the sack" with Karl. Now, in light of her own actions, she began to wonder if any of them just might have done that. While it was always said in a joking manner, she also knew her friends weren't above doing such a thing if the opportunity presented itself. Isn't that exactly what she had done, taken advantage of the opportunity? Of course, in her case it was more like taking advantage of an opportunity that she herself had made. What had she been thinking going up there like that and at that hour of the night? Had she actually gone up to his apartment with the intention of sleeping with him? The fact she had left her house without a bra on pretty well answered that question. So why, Anne wondered, wasn't she feeling even a semblance of guilt for what she had done?

It was only while dressing that it dawned on Anne how little she had actually taken Karl into consideration in all of this. Had she just assumed he'd want to sleep with her? She had been aware for some time of the way he watched her as she worked about the place in her shorts; he tried not to be obvious but it proved impossible to miss. Well, it was all too late now; she had slept with him. She did have to admit though that Karl had turned out to be a surprisingly gentle, patient lover. Just thinking about it as she lay there in the tub caused her to become aroused. It had been a long time since she had experienced anything quite like it. And, she was right not feeling guilty about what she had done. She was a single woman for gosh sakes.

For the moment she decided she was just going to enjoy the sensation. Of course, that didn't change the fact that as enjoyable as the night with Karl might have been, under no circumstance could she let it happen again. One such encounter was excusable, she rationalized; any more than that would be dangerous. She could only imagine what her friends would say if they were to find out about it. They would pretend to make light of it, congratulate her even, but they'd also gossip about it as well.

Once the word spread around town that Anne was keeping a lover at her house, she might just as well begin wearing a scarlet A on her chest. As for her son, there'd be absolutely no way she could ever explain it to him; she'd already had a good indication of his reaction. No, she definitely could not let it happen again; nothing good could possibly come from it.

The sound of tires crunching on gravel roused Karl from his slumber. Rolling over he saw that Anne had gone, though the impression made by her body while she slept was still visible on the mattress. Her smell had also lingered or was that only his imagination. Her coming to his apartment in the first place had truly surprised him, but an even greater surprise had been the unexpectedly passionate and uninhibited nature of her lovemaking; he found himself smiling just thinking about it.

Ironically, it was Karl who felt most guilty, though for very different reasons that Anne's. Bolting up from the bed, he headed straight for the shower. What was he thinking, he had work to do and there was no way he could let this woman interfere with it. A relationship with Anne was the perfect way to blow his cover since if it became public knowledge inevitably people would become curious to learn more about him. He had to get down to the beach immediately and begin retrieving some of his supplies. Time was passing far too quickly and the war was entering a difficult phase; if his mission were to have any success, he had to move now.

Karl had already decided that early afternoon would be the best time to go down to the beach because that's when the largest number of people would be there and he could move about without appearing conspicuous. Since he would have to make several trips to retrieve all the materials he needed, he would employ different means of traveling back and forth to avoid attention. For the first trip he concluded the most obvious means would probably be the least suspicious, and nothing could be more obvious than simply bicycling down to the beach in broad daylight.

His main concern was the explosives. How would he carry them back from the beach? Then he remembered an old khaki knapsack he had seen hanging in the barn; he quickly went in search of it. He found it with little difficulty covered with dust and cobwebs. Cleaning it off, he noticed it was stamped with the words Boy Scouts of America. On one of the flaps he found the name Robert Westbrook printed in boyish lettering. So, this had been her son's knapsack. Karl suspected he wouldn't be very pleased if he knew what his knapsack was about to be used for, nor would his mother for that matter. For some reason the thought amused him. Could it be he resented Anne's son?

By early afternoon Karl was ready. He had dressed in a pair of khaki pants, the legs of which had been cut just above the knee to make shorts, a white t-shirt and an old pair of tennis sneakers. If he were to be spotted walking through the dunes, he wanted to look as if he belonged there. It was also practical given the steamy weather that was predicted.

Setting out on his bike he immediately began to feel the humidity, and he was thankful for the breeze that refreshed his face as he coasted down Argilla Road. With the exception of the last quarter mile, the entire trip from Anne's house to the beach was downhill. That meant, of course, the entire return trip would not only be uphill, but his knapsack, now containing only an extra shirt and some lunch to fill it out, would be stuffed with detonators and incendiary devices. He'd have to be very careful to conceal just how heavy his load really was.

Pedaling into the beach's small parking lot, he was relieved to see several cars there. The gravel parking lot proved too bumpy for the bike so he dismounted and pushed it over to a small clump of trees near the edge of the sand dunes. Setting his bike down in the shade he glanced across to where the cars were parked to be certain no one was watching him. Concluding no one was, he headed out across the sand, keeping a ridge of dunes between himself and the beach. It was his first opportunity to see the dune area he had crossed on the night he had come ashore; it looked so different during in daylight.

The dunes had been formed by the prevailing winds into a series of parallel arcs, resembling a procession of gigantic amphitheatres. The outer slopes tended to be steep and firm and easy to climb, while the sand on the interior slopes was soft and his feet sunk in well over the ankles as he slid down. Periodically he came upon clumps of pitch pine that were in the process of being buried by the encroaching dunes and in a few places Karl noticed the trees had been so completely covered that only a few dead branches remained visible. Schussing down one slope he actually came to a small pool of water, not unlike a tiny alpine lake. The water was brownish in color, almost certainly undrinkable, but that didn't stop a variety of plant life from flourishing around it; there were also raccoon and deer tracks everywhere.

Karl kept walking. After about fifteen minutes he decided it might be wise to check the beach for any possible Coast Guard patrols. Climbing to the crest of a high dune covered with clusters of sharp-pointed beach grass, he found the beach suddenly spread out before him. The tide was out and scores of sea gulls dotted the shoreline. As he scanned the area he couldn't help but notice the network of sandbars that formed a protective shield to the beach. These were clearly what Captain Frisch had been concerned about and the reason why he couldn't bring his submarine any closer to the shore. Otherwise, everything appeared peaceful and relaxed; one would never have guessed the country was at war, Karl concluded.

There were perhaps thirty people on the beach, some picnicking, a few more lying stretched out on blankets enjoying the sun, and the rest seemingly attempting to stay cool by standing ankle deep in the water. Yes, from his vantage point everything looked so normal, he actually found the scene annoying. How could they be so indifferent to the war? Americans never ceased to amaze him. Having decided there was no immediate threat, he slipped back down the dune; time to see if he could find the spot where the chest was buried.

Walking deeper into the dunes Karl found himself sweating profusely; the temperature was clearly several degrees hotter here than it was in the parking lot. To make matters worse the reflection of the sun's rays off the brilliant white sand was nearly blinding. He cursed himself for not bringing a hat or a pair of sunglasses. Nevertheless, after about twenty minutes Karl spotted a familiar grove of trees down to his right. He was certain it was the place. Glancing around, he could see no one. He waited a few seconds just to be sure, then, slid quickly down the side of the dune and into the protective cover of the trees.

The pine trees provided some badly needed relief from the sun. He also noticed he was not the only one to find shelter among the pines. The same animal tracks he had observed at the pool of water he had passed were all around him. Studying the surrounding trees he quickly spotted the notch he had cut into one of the pines with his shovel. After that it took only a few seconds to determine where he had buried his supplies.

Kneeling down, he began to probe the soft sand with his fingers. Almost instantly he struck something metallic; it was the shovel he had used to bury the chests. Certain of his discovery, he stood up and walked to the edge of the pine grove for one last look around. He had already decided it was far too hot for anyone to be strolling through the dunes, but he was there, wasn't he. And, if anyone were to spot him out here, it would almost certainly arouse suspicion, especially after the disappearance of the Coast Guardsman and his dog.

It required about half an hour to completely unearth the two chests. Carefully, he lifted the one marked with an X from its resting-place, though such caution was unnecessary; the explosives packed inside the chest were quite stable. Prying loose the top of the chest with the entrenching tool, he removed several individually wrapped blocks. He knew from having been present when the chest was packed that each block had been painted black and now looked exactly like a lump of coal, except for the small detonator inside. In fact, he intended to drop one of these lumps in the coal pile near the machine shop. When ultimately it was shoveled into the shop's boiler, the resulting explosion would probably destroy the entire structure along with anyone in it at the time. It was amazing, he mused, how anything so innocuous-looking could be so destructive.

After securely replacing the top on the first chest, he lifted out and opened the second one. Carefully wrapped in oilcloth was a 9-mm Pistolen-08 that he removed along with several eight-clip magazines. He decided to take the gun back to the apartment just as a precaution. He also withdrew a timer and several incendiary devices made to look like simple pen-and-pencil sets. The latter required sulfuric acid fillers to operate, but he decided to leave the fillers for another trip. No need to tempt fate any further, he concluded; he was tempting it enough just being here at the beach.

Satisfied that he was carrying as much as he safely dared, he placed the chests back in the hole and covered them over. He then dropped the shovel in what remained of the depression and covered that over with his hands. Finally, he smoothed the entire area with an old pine branch he found lying on the ground. It was the best he could do for now. He'd just have to hope no one came up here until after the deer had had an opportunity to tramp about the place; only then would the remaining evidence of his activities be obliterated.

To his relief, the return trip proved as uneventful as the trip down. He never saw any of the Coast Guardsmen and only a couple of cars passed him on the road. Riding into the yard he found his luck had not deserted him; Anne had yet to return home. Quickly, he hid the explosive devices under some loose floorboards he had discovered in the barn. He covered the boards with loose hay and returned the knapsack to the nail on which it had been hanging; he threw a little dust from the floor on the knapsack just on the chance someone noticed it had been cleaned. The Pistolen-08 he took with him back to the apartment. Going directly to the foot of his bed, he lifted the mattress and inserted the gun and clips into a nearly invisible slit. He was sure no one would discover it unless the person was intent on tearing the place apart.

It was just getting dusk when he heard Anne's car drive into the yard. He listened as she went into the house and closed the door. He was pretty certain there would be no knock on his door tonight.

Chapter Eighteen

Mack McCarthy had gone off to Cape Cod for the July Fourth weekend without leaving a phone number where he could be reached, so Eddie had to wait until Monday morning to contact him. But, when he did finally relay the news to him that they had found two people who had heard the sound of automatic weapons fire on the same night the Coast Guardsman had disappeared, Mack was elated.

"Great work, Eddie," he exclaimed. "Now that might just be the break we've all been hoping for."

"My sergeant here, Mike Bradford, deserves all the credit for finding the two guys. If he hadn't been so dedicated, so willing to go beer drinking after a long day on duty, we might never have found out about them," laughed Eddie.

"Well, tell Sergeant Bradford that I personally owe him one. In fact, I can probably tell him myself since I should probably get up there and talk to these guys. Will you be around this afternoon?"

"When am I not around," replied Eddie with a sigh. "Sure, I'll be here."

"You know, it would really be great if you could get those two guys to meet us at the beach this afternoon. That way they could show us exactly where they were when they heard the gunfire. Any chance you could set it up?"

"Don't see why not. Assuming I can get in touch with them, I'll try to arrange it for about two o'clock. How does that sound to you?"

"Two o'clock sounds perfect."

"Then why don't you meet me here at the office about one thirty.

That'll give us a little time to talk and still get us to the beach by two. I'll have them meet us there."

"Sounds good to me and, look, while I have you on the phone let me update you on what's been happening in Washington. As I think I told you, one of the German agents died so there will be only one going to trial. He'll be tried before a military tribunal and that trial should start sometime in the next few days; it'll be held in the Justice Department Building in downtown Washington. Unfortunately, there will be no press coverage, which means the only thing you'll hear is what the Government wants you to hear and that won't be much. The press is really riled up about the secrecy issue. For whatever reason people seem fascinated by spies and spy trials. I guess they have this image that spying is somehow glamorous, though from what I've seen it's anything but."

"Has this guy provided any additional information about his mission?" asked Eddie hopefully.

"Not yet, but I'm sure he will if for no other reason than to save his own neck. Of course everyone in Washington, including members of Congress, is calling for the death penalty. It's all up to President Roosevelt, however; he's the one who'll have to ultimately decide. But, if I were a betting man, I'd put my money on the electric chair for this guy. Rumor has it that Roosevelt wants to make an example of him. So, see you about one-thirty?"

It was just before two o'clock when Eddie and Mack drove into the beach parking lot. The day was humid with a heavy overcast so only about a dozen cars could be seen in the lot, along side one of which three men stood talking. Two of them were clearly civilians, the other, however, was dressed in the uniform of the United States Coast Guard.

"Oh, I almost forgot," Eddie explained, "I called the Coast Guard station down here and asked if one of the men would be willing to accompany us down the beach. I think the guy joining us will be Boatswain's Mate Jim Barry; he's the acting officer in charge of the station down here. You don't mind, do you?"

"Not at all," replied Mack. "Good thinking, in fact."

Eddie pulled the cruiser up next to the three men and he and

Mack climbed out. After everyone had been introduced, the five started towards the beach.

"You're in charge, Frank, so why don't you lead the way," said Eddie lightheartedly.

As they walked along the beach, Eddie and Mack took turns asking questions of the Coast Guardsman. Did he remember exactly what time it was when Frankie had left on his patrol? What was he wearing? How was he armed? What was the weather like? Had there been any kind of unusual activity at the beach that day?

They were all questions that had been asked many times before and both Eddie and Mack were familiar with the answers. Still, it was good to go over the information again, especially out here on the beach itself.

They had walked about two miles when Frank suddenly stopped. Pointing to what appeared to be nothing more than a mound of sand, he said, "That's where we were, right there."

"How can you be so certain?" inquired Mack. "It was dark, after all."

"I've been fishing off this beach for years. I know every sandbar, sand dune and piece of driftwood by heart. That mound of sand over there is actually an old lobster pot that was washed up on the beach during the big northeaster we had last February. That's what we dove behind when the shooting started."

It was an old lobster pot though nearly completely buried by sand and other detritus.

"Show us if you could, how you hid behind this mound and then indicate from where you think the shooting originated," Eddie asked.

They both crouched down and pointed in a general direction back up the beach.

"We kept our heads down for some time after the shooting ended. Then after everything seemed to have quieted down we raced back down towards the Essex River where our boat was moored," the nephew volunteered.

The uncle didn't appear too happy about the comment since it certainly didn't make them appear especially heroic.

Sensing his annoyance Mack quickly asked the uncle how far away he thought the shots had been coming from?

"A quarter of a mile," Frank answered.

"You agree with that estimate?" he asked the nephew.

"Yeah, a quarter of a mile, maybe a half a mile. There was a pretty good breeze blowing that night and we were downwind. The sound carried pretty well."

"But you saw nothing. No flashes from the muzzles, no lights of any kind," Eddie probed.

Frank looked at his nephew. They both indicated they hadn't.

"And, what about other sounds," Eddie asked. "Did you hear anyone shouting or crying out in pain as if struck by a bullet? You just said that sounds were carrying well that night."

"The wind that night was actually on-shore, which means it was not really blowing in our direction," Frank explained, giving his nephew an annoyed look. "On top of that the surf was very loud; you couldn't have heard anyone talking ten yards away. So, I'm not sure why we were able to hear the shots but we did, and there were a lot of them."

"All right," said Mack, "there's nothing more we can do here. Let's go back up the beach to where you think the gunfire may have come from."

When they had walked back about a quarter of a mile or so, Mack stopped.

"They must have come from about here," he said, glancing around.

Without another word they all began searching the area, though it was uncertain what they were looking for. Eddie headed off in the direction of the dunes.

"What's on your mind," Mack yelled over to him.

"Nothing really. I was just thinking that if anyone did come ashore here he, or they, would not have walked directly up the beach towards the Coast Guard station but would probably have sought cover in the dunes until someone came to collect them."

"So you think he, or they, let's call them 'they' since they're probably working in teams of at least two, have somebody helping them around here?"

"It's certainly possible. I mean, no one has reported seeing anyone suspicious and until we heard about the shooting, we'd come up with nothing. So if German agents really did come ashore here, one possible explanation for our inability to find them is that someone was waiting for them and has them in hiding."

"Can you think of anyone in your town who'd be prepared to engage in such activity," asked Mack. "I mean, hiding an enemy agent is pretty serious stuff; it can get you life in prison at a minimum."

" I can't think of anyone off-hand, though I certainly know people who are not especially enthused about America's involvement in the war. None of them, however, would be prepared to actively support the Nazis. That's one thing I'm sure of. Anyway, it would be too difficult to hide out in a small town like Ipswich. My guess is that they'd immediately be transported to a place like Boston where they could move about freely without arousing any undue suspicion."

"I agree completely," replied Mack. "And that's the assumption the Bureau is working on. We've alerted every police department in eastern Massachusetts to be on the lookout for any suspicious individuals. Unfortunately, there's no shortage of people whose behavior falls into that category."

"Don't I know that," admitted Eddie with an audible sigh of resignation.

"But let me ask you something else," said Mack pressing on with his questions. "What do you think they came here for? Was it to gather intelligence on ship movements? To buy or steal plans for new weapons systems, to commit sabotage? If we could only figure that out, you know, we'd have a much better idea of where to start looking for them."

"That," said Eddie, "is what I thought you guys were supposed to do. You've got this guy sitting in jail right there next to FBI headquarters and you can't get anything out of him? Sweat the guy, use drugs on him, do something. I mean, we are at war aren't we?"

"Oh, we'll get something. I just wanted to hear what you thought; you seem to have incredibly good instincts about this kind of thing. As for the guy in jail, he apparently acted really tough when they first arrested him, but I can tell you from experience it's mostly bluff. After a few days in jail with no outside contact a person begins to wilt. He wants to talk to someone, anyone. That's when we start to squeeze him. In this case we'll begin by explaining to him how an electric chair works, what it does to the human nervous system. It won't take long for him to realize his only hope is to tell us everything, though I suspect his execution is a certainty whatever he says."

"And in the meantime, of course, some other German agent could blow up a factory and dozens of innocent people could be killed," Eddie replied angrily.

Mack let it go; there was really nothing to say since Eddie was right. It could happen anytime. There was a war going on and even if they were able to catch these agents, more would be sent. They walked back to join the others.

"Look," Mack began, "we're not going to accomplish much ambling about like this so I suggest we organize a systematic search of this area for tomorrow if that's possible. Eddie, is there any way you could get about a dozen men down here armed with rakes and shovels? Maybe you could get them from the Highway Department or something. I know it's short notice. I'm pretty sure I could get a few guys to come down from the Boston office. They'd be only too happy to spend a day at the beach."

"I've got an even better idea, Mack. The commander of the Army boot camp uptown owes me big time for all the trouble his guys keep getting into. Maybe he can put a down payment on the balance by having some of his men come down here and help us. Plus they'll have a little better idea of what we're looking for. And while we're on the subject just what are we looking for?" laughed Eddie.

"Getting those army guys down here is a great idea. As for what they should be looking, I'm not entirely sure. It's been at least three weeks, but maybe spent cartridges, fragments of clothing, anything that might confirm our suspicions. Unfortunately, I suspect these guys were professionals, who did a good job of cleaning up after the firefight, so we probably won't be finding much. Still, anything is better than nothing!"

"All right, let's get back so I can set up this scavenger hunt."

Returning to the parking lot, Eddie and Mack thanked the Coast Guardsman for joining them and asked Frank and his nephew if either of them could be at the beach the next day. The nephew replied he could.

Once in the car Eddie turned to Mack.

"There is one thing I'd like to do on the way back. Only take a minute. Someone I'd like you to meet. It'll be worth it."

"Judging from the smile on your face it must be a she," replied Mack grinning.

"As I said, it'll be worth it."

It was almost time for Karl to leave for work and he was hurriedly rinsing off some dishes in the sink. Anne had not been around for much of the morning so without any instructions from her he had settled for splitting wood. He chose it for the exercise more than anything else. Certainly she was not going to be using her fireplace, not with the warm weather they'd been having. It occurred to him that he had not seen Anne to speak to since they had spent the night together and he was sure she had been consciously doing her best to avoid him. Sooner or later she would have to talk to him, he mused, if only to tell him what she wanted done around the place.

Any further thoughts were suddenly interrupted by the sound of a car driving into the yard. Glancing out the window he was surprised to see it was a police car with two men in it. Taking great care not to be seen, he watched as the two men climbed out and looked around. Karl quickly recognized the driver; it was the local police chief whom he seemed to be running into everywhere. The other man was not anyone he had seen before; neither was he wearing a police uniform, though he carried himself erect and with a sense of authority that had military intelligence or FBI written all over it. Regardless of who he was, however, one thing was certain-- they had not stopped by just for a social call.

As he watched they both stopped and looked in the direction of the marshes. They appeared to be admiring the view, though it could be just a ruse. Karl breathed a little easier. The two were not acting as if they had come to arrest anyone. Still, he'd better remain on guard. If he had to get away quickly, his only means of escape would be jumping from one of the back windows. Just at that moment they turned and headed for Anne's back door. Even before reaching it, however, Anne had come out on the screened porch to greet them. Though Karl couldn't hear what was being said he could tell the police chief knew Anne and was introducing her to the other man. A minute or so later they all entered the house.

Karl decided to stay out of sight until they left even if it meant being a little late for work. He kept his eye on the house though he could see nothing. Why, he thought, would they want to talk to her? And who was that guy with the chief? Perhaps those stupid crewmen dumped the bodies over the side before reaching the sub and they've been found. Or maybe they've arrested some of the other members of the operation. Still, if his cover had been blown they'd almost certainly have come to arrest him and that didn't appear to be their intention. He'd have to find out from Anne just what they had come for.

About fifteen minutes after entering the house Karl saw the two men coming back out onto the porch. Judging from the laughter it had been a pleasant visit. Anne walked them to their car and waved as they disappeared down the driveway. Only then did she go back into the house. Odd, he thought to himself, but in that entire time no one even glanced up in this direction though he was certain the chief knew he was living here. I wonder if he suspects me of something. But if so, what, that was the big question?

Chapter Nineteen

There was something about this Karl Stoner that was beginning to get on Eddie's nerves, but he couldn't figure out what is was. It had started the night he interviewed him about the fight; he was so sure of himself, so arrogant. But, it had to be more than that. The little checking Eddie had done on him had turned up absolutely nothing, just the opposite, in fact. The few people he could find that actually knew Karl had only positive things to say--he was a hard worker; he was not a heavy drinker; he went out of his way to look after Tom O'Malley. The only blemish on his record that Eddie could find was the fight and even that did not appear to be Karl's fault; the evidence clearly suggested he had done his best to avoid it. So, what was it about this guy? Reluctantly, Eddie had to concede that it was his relationship with Anne. It was bad enough that he was living at her place and appeared now to be acting as her chauffer, but Eddie couldn't help wondering if they might be sleeping together. He couldn't get the thought out of his head and it was driving him crazy. And making it even worse, it was not the kind of thing he could talk to anyone about.

Eddie had arrived at the beach early and was now sitting slouched in the cruiser waiting for Mack and the enlisted men to show up. He was thinking about Karl, something that was not putting him in a good mood though he had every reason to be. The commander of Camp Agawam had agreed to his request without hesitation. He would send down two-dozen men along with an NCO. That way, he explained, he could always say it was a military exercise if anyone later asked what they were doing down there. As for the rakes and shovels, the Highway

Department had dropped off everything he needed about an hour before.

Eddie was almost asleep when he detected the rumble of a large truck coming his way. Looking into his rear-view mirror he saw a military green lorry bumping across the parking lot followed closely by a black Plymouth sedan. As they pulled up he recognized Frank Storey's nephew in the Plymouth. Beyond he could see the enlisted men swarming out of the truck like a group of children heading for a day at the beach. Eddie climbed stiffly out of the cruiser and wandered over towards the truck. Spotting the NCO, he introduced himself and briefly went over what his men were to do with the rakes and shovels.

As he completed giving the NCO his orders, Mack roared into the parking lot raising a cloud of dust.

"Sorry, I'm late," he grumbled, as he scrambled out of his car. "Between phone calls and paper work, I just couldn't get away as early as I wanted."

"No problem, we all just got here ourselves," Eddie lied.

After Eddie had made the necessary introductions, they all set out down the beach to where Frank and his nephew had heard the gunfire. When they reached the spot, Mack had the sergeant line up his men between the high-tide line and the dunes in order to rake the sand for any man-made objects they might uncover. Whenever anything was found, it was placed in a bag Mack had given to each man for just this purpose.

Although there was not much sun, it was very humid and the men had responded by stripping to the waist. Soon they had removed their boots and socks as well. As they raked, they maintained a steady banter of insults and wisecracks and whenever something was found it provided an additional cause for joking and laughter before it was finally deposited in one of the bags. While all this was going on Eddie and Mack took the opportunity to explore the adjacent dune area.

"One thing I'm almost certain of, if a person was going to bury something around here it would probably be somewhere down there," Mack postulated, pointing to a grove of trees in a valley between the dunes.

"Otherwise," he continued, "it would be too difficult to find the spot again and anyway the person would be too exposed while he was digging. He'd want the trees for cover."

"I suspect you're right," replied Eddie. "Let's go down and have a look."

The trees, a mixture of pitch pine, black cherry and poplar, provided a respite from the heat in the dunes. It was also easy to move about for there was little in the way of underbrush.

"This place must be crawling with deer. Look at the tracks and deer droppings. Is it legal to hunt around here?" asked Mack incredulously.

"Sorry to disappoint you but hunting isn't allowed on the beach. That's one reason why there are so many deer around."

"I don't know why I asked; I'm not a hunter myself, I prefer deep-sea fishing. How about yourself?"

"Don't do either," Eddie replied. "I never seem to find the time to do much of anything, to be honest."

They continued to search the area but found nothing to suggest anyone had been hiding out there or had buried anything recently.

"What do you say," suggested Mack, "should we head back to the beachfront and see if they've had any better luck? We're not going to find anything around here. I'm not even sure there's anything to find."

They slogged back through the sand and met up with the sergeant.

"Anyone find anything of interest?" asked Eddie.

"Doesn't appear so," he replied. "I mean, they have found stuff, you know like shell casings, a jackknife, some coins, things like that, but nothing that really stands out. Do you want us to keep going? We've pretty well finished the area you wanted searched."

"No," Mack responded. "It was just a shot in the dark anyway. I'll just collect what they've found and take it back to the lab with me. I really appreciate your help."

"And, I'll call your commander and personally thank him," Eddie added.

"Hey, it was like recess for these guys. Probably the only time in weeks I haven't heard them complaining about what they're doing," laughed the sergeant.

Mack gathered up the booty. He and Eddie followed the men back up the beach to the parking lot. The nephew's car was gone by the time they got there.

"Probably didn't really need him to come back here today," Eddie mused.

"I suppose you're going to stop by to have a visit with that woman we met yesterday. Anne was her name? She's some woman. I wouldn't let her run around loose if I were you. Someone's going to catch her before long, you can bet on that."

Eddie laughed but it was Karl's image that flashed through his mind, not Anne's.

"I've run out of excuses for stopping by," Eddie offered wistfully.

"A woman like her? That's excuse enough. Let's be honest, she has to get bored kicking around that house all day."

Mack could tell by the expression on Eddie's face that he was touching on a sensitive issue so he quickly changed the topic.

"If the lab finds anything interesting here or, even better, if we get some information from our favorite German spy, I'll give you a call."

"Thanks, Mack, hopefully I'll be talking to you soon."

The humidity had only gotten worse during the afternoon and by early evening the metal structure in which Karl was working had become stifling. Every door and window had been thrown open in the vain attempt to capture the slightest movement of air. Karl was sweltering even more than most of the workers because of the clothes he had to wear when he was welding. In addition to the large bulky helmet that protected his face and, especially, his eyes from sparks and hot molten metal, he wore thick gloves along with a heavy leather apron. But however difficult work conditions were for Karl, they had become impossible for Tom O'Malley, who looked as if any minute now he was going to pass out. His face was scarlet and his breathing had become increasingly more labored as the evening wore on. Karl finally convinced him to go outside and get some fresh air before he had a heart attack.

As with much of Karl's concern for Tom, there was a measure of ulterior motive to it. Though he was under orders not to commit any acts of sabotage within the first two months of his arrival, he was realistic enough to know his presence could be uncovered at any moment. He had begun to devise a plan of sorts, one that would hopefully destroy the shipyard while keeping casualties to a minimum. The purpose of the mission was after all to make a statement—that Germany had the capability to bring the war to America. And, while he was having some doubts about the wisdom of the mission, that is, whether it would actually accomplish anything, he intended to go through with it.

The first step in his plan was to begin smuggling in some of the explosives and incendiary devices he would be using; he just needed a secure place to hide them. Even with the shipyard's relatively loose security, it would not be wise to bring more than one or two devices in on any given day; he would do it over a period of a couple weeks smuggling them into the yard in his lunchbox. And it was for that reason he needed to find a place to conceal them. It turned out to be easier than he expected for within only a few minutes of poking around he'd discovered several potential sites.

For much of the evening the rumble of distant thunder could be heard over the pounding and rattling of the shipyard. By quitting time, however, the thunder had taken on a new intensity while bolts of lightning followed one after another across the pitch-black sky. Racing out the gate on his old bicycle, Karl could only hope he'd be able to reach home before the full force of the storm hit, though as he pedaled furiously up the road he realized there was no chance of making it. He resigned himself to getting thoroughly soaked.

Karl had just passed Clark's Pond when the first few droplets of rain splattered against his face. Within seconds the storm was upon him with a fury that made it almost impossible to see the road in front of him. Ultimately, the rain became so heavy he had no choice but to dismount and push his bike through the monsoon-like downpour. As he made the turn and started up Anne's driveway, the night sky was suddenly illuminated by a blazing flash of light, followed almost instantly by a thunderous crash. A nearby tree exploded into flame as if struck by an artillery shell. Instinctively, Karl cast his bicycle aside and threw himself onto a thick blanket of wet pine needles. As he was lying there, catching his breath, an image of his father began to take shape in his mind. It was strange because he only knew what he looked like from photos, but he was certain it was his father huddled there in a mud-filled trench trying desperately to escape the endless rain of artillery shells pouring down on him and his regimental companions. Even in his mind Karl could see it was hopeless; there was no way for any of them to avoid being torn apart by the fragments of jagged steel exploding among them. Karl even imagined he could see the body of his father lying twisted and bloody among the indecent tangle of dead and dying men.

Shaken, and just a bit dismayed by his reaction to the lightening strike, Karl dragged himself to his feet and, picking up his bicycle, began pushing it up the driveway using the occasional flashes of lightning to find his way. Reaching at last the safety of the barn, Karl leaned the bicycle against the wall and returned to the doorway where he stood for several minutes waiting for his heart to stop pounding. As he watched the storm slide steadily off to the southeast, he suddenly detected a faint light moving uncertainly about the downstairs of Anne's house; the rest of the house was in complete darkness. He immediately suspected a prowler, having just read in the local newspaper that several empty houses in the area had been broken into. And, though the police were fairly certain the break-ins had been the work of high school kids, they had no proof of it. But, even if it were only high school kids Anne could find herself in a potentially dangerous situation if she tried to confront them.

Between flashes of lightning Karl slipped noiselessly across the yard and cautiously opened the screened door onto the porch. The intruder was now moving about the kitchen. Concluding there was only one person inside and that he was unlikely to be very heavily armed, Karl moved towards the kitchen door. As he was reaching for the knob, the door suddenly opened and he found himself staring into the flashlight's blinding beam.

He heard a startled cry and then a frightened voice say, "Karl, what are you doing?"

It was Anne.

Standing there in front of her soaking wet, poised to attack an intruder, he suddenly realized how foolish he must look.

"I'm sorry to have frightened you. I was coming in from work and saw the light. I thought it was a prowler."

She laughed with obvious relief.

"The storm woke me up and I was so frightened by it, I turned on some lights. Then there came a loud crash and the lights went out. I finally found a flashlight and was just coming out on the porch to see if I could figure out why the power went out."

Karl now saw that Anne was wearing only the briefest cotton nightgown and she was beginning to shiver.

"You should go in," he advised. "You're getting cold."

"So are you. Please come in. I'll make us some hot tea or something."

She had that fragile, vulnerable look again.

Karl stepped forward and put his arms around her. There was no hesitation in her response this time. She met his mouth hungrily.

"You're soaking wet," she murmured. "Lets get those things off."

She took his hand and feeling her way along led him up the stairs and into her bedroom. She fumbled with the buttons on his shirt but they were impossible to undo. He took over while she undid his belt. Finally, free of his wet clothes he drew her to him. They were both shivering as he slipped the nightgown over her head. Anne backed up to the bed and pulled him down on top her. As he slipped into her she let out a soft moan. There was something about this night, perhaps the residue of her earlier fright that heightened her sense of arousal. It was a reaction, she later decided, similar to that experienced by many Londoners during the Blitz who found themselves seized by an almost uncontrollable urge to make love even as German bombs were raining down death and destruction all about them.

They made love several times that night but it was quite unlike their first encounter. They were far more patient, gently exploring every intimate spot in an attempt to discover in each other new sources of pleasure and excitement. Later, as they lay relaxed, entwined in each other's arms and legs, Karl whispered, "Tell me about your husband. What was he like?"

Anne was surprised by the question and it took her a few moments to think about her response.

"He was a really good man," she said finally, her voice barely audible. "He was the only man I guess I ever loved and I was devastated when he died."

She didn't add that she had become terribly lonely and that her marriage had come to feel empty.

Karl remained silent. She was obviously thinking about her husband

and he had no desire to intrude on what he assumed was her sadness for his passing. When she did speak again it was obvious she had decided to take the conversation in a slightly different direction.

"My father never completely approved of him, you know, not even in later years when Bob had demonstrated how devoted he was both to me and our son. I've never quite forgiven my father for that."

"But why didn't your father approve of him?" asked Karl, genuinely curious about her answer. He tried to picture his own father but all he drew was that strange image of his father crouching in the trench during an artillery barrage.

"Oh, for silly reasons. The kind only New Englanders would really understand. I guess the best way to put is to say my father was a snob; he still is a snob for that matter."

"But what did his being a snob have to do with it," he asked, clearly confused.

"Well, being the snob he is meant he didn't approve of the fact I was marrying someone whose ancestors didn't come over on the Mayflower. The Mayflower was the ship that brought the first English settlers to this country and Bob's family didn't trace its roots back to anyone on that ship. Silly, huh? And, then, Bob's family didn't come from old money; they weren't robber barons or slave traders. But, the single biggest reason he disapproved of him, and by far the stupidest, was because he didn't go to Harvard; not that he couldn't have gone by the way."

"You're right, I don't understand a lot of what you said but it does seem your father wasn't very fair to your husband; I can also tell you're very bitter about it and I can't say I don't blame you."

Anne was too upset to continue with the conversation though she wasn't entirely certain why. Instead she drew Karl's arms more tightly around her and closed her eyes. They didn't move for the longest time and when finally they drifted off to sleep they didn't even notice that the first faint glow of daylight was already making its way over the watery horizon.

Chapter Twenty

On this morning it was Karl who awoke first, roused by the bright sunlight streaming through the open windows. The air was completely still; the curtains hung lifeless. The day was going to be what the locals called a "scorcher." Glancing at his watch he was astonished to see it was nearly noon. Good God, he thought, how undisciplined he had become; he should have been up hours ago. Once again he was struck by a feeling of guilt, especially when he compared his situation to that of his friends so many of which were serving and dying on the Eastern Front. Of course, he was doing what he had been trained to do, and if he were caught he would die just like them. Unfortunately, he just couldn't help feeling there was an element of futility to all they were doing and it wasn't only his mission but the whole campaign against the Russians as well. He was rapidly coming to believe it was going to take a miracle for Germany not to suffer another disastrous defeat, and he was not one to believe much in miracles.

Thinking like this did little to push him out of bed. Instead, he continued to lie there with his hands clasped behind his head, surveying Anne's bedroom. He realized he had never really studied the framed photographs Anne had placed everywhere--on the walls, the bureau, even on the night table next to the bed. The only face he actually recognized other than Anne's was her son though it didn't take much to figure out which one was probably Anne's late husband. The others, he concluded, appeared to be either her parents or his. Staring at all those smiling faces, he wondered what it would be like to be married and have a family. Not the sham marriage encouraged by his superiors in the Abwehr but a real marriage with children of his own. Until this moment he had never really thought much about it. His own childhood had not been an especially happy one and, then, what with the war, well, it just hadn't seemed like a wise thing to do. But looking over at Anne, the idea didn't appear quite so far-fetched now. And, he even had money, fifty thousand American dollars to be exact, just sitting there in one of the wooden chests buried at the beach. But enough of these thoughts, he reminded himself, they were not only foolish, they were dangerous.

He looked down at Anne who appeared to be sleeping soundly; only a few strands of her hair were visible on the pillow. She had obviously pulled the sheet up in an effort to ward off the bright sunlight but it also served to highlight the soft contours of her body. He had to admit he'd never known a woman quite like her. In Germany a woman was discouraged from acting independently even if she had the means to do so. But Anne was more than just independent. She was attractive, intelligent and possessed an uninhibited and passionate approach to lovemaking that continually surprised him. He wondered if marriage would change all that. There was that word again, marriage, he had to stop thinking about it, and anyway, marrying Anne was out of the question for a host of reasons, not the least of which was the age difference; she had to be at least a dozen years older. The greater obstacle, however, would probably be the fact that her son was only a few years younger than himself. He decided it was a good time to get up; the whole thing was beginning to depress him. Easing himself to a sitting position, he was about to stand when a hand gently took him by the arm.

"Going somewhere?" asked a rather groggy voice.

He turned. Anne had thrown back the sheet and was now lying on her side looking up at him with a soft smile. She was bare from the waist up and made no attempt to cover her breasts since modesty no longer seemed necessary. Furthermore, Anne was very proud of the fact that her breasts were still firm and full, something she suspected few women her age could truthfully say. Glancing at Karl she could see he was staring at them and she suspected he was struggling with the urge to lean over and kiss her dark inviting nipples. Just watching him she could feel herself becoming aroused. Why didn't he respond, she wondered. In fact, Karl could barely resist burying himself in her but he knew she was teasing him. It was now a test of wills only he wasn't certain how badly he wanted to win this contest.

"Well, I have some things I really should get done today," he offered, knowing full well Anne was not about to let him leave.

Anne responded by rolling onto her back, allowing the sheet to slip further down her body. It was not a fair test, Karl concluded, as his eyes moved admiringly down her smooth flat stomach, stopping only when he came to the line of dark hair protruding invitingly from beneath the sheet. She was watching him just as intently, hoping to detect the first hint of weakness.

"Now let me see," she said mischievously. "You don't have to be at the shipyard until nearly four and until then you're supposed to be working for me. So, if I give you the rest of the day off, we still have several free hours, do we not?"

He couldn't help smiling and whatever qualms he had about their relationship no longer seemed quite so important. He rolled back onto the bed and took her in his arms.

"Now doesn't this beat whatever it was you had to do?" she sighed.

It was nearly one-thirty before Karl made it back to his apartment. Before he left, Anne had informed him, almost apologetically to be sure, that she'd be leaving for Boston later in the afternoon and she wasn't sure exactly when she'd be returning? Her mother was very ill and her father had asked if Anne could come and spend a few days with her. He had made it sound serious so she had agreed without hesitation, she explained, but now that it was time to say good-by she was having second thoughts. She promised she would not stay away very long

For his part, Karl had also found her proposed absence unwelcome but his concern was very different. For one thing, Anne had mentioned that one of her friends had been annoyed by his seemingly arrogant attitude at the cookout, a comment he couldn't believe coming from that group. And while it was true Anne had said it jokingly, there was still something strange about it. Also strange was the fact her unexpected visit was occurring only a day or so after the visit by the police. Could it be they were suspicious of him and that her trip was an excuse to get her safely away while the police placed him under surveillance? It had been stupid of him not to ask her what they had wanted. It wasn't that he hadn't thought about it, only that he hadn't figured out how to do ask without making her suspicious. Now she was leaving and it would probably be several days, at least, before he would be speaking with her again. He decided it might be wise if he rigged a small trap or two just to be certain no one was entering his apartment while he was away at the shipyard. A couple of strategically placed hairs on the only entrance to the apartment would probably do the trick.

Eddie glanced at his watch; it was almost two-thirty and at the moment he was the only one on duty at the police station. For the third time since noon he had gotten up and poured himself a cup of coffee. He did it largely out of habit since he seldom drank much of it. The only coffee available since the war had begun was of such poor quality Eddie likened it to drinking muddy water. Still, he liked the idea of having a cup of coffee at hand for it seemed to relax him even if most of it would just end up in the sink.

As he was walking carefully over to his desk, for as usual he had filled his cup literally to the brim, the phone rang. Reaching for the receiver Eddie let out an expletive as the liquid slopped over the edge of his cup and down the front of his pants.

"Some greeting for a guy who's calling with great news," came a voice from the phone. Eddie instantly recognized Mack McCarthy's laugh.

"Sorry about that but you just made me spill coffee all over myself; of course, I drink too much of the horrible stuff anyway, though there are probably better ways to cut back than dumping it on my pants. So, what's the great news?"

"All right, let's start with the captured German agent. It's finally sunk in to him that he's facing the electric chair so he's hurriedly trying to tell us everything he knows as a means of saving himself."

"So, will it," asked Eddie quickly.

"Not a chance," Mack replied bluntly. "But, he has given us valuable information. For example, he told us that he, and the guy that died, though he still thinks he's in the hospital, had been sent here as part of a larger operation, code-named Firestorm, to conduct sabotage against East Coast military bases and industrial facilities. Apparently Germany's military leaders had wanted to undertake such an operation for several years but Hitler wasn't interested; he worried it would provoke us into entering the war. Of course, then he went ahead and declared war on us anyway so he had no good reason not to implement the plan."

"I don't get it," said Eddie. "Does Hitler really think he can do enough damage to affect the war effort?"

"Probably not, but by bringing the war into America's backyard, so to speak, he may score some propaganda points. It's a way for him to demonstrate that Germany's military might can be projected anywhere on the globe, even to America."

"So, what does the FBI think? Are these guys really capable of doing any serious damage?"

"Well, not these two certainly, but from what our songbird says about a dozen were sent here, so that leaves at least ten unaccounted for. Apparently they all trained together for this operation at a special school the Abwehr has established for this sort of thing on the outskirts of Berlin. He referred to it as Quenz Farm. Anyway, as part of their training these guys were taught how to make surprisingly sophisticated bombs and incendiary devices out of simple ingredients like sugar, oil and potassium chlorate. They were even taken to various industrial sites around Berlin and shown what kind of explosives to use and how to place them for maximum effect. So, in answer to your question, if everything he's told us is true, they are well trained and with a little luck they could do some real damage if we don't catch them quickly."

"How do you go about looking for such guys?" Eddie inquired anxiously.

"It's not going to be easy. Apparently to qualify for the operation a person had to have lived here in the States for at least five years and to speak English fluently. Furthermore, once they made it ashore they were expected to go about finding jobs, buying homes, and even getting married as a way of assimilating into American society. Clearly, this was planned as a long-term operation. The good thing, if I may use that term, is that these guys were probably not sent here as decoys to mask an even more elaborate operation."

"Well, I guess that's some consolation but were you able to find out anything from this guy about the possible whereabouts of our missing Coast Guardsman?"

"No, we didn't. The only thing this guy said in that regard was that they had been trained in the use of a variety of weapons as well as in hand-to-hand combat. However, while he couldn't help us, our little search party at the beach yesterday came up big."

"What do you mean, did they really find something?" Eddie desperately needed better news than the fact there were ten more German agents on the loose.

"Among the numerous shell casings we found there was one quite different from all the rest. Our lab guys have identified as coming from a German-made Bergmann MP34 submachine gun. It's a common enough weapon in Germany, but it isn't one you'd expect to find here in the States."

"So," interrupted Eddie, "the Essex guys were not imagining things after all."

"They certainly weren't," Mack continued. "It's very possible that German agents coming ashore may have surprised the Coast Guardsman and killed him along with his dog. The bodies were probably taken back in the same dinghy that brought the agents ashore and dumped well out to sea. That's why we haven't been able to find any trace of them."

"How come we didn't find more shell casings, then?" asked Eddie.

"Oh, I'm sure they were under orders to collect all shell casings so there'd be no evidence of a crime; they just missed one. If it hadn't been for the two Essex guys, we would have missed it too. Oh yes, and there's one more thing I forgot to mention. The agents sent here brought with them a good supply of explosives. Our German captive is going to take us to the spot where he hid his supply. Once we see what they brought with them, we'll have a better idea what to be on the lookout for."

"Look, don't get me wrong, I think this is all great," Eddie admitted ruefully, "but couldn't this guy have given you some information on these ten guys, like what are their names and what do they look like?"

"Hey, give us a break, Eddie, of course we got such information from him. We're checking on the names right now, but as I'm sure you must realize they're all probably operating under false identities. Apparently, they didn't even use their real names during training. As for their physical descriptions, those could fit just about anyone. This is no amateur operation; these guys are pros."

"So, are you telling me that with all the information you've been able to acquire, you guys are no closer to nailing the other agents than you were before?"

"I'm not saying that at all. Armed with this new information we now have hundreds of agents scouring the East Coast from Maine to Florida, which admittedly is a huge area. In addition, we've issued warnings to all major defense plants to increase their security and let us know immediately if they detect any activity they deem unusual."

" But do you know how many potential targets there are just in New England alone?" Eddie asked incredulously. "There are hundreds. There are even targets in this town."

"We're well aware of that." Mack replied. "For the moment all we can do is keep our eyes open for anything that seems amiss. Hopefully, they'll make some kind of mistake that will reveal their whereabouts before they can do any serious damage. Still, there is one thing I'm going to request of my boss."

"And what's that?"

"I'm going to request that the Bureau assign some men down here to keep the beach under surveillance. There's just a chance, a small one admittedly, that our German agents may have buried some of their equipment when they came ashore and they may now need to get it. If they do, I want to be there to grab them."

"Isn't it possible they've already gotten their stuff. It's been three weeks or more since they landed."

"They may have. Like I said, it's a long-shot," responded Mack with a grin. "However, I owe my last two promotions at the Bureau to betting on long-shots and I feel it's about time I received another promotion."

Chapter Twenty-One

The several days immediately following Anne's departure were anxious ones for Karl. The suddenness of the whole thing--her mother's illness, her father's request for her to visit--seemed far too coincidental. Consequently, he found himself checking and re-checking the small traps he had set to detect whether anyone was entering his apartment while he was away at the shipyard. If there were, the person had to be a professional, he decided, since the traps appeared undisturbed. Gradually, as the days passed, he began to breathe more easily, although as he did so he found to his surprise he began to miss Anne. He chided himself for acting like a lovelorn teenager, but it did little to suppress his growing unhappiness with her absence.

By Friday Karl concluded he had been mistaken; he was not under surveillance. It was time, then, to begin smuggling the blocks of explosive into the shipyard. Security, Karl had long since noticed, became increasingly lax as the weekend approached; security guards were clearly no different than the rest of the workers there. Smuggling his first block through the main gate proved to be no problem. Karl was a little surprised but relieved. Had he been asked to open his lunchbox, he had no ready answer for why he had a piece of coal in it. In that sense it would be much easier smuggling in the pen-and-pencil incendiary devices. On the other hand, if he were discovered with a cache of pen-and-pencil sets, it would be no small task explaining them away either since his work did not require any kind of writing. Clearly, he had to make certain he did nothing to arouse even the slightest suspicion about his activities.

Saturday morning arrived without any sign of Anne. Karl decided to drive the truck to town; he needed to purchase some food items, but he especially wanted to get copies of the local newspapers. The radio kept him reasonably well informed on national and world affairs but for the report he was preparing to send to Berlin he needed far more information on the kinds of issues New Englanders were concerned about. Local newspapers were also the only places where he could pick up information on ship launchings, for example, though because of the government's partial ban on publishing such information one had to be able to read between the lines to obtain it.

Karl was able to buy several newspapers, among them the Boston *Post*, the Salem *News*, and the Ipswich *Chronicle*. The banner headline on the *Post*, Brits Halt German Advance, captured the tone of the latest news. The story accompanying the headline made it fairly clear that Rommel's drive towards the Nile had been blunted and with it all hope of reaching the Persian Gulf. If the story were accurate, Karl concluded, it was a setback almost as serious as the Nazi leadership's failure to mount an invasion of England. As for the other news it was no less discouraging. There was an item describing how the bombing of German cities by the British and Americans was forcing the diversion of air support from the Eastern Front, where it was already in short supply, to the home front. And then there was the picture of a military funeral, the caption of which read--twenty-nine German crewmen of a U-boat sunk by an American destroyer were buried with full military honors in Hampton, Virginia. Could it have been U-128, the U-boat he came over on? He thought about Captain Frisch. One of the war's unsung heroes and a real German patriot, he mused. How many such men will have to die before this war ends? And Thomas? Was he one of the twenty-nine buried with honors? He hoped not. Thomas deserved a better fate; they all did for that matter.

For a time he stopped reading, giving himself over to thinking what it must be like to die several hundred feet down in the waters of the Atlantic. But, it was too disconcerting to even contemplate. Eventually, he went back to the newspapers scanning many of the smaller items appearing on the inside pages. One discussed the probability that gasoline rationing, now limited to the East Coast, would be extended to the entire country by fall. It also added that rubber, the only other commodity presently rationed, would soon be joined by shoes, canned goods, aluminum, sugar, and butter--to name just a few.

An article that particularly caught Karl's eye concerned complaints by submarine commanders of a shortage of torpedoes. Until now apparently the navy had possessed a monopoly on torpedo production, which was conducted at two factories--Newport, Rhode Island, and Alexandria, Virginia. Unfortunately, even working at full capacity the two plants were unable to keep up with demand so the government was considering contracting additional torpedo production out to the private sector. In the meantime, however, the shortage would continue. Karl quickly decided the Newport torpedo plant might make an excellent next target. Shutting down that plant could have a major impact on the war effort. How often did one find targets like this? For a moment he wondered if perhaps he shouldn't even bother with the shipyard and instead go for the torpedo plant, but he quickly concluded he had put too much preparation into the shipyard to give up on it.

Karl had nearly completed his reading of the newspapers when another item, this one in the Salem *News*, caught his attention. Within a rather rambling article describing how local civic organizations like the Chambers of Commerce, Civil Air Patrol and Boy Scouts were pitching in to aid the war effort there was an interview with the commander of the Salem Coast Guard station. In response to a question about how ordinary citizens could contribute to the war effort, the commander mentioned that everyone should be on the lookout for spies. The FBI, he reported, had evidence to suggest that U-boats may have dropped several German agents off at various places along the New England coast. If anyone, therefore, were to see anything suspicious, it should be reported immediately to local authorities. That was it; there was no elaboration and no further mention of German agents in the article.

So, Karl thought, that's why the police had probably stopped by to see Anne and that guy with the chief was almost certainly FBI. But what evidence could they have found? He was not surprised there was no mention in the article of anything. On the other hand, it did seem to suggest the FBI was looking for more than one person. That was at least a little consolation. In fact, it was about the only encouraging piece of news appearing in any of the newspapers, though by itself it was hardly a reason for celebration.

As for Anne the days away from Ipswich were turning out to be difficult ones for her as well. Although she had gone to Boston because of concern over her mother's health, she found she couldn't stop thinking about Karl even as she sat by her mother's bedside. It made her feel incredibly guilty for she knew how hurt her parents would be if they found out about her affair. Even her mother, who had always prided herself on being just a bit of a rebel, in thought at least, if not in deeds, would be shocked at the idea of her grown daughter having an affair with a stranger only a few years older than her son. It probably wouldn't do much good, she decided, to remind her mother she had once remarked, with more than a hint of sarcasm, that while society scorned women who had extramarital affairs, it appeared to reward men who did so. In her defense, of course, Anne could rightly point out she was not having an extramarital affair; she was not married, neither of them was, although to be honest she really didn't know for sure about Karl. It probably wouldn't matter to her parents in any case.

Of course, it wouldn't be only her parents who'd be hurt; she already knew how her son felt. Just the suspicion that there might be something going on with Karl had been sufficient to trigger off a surprisingly bitter exchange. He would never understand nor would he ever forgive her, she was certain of that.

And, then, there were her friends, whom she knew would be outwardly appalled. On the other hand, they were also the biggest hypocrites. She knew for a fact that at least two of the men whose wives she hung out with were having affairs with women in Boston. She had heard it from a mutual friend. As for the wives themselves, her so-called friends, they'd spread word of her affair all over town even while secretly envying her. Sex seemed to be their favorite topic of conversation these days. They were forever talking about how uninterested their husbands were in having sex. No wonder, she thought bitterly, their husbands were getting all the sex they wanted here in Boston.

Anne knew she was trying to rationalize her behavior and when all was said and done her affair was unwise, if not wrong. Ultimately, she would hurt everyone who was close to her if word about it got out, and inevitably it would. She wondered if, in fact, the whole affair was really just about sex anyway. While she felt guilty even thinking it, the truth was her husband had never been an especially imaginative lover. Dutiful maybe, but he had never displayed much passion for it. She had always blamed herself having been a virgin when she slipped into bed on her wedding night. Yet, in just that one time with Karl she realized how much more there could be to lovemaking than what she had ever experienced.

But the more she thought about it, the more she came to the realization that it was more than just sex with Karl. Some people, she had concluded, could live contentedly by themselves, but she was definitely not one of those people. She needed someone with whom to share her life; she didn't enjoy being on her own, even though she often told people she did, and it was not just middle age looming. She had never liked it. That was the reason she worried about ending her relationship with Karl. What if no other man ever appeared in her life? It was a frightening thought. And, it would be so easy just to continue her relationship with him, so easy and so pleasurable. But, in the end it all came down to the other people in her life; was she really prepared to hurt them?

Chapter Twenty-Two

By Sunday afternoon Anne's continued absence was beginning to anger Karl, especially after learning there was a search underway in the area for possible German agents. And while he kept reminding himself he hadn't been in any kind of trouble since arriving in town, other than that stupid fight, he still had the feeling he was under some kind of surveillance. For some reason he felt less exposed when Anne was around, probably because he suspected she would alert him if she learned he was in any kind of danger. Of course, she might be ordered by the police not to do so. But, even then he was sure she would say something. For the moment, at least, he had no choice but to operate on that assumption.

There were, however, a couple of things about his relationship with Anne that were beginning to make him feel a little uneasy. For one, it seemed he was becoming dependent on her to protect his cover, perhaps too dependent. On the other hand, there was also the issue of what would happen to her if he were caught and exposed as a spy. Could she be arrested for harboring him even if she were totally ignorant of his mission? Until this moment he had never really given it much thought. No, that wasn't quite true, he had thought about the possibility of her being arrested, but until now that possibility had never really bothered him. Now, suddenly, it did and it greatly complicated his situation. He had to find a way to protect her though he suspected it might already be too late for that; she would be found guilty just through her association with him, if not in the eyes of the law, almost certainly in the eyes of most Americans.

To help relieve some of his anxiety Karl decided to retrieve his short-wave radio from the beach. At least if his cover were blown, the radio would enable him to quickly contact Abwehr headquarters in Berlin and request a U-boat be sent to rescue him. And, while he realized that the chances of successfully conducting such a rescue were slight at best, it was still a plan and in that sense it provided a boost to his morale. Of course, retrieving the radio from the beach posed its own set of risks. It was too bulky and obvious to transport by bicycle, so he would probably have to use the pickup truck to get it back to the barn. For this reason it was best if he retrieved the radio while Anne was away. It would save him having to explain why he needed to drive down to the beach in the truck.

The day had started out sunny and seasonably warm but by late afternoon it had clouded over as the wind shifted into the northeast; there was now a distinct chill to the air and just a hint of rain. As Karl drove into the beach parking lot he noticed two lone cars there; he had been hoping to have the beach to himself but two cars was probably the next best thing. Parking his pickup truck as far away from them as possible, he shut off the engine. Almost immediately he saw two men climb out of one of the cars and glance over in his direction. With their dark suits and fedoras they had G-men written all over them. You could never mistake them for they dressed the same the world over, he thought. These guys must have the beach under surveillance. Luckily he had come by truck. Had he biked down he'd have a much more difficult time explaining what he was doing there.

He climbed out of the truck as if nothing were amiss, though the pounding of his heart provided a healthy reminder of the potentially dangerous situation he was in. He stood motionless as the two men slowly approached. The expression on their faces spelled trouble. "Excuse me, I'm Agent Ben Smith, FBI," said one of the men flashing his identification. "And this is Agent Silvestri. Mind if I ask you your name?"

"Not at all," responded Karl, mustering up a weak smile. "It's Stoner. Karl Stoner."

"May I see some form of identification?"

Karl reached into his wallet and drew out his driver's license; he was not worried they'd be able to recognize it as a forgery just by inspecting it. Karl did notice that both agents appeared to be wearing shoulder holsters; it was impossible to completely hide the bulge in their jackets.

After examining the license for several seconds, Agent Smith moved as if he were about to hand it back only instead it slipped from his grasp and fell to the ground; he made no attempt to pick it up. Karl instantly understood he had done it intentionally. Clearly the agent was trying to provoke him. Without a word Karl bent down and retrieved his license, sliding it back in his wallet.

"So what brings you down here," Agent Smith asked with a smirk. "Certainly not much of a beach day."

"I just came down for a load of sand. I need it for a patio I'm building. Nobody's ever objected to my taking sand before. Is that what this is about," asked Karl feigning innocence.

"We could care less about your taking sand," Agent Smith responded, the same bemused smirk never leaving his face.

Karl was familiar enough with men like these to realize they invited trouble; he needed to be very careful. It was obvious they had taken an instant dislike to him and were doing their best to make him feel uncomfortable. The two stood appraising him, neither saying a word, nor taking their eyes off of him. After a time it was Silvestri who moved, walking slowly over to the truck and glancing in the back. He nodded to his partner. Smith turned back to Karl.

"You live around here?"

"Just up the road about a mile from here. Now, could I ask you a question?"

"Depends," replied Smith without expression. Karl knew he wouldn't be getting much information from these two. They were becoming more hostile to him by the minute. Be careful, he thought to himself.

"I was just wondering who it was you were looking for? Obviously, you guys wouldn't be down here unless it was important." Karl tried his best to hide his sarcasm though he was fairly certain it wouldn't matter anyway.

By this time Agent Smith was standing directly in front of Karl, Silvestri somewhere behind him. Karl understood the situation perfectly, they were hoping he'd do something stupid that would give them an excuse to arrest him, though they'd probably rather just rough him up a bit.

"That, my friend, is none of your business," Smith declared flatly. "Now if you're not out of here in fifteen minutes we're gonna arrest you for trespassing on government property. You do know the government has taken over this beach? So get your sand and get outta here. Come on Silvestri, let's go."

Assholes, thought Karl, as he watched them stride back across the parking lot. What he'd give to meet that Agent Smith alone some dark night.

Karl threw a few shovels of sand into the back of the truck and headed back home. These were not the kind of guys to mess around with that was obvious. Not only did these two guys have the full weight of the government behind them they would probably be allowed even further liberties with suspects because it was wartime. But he was right about being under surveillance except now it appeared everyone was. He would have to be extra careful retrieving his transmitter; it was going to require a whole new plan for there was no telling how long they intended to keep the beach under surveillance. His maneuvering room was shrinking quickly.

Pulling into the yard he was surprised to see Anne's car there. For some reason he had just assumed she wouldn't be there. How was he going to explain why he had a load of sand?

By the weekend her mother's health had sufficiently improved that Anne felt comfortable returning to Ipswich for a few days. She assured her father she could be back in a matter of hours if her mother's condition worsened. Anne had spent countless hours at her mother's bedside, seldom even stepping outside for a breath of fresh air. But, right now she needed a break; she simply wanted to get back to her house, the marshes, the beach, though deep down she recognized the real reason for wanting to return home.

It had been an especially painful week for her. Finding her mother looking so frail and helpless was difficult enough but thinking about how hurt her mother would be if she learned of her affair with Karl only made the pain worse. She had decided almost on the spot that on returning home the first thing she would do is explain to Karl it was over, that it was impossible for her to continue the affair. The guilt was simply too much for her. But that was early in the week. Now, as she preparing to leave, what previously had seemed so clear was becoming clouded by doubt; she was beginning to wonder if she could actually go through with it. Why, she constantly asked herself, should she so peremptorily end an affair that was bringing her more pleasure than she had enjoyed for years. The problem was, she knew the reasons; she just didn't want to accept them. So, she rationalized to herself that the affair couldn't last anyway. She had no idea what Karl thought of the whole thing; they'd never really talked about it. He was probably just in it for the sex. And then there was the age difference. No, the affair would end and probably sooner rather than later. Why not just let time resolve the issue?

Thinking about Karl in this way served only to dampen her spirits, however, and her mood wasn't improved when pulling into the driveway she saw no sign of him. She didn't have sufficient nerve at that moment to go directly to his apartment so instead chose to make a big production of retrieving her suitcase from the trunk and lugging it into the house. It was only on coming back out that she noticed the pickup truck was gone. Her immediate reaction was one of annoyance until she reminded herself she had never given him the slightest clue on when she'd return. All at once she felt a pang of jealousy. What if he had met another woman while she was away, or worse, what if it was someone she knew, like one of her good friends. Admittedly, she had no claim on him. Still, the idea of Karl being with another woman hurt deeply enough for a second it actually took her breath away.

As she stood there, fearing the worst, she became aware of the sound of a motor vehicle speeding up the driveway. Suddenly, her black pickup came hurtling into the driveway with Karl at the wheel. The look of surprise on his face upon spotting her made Anne wonder if, in fact, she had been right about the possibility of another woman. She watched as he backed the pickup into the barn, then, slipped effortlessly from behind the wheel. He walked directly to her and took her in his arms.

"I missed you," he whispered, kissing her with the passion she had come to expect of him.

Whatever remaining doubts she may have harbored about Karl were swept away instantly. The week apart had only served to heighten their desire for one another and to her it was like a second honeymoon; actually, a first honeymoon, she corrected herself, although without the awkwardness and tentativeness to the lovemaking. It was just so spontaneous. And afterwards, flush with the contentment that only lovemaking can generate, she would lie securely wrapped in his powerful arms.

Anne also began to notice subtle but encouraging changes in their relationship. Karl's reserve was gradually beginning to thaw and for the first time he spoke about his past. Her relief was almost audible when he confided not only that he had never been married, he had never even had a serious affair. And the care with which he revealed details of his childhood only strengthened her conviction that he truly had come to love her, though she could not know the only truth was that part derived from the years spent in Chicago with his aunt; the rest was the product of those in the Abwehr responsible for creating credible cover stories for their agents.

Anne tried to remember if she'd ever felt any happier. Even some of her friends noticed and one went so far as to wryly suggest she had to be having an affair with "the gardener," her condescending way of referring to Karl. Anne had ignored the woman's comment suspecting it was probably made out of envy. This was the woman who had she been having sex with someone outside her marriage she'd be telling them every excruciating detail about it. And that was another thing about her relationship with Karl, while she always referred to her friends as having sex, in her mind she and Karl made love. It was something special and beautiful; she could only hope that Karl felt that way too.

Chapter Twenty-Three

"So explain this to me again. It looks like an ordinary lump of coal but, in fact, it's actually dynamite," Eddie was saying, leaning back in his chair, hands clasped behind his head. Mack was resting against the counter that ran nearly the length of the room and separated the desk area from the public; he had a cigarette in his hand. It was the first time Eddie had seen him smoke. With his typical wide grin Mack explained he was a social drinker and a social smoker--one or two a day of each.

"Exactly. It's a block of explosive encased in molded plastic and painted to resemble a lump of coal, and unless you examine it carefully and happen to notice the tiny detonator inserted into it, you'd never guess it was anything but a lump of coal," Mack explained. He had driven down from Boston to brief Eddie on what the FBI had found when they uncovered the wooden chests buried by the German agents near Norfolk.

"And you can handle this stuff without it going off? I'll be the first to admit I know almost nothing about explosives."

"Apparently, this particular type of dynamite is incredibly stable. Our lab guys said you could drop it, hammer it, do almost anything you want to it and it wouldn't explode. Only intense heat will actually detonate it. So, these guys could have gone around the Norfolk area dropping lumps of this stuff in the coal piles of power plants, factories, anywhere and done one helluva lot of damage without us ever knowing what exactly was happening. And they had a chest filled with this stuff."

"What else did you find," asked Eddie, overwhelmed at just the thought of such devices. "Was there anything in these chests that might lead us to the whereabouts of other German agents?"

"There was the usual equipment needed for this type of sabotage operation---wire, timers, detonators, that type of thing. But there were also these ingenious incendiary devices that were made to look like pen-and pencil sets. The Abwehr was not fooling around. They've mounted what appears to be a first-rate operation."

"Pen-and-pencil sets?" Eddie asked curiously. "How do those work?"

"Oh, there's these sulfuric acid cartridges that fit into the sets when they're readied for use. The acid burns through and causes the kind of intense fire needed to detonate the lumps of coal, for example. Very simple devices, really, but if placed properly they could do an incredible amount of damage."

The telephone on Eddie's desk began to ring.

"That could be for me," Mack explained. "I told the office I'd be down here and I took the liberty of giving them your phone number. I hope you don't mind?"

Picking up the receiver, Eddie shook his head. "It's Sergeant Bradford."

After a pause during which Mike was clearly making an excuse for something, Eddie responded, "It's all right, Mike, just get here as soon as you can."

Eddie hung up shaking his head.

"You know, Mike lives only three houses down the street, yet he's late coming on duty at least half the time. I'd say it was because he lived alone with his mother but, then, I do, too. It may have something to do with that Irish stubbornness of his."

"Careful now, Eddie, you're treading on dangerous ground. You know I'm Irish, what with a name like McCarthy," replied Mack laughing. "But you may have something there. We Irish don't like having people tell us what to do or when to be someplace. I guess it stems from all those years of having to take orders from the British, or maybe from our mothers. On the other hand, maybe it's just our nature."

" I was only kidding, Mack. There's no way anyone could mistake you for anything but an Irishman. As my mother would say, you have the map of Ireland on your face, of course, she always says it in Polish, which never makes it sound quite so funny."

"I'm supposed to be the spitting image of my father, Michael Sean McCarthy, God rest his soul. He was a good father; as a husband, well, let's just say he could have worked a little harder at it."

They were both quiet for a moment before Eddie spoke. "So, getting back to business, I guess it was pretty lucky you were able to arrest those guys down in Virginia before they could do any damage. I just hope if there are German agents around here somewhere, we can do the same."

"Oh, we will; you can bet on it," said Mack encouragingly. "And, by the way, there was one other thing we found that may be of some interest to you."

"And what might that be?" inquired Eddie eagerly.

"Money, lots and lots of money. We found nearly seventy thousand American dollars, some of it in crisp new fifties and hundreds. And though the bills appeared to have been shuffled, the serial numbers indicate they came from a shipment of bills the Treasury Department sent to Germany several years back. So it gives us something else to be on the lookout for. You certainly don't see many hundred dollar bills around these days."

Eddie sat there quietly trying to absorb all this new information. Clearly, the Germans had a major operation underway.

"So what's going to happen to this guy now that he's led you to the buried treasure; will they reduce his sentence?" Eddie asked, looking directly at Mack.

"I seriously doubt it. He's back in the DC jail right now and I'm willing to bet he'll be having a visit from the prison chaplain sometime in the next few days. Roosevelt has every intention of executing the guy; I'm convinced of that. Letting him think he's going to get a reprieve is just a way of giving the guy a little more time to decide if there's something else he should be telling us. Anyway, I'm certain you'll be hearing about whatever they do in the next day or so even way up here in Ipswich. Roosevelt will want maximum publicity. It'll be his way of saying to Hitler 'Don't try to export your conflict to this country.' At the same time he'll hope the publicity will cause other agents sent here to have second thoughts about actually going through with their missions whatever they may be."

"President Roosevelt's not fooling around, is he? And to be honest, that's fine by me. Those Nazi bastards killed my only brother and Lord knows how many of my relatives back in Poland. My mother still has two brothers back there though she's apparently lost contact with them." Eddie could feel his anger rising.

"Roosevelt wanted to get us involved in stopping Hitler several years ago but Congress wouldn't hear of it," Mack replied, the disgust audible in his voice. "We'd have been a lot better off right now if only we'd listened to him. And, of course, those same critics are now saying Roosevelt knew before it happened that the Japanese were going to attack Pearl Harbor but said nothing so we'd have to declare war on them. Do you believe that? In fact, had Hitler not proceeded to declare war on us after our declaration of war on Japan, Congress probably still wouldn't have voted to go to war against Hitler. It's amazing!"

"I couldn't agree with you more. Oh, and have your surveillance teams down at the beach picked up anything," asked Eddie, anxious to change the direction of the conversation.

"No, not really, though they have pulled together a list of people they questioned and I have it right here." Mack pulled a folded sheet of paper from his inside pocket. "Actually, I'm glad you mentioned it; I'd completely forgotten about it. Here, see if there's anyone on the list you know?"

Eddie scanned the list. "Yah, I know several people here. They're local people, most of them born right here in town; I'd probably be willing to vouch for all of them. But wait a minute. Now, here's a name. Karl Stoner. That name seems to be popping up everywhere these days. I wonder what he was doing down there?"

"Stoner, huh? I remember one of my colleagues, Ben Smith, mentioning something about him. I don't think they liked him very much. If I'm quoting Ben correctly, he described him 'as an arrogant, friggin', son-of-a-bitch.'" But his explanation for being there seemed solid enough. So what is it about this guy that bothers you?"

"It's like your colleagues said, he's an arrogant son-of-a-bitch. I met him, you know. He got in a fight with a couple of enlisted men up near the railroad station. There's nothing unusual about that, of course, since these guys are getting into fights all the time. Apparently, they just can't wait until they get sent overseas. But, what was different about this fight was that Stoner did a real job on the two guys that started it; if you can believe it, they both needed medical treatment. He said he learned to fight like that on the streets of Chicago, and while I've heard Chicago can be a rough town, what I got from a couple of guys who witnessed the fight, this guy is more than your run-of-the-mill barroom brawler. I don't know, it's probably nothing, but there's something about this guy that just doesn't feel right. On the other hand, except for that fight he's been a model citizen."

"And if he were an enemy agent, that's exactly what he'd try to do, wouldn't he--be a model citizen, not get mixed up in some stupid street brawl. Just the same, I'd keep an eye on him," suggested Mack.

Eddie still hadn't mentioned that Stoner was living at Anne's place, though he wasn't quite sure why. He decided he was probably being protective of her; if Stoner was involved in something, he wanted to make sure Anne was kept clear of it. Had he known the whole story, he would have been far more concerned not to mention a lot more jealous.

If the long, hot days of July were proving blissful for Anne, they were becoming increasingly problematic for Karl. What had begun as an affair of convenience had now evolved into something more serious. He had clearly fallen in love with Anne and it was proving to be a whole new experience for him. Ever since that day he had blurted out "I missed you" he found it more and more difficult to deny his true feelings. For a brief period he convinced himself he had only made that comment to deflect her attention away from the truck. But the truth of the matter, he came to recognize, was that he really had missed her and not just because her absence had made him feel vulnerable.

In fact, his relationship with Anne should have been bringing him nothing but pleasure. Ironically, if his Abwehr masters were to learn about it, they would most likely be commending him for his incredible success. To have a wealthy American widow fall madly in love with him was the perfect cover for his activities. In this regard, at least, he had probably exceeded their wildest expectations; they could safely depend upon him for information and the development of potential saboteurs for years to come.

The problem, Karl recognized, was not the affair per se but what it was doing to him. He had joined the Abwehr enthusiastically and had trained hard for this mission. Suddenly, he found himself wondering what would happen if he didn't go through with it, if he just called it off. He knew it was dangerous, even treasonous, to think like this but he couldn't help himself. It wasn't just the affair; there was more. In the past few weeks he had begun to have grave doubts that Germany would be able to win this war. America was far stronger than he had imagined when he volunteered for this mission; you could see indications of it everywhere, even at the tiny shipyard where he worked. And once the country's factories got going at full capacity, they would be producing military goods in such quantity as to overwhelm any adversary. Unfortunately for Germany, the Nazi leadership had blinders on when it came to America. They did not seem to understand, for example, that the tide of battle in the Pacific was already turning in America's favor. What had the Japanese lost at Midway, four aircraft carriers? Militarily, there was no way they would ever be as strong again.

As for Europe, Germany had not even begun to feel America's might because her attention was focused on the war with Japan. But, once American did turn its attention their way, Germany's defeat would only be a matter of time. Tragically, no one around Hitler would even dare suggest such a possibility; he'd be immediately sent to the Eastern Front for doing so. Unlike the previous war when the German nation suffered little in the way of physical damage, this time it was going to be far different. The victors would see to it that the country was so laid waste, it would take generations to recover.

And, there was no question that Hitler himself was the main problem. Had he only confined himself to ridding Germany of the odious restrictions imposed by the Versailles Treaty it was doubtful anyone would have challenged him. Even most Western leaders were prepared to admit they had been excessive in their reparation demands. But that wasn't enough for Hitler. He now wanted to dominate Europe from the North Sea to the Ural Mountains. And, if that were not enough, there were his bizarre racial policies. Karl couldn't help thinking back upon the horrendous night in November of 1938 when he witnessed mobs of Nazi supporters taking to the streets to burn synagogues, smash windows and loot stores owned by Jews. He remembered clearly watching a brown-shirted Nazi tacking up a sign in front of one burned-out store that read *Kauft nicht bei Juden*. And everywhere there were members of the Gestapo pulling screaming Jews from their homes and beating them in front of cheering crowds. This so-called "night of the broken glass" was allegedly a spontaneous response to the murder of a young German official in Paris by a Jew, but Karl had later learned the incident had been planned and carried out by the Nazis.

The shame Karl had experienced over the incident was only made worse by the knowledge he had sworn an oath to Hitler personally and was, therefore, a part of the very system responsible for this horror. Still, he believed at the time that the Nazis had gone too far and that the German people would cast them aside. But, of course, it hadn't happened, because Germans like him had gone on about their jobs, pretending to believe the explanation provided by the Nazi leadership.

So, if Germans did nothing in the face of such atrocities, why should Hitler give a damn about the Americans, he didn't understand them anyway. While he was probably correct in his assessment that they had played only a marginal role in World War I, he clearly misjudged them in other more important ways. He truly believed they would never intervene in another European war. In his mind they had become too disillusioned by their experience in World War I. And even if they did decide to intervene, Karl had once heard him state, America was simply too far away to play any decisive role in the war's outcome. It had yet to dawn on Hitler that improvements in transport technology had drastically reduced distances between America and the various nations of Europe.

Fortunately, for Hitler, and contrary to his orders, Canaris had established an excellent intelligence network in America. The information flowing to Berlin was incalculable though it didn't appear to be having much impact. So, while he realized he should be doing everything possible to support Canaris in his efforts to influence Hitler's policies, deep down he suspected it was already too late. But did this mean it was all right to become a traitor, to bring dishonor on his family name? Was he prepared to turn his back on the country to which he had taken an oath and for which his father had given his life in combat? The answer should have been an easy one, that it wasn't gave him only greater cause for concern.

Try as he might he couldn't stop thinking about deserting, for that's what it would be, deserting his post in the middle of a war. And, what if he were able to learn to live with his guilt, his shame. Was there after all of this a life for him in America? Would Anne, for example, seriously think about marrying him? When they were lying together in bed it was so easy to believe she'd marry him without hesitation, but in the bright light of day that possibility always seemed to fade. And what if she did marry him, how would he support himself here? Would he continue to work at the shipyard after the war ended? He certainly could see himself building those beautiful sailing ships for which the shipyard was famous. One thing he couldn't do, at least not for years, would be to use any of the money stashed at the beach. Crisp new hundred dollar bills were not common and would immediately attract attention; even Anne would wonder where they were coming from. That money would unfortunately have to remain buried along with his past.

His past would be his greatest problem; how long could he hope to keep it buried? His papers wouldn't hold up forever. Sooner or later someone would discover they were forged. He wouldn't even be able to contact his aunt in Chicago. And then, of course, there was always the question of his wartime espionage even if there were some statute of limitations. The more he thought about it, the more impossible his situation appeared.

The only thing that remained clear was his need to keep Anne from detecting his distress. Under no circumstance must he give her any reason to start asking questions. Even the slightest knowledge of his mission would prove as dangerous to her as it was to him, maybe more so since this wasn't her fight.

He decided he had no choice; he would have to try once again to retrieve his transmitter from the beach. He had this gnawing sensation that time might be running out, and it would be in his best interest to quickly prepare an escape plan.

Chapter Twenty-Four

Mike Bradford was hunched over his desk, the newspaper spread out before him, a cup of coffee in his hand, a cigarette in his mouth. This was the image of Mike burned into Eddie's brain if for no other reason than this was typically how he found Mike when he entered the office first thing in the morning.

"You know, just one of these days I would love to come through the door and see you doing something other than reading the newspaper," Eddie snorted, shaking his head.

"Like what," muttered Mike, grinding out his cigarette in an ashtray overflowing with the butts of old cigarette.

"Like work, that's what. You must be at least two months behind in writing up your arrest reports." In spite of himself Eddie had to smile. He found it next to impossible to get mad at Mike; he was a good guy. They had worked together now for nearly ten years and they had had few serious disagreements in all that time. Mike was neither the most exciting guy nor the most imaginative, but he was dependable and Eddie liked that quality in him. You could count on Mike being there when you needed him; there were never any unpleasant surprises.

"I have been."

"You have been what," Eddie replied, having not the slightest idea what Mike was talking about.

"I have been working, isn't that what you were complaining about? Reading the newspaper is a very good way of gathering information. For example, have you seen the front page of today's *Globe* yet?"

"No, I haven't had a chance. So what have I missed?"

"Take a look," said Mike, handing Eddie the front page of the newspaper. "Lower right."

Spreading the newspaper flat on the reception counter, Eddie scanned the front page. The bold lettering caught his eye immediately--German Spy Found Guilty Will Be Executed. Eddie quickly read the tersely written article.

A spokesman for President Roosevelt today announced that Hans Oberg, a German national, found guilty by a military tribunal of secretly entering the United States with the intent to conduct sabotage against defense plants and military facilities would die in the electric chair. In announcing the decision the spokesman reiterated President Roosevelt's warning that any person found guilty of conducting or attempting to conduct espionage or sabotage against American interests could expect to be tried in similar fashion with a similar result. A second German agent, who was with Oberg at the time of his arrest, was shot and killed by the FBI as he attempted to avoid capture.

The phone rang while he was reading and Eddie winced as he heard Mike exclaim, "Mack, how the hell are ya." Once Mike got to know someone, and that might mean having only met the person once or twice, his initial sense formality seem to abruptly disappear.

"Yeah, we were just reading it. Why don't I let you talk to Eddie?" He handed the phone over. "Its Mack," Mike explained as if Eddie hadn't been there during their conversation. Eddie could only roll his eyes, but if he thought it would have any impact on Mike he was disappointed. Mike had already buried himself back into the sports section.

"Good morning, Mack, well you certainly had your information right about the German agent. Now, when are they going to carry out the execution?"

"That soon? Boy, that's quick. Where will they do it?"

"They have one right there in the DC jail? Never occurred to me that Washington would have one. I don't even know where the nearest electric chair is around here. Salem, I guess. It's never been anything I've had to think about until now."

Eddie stood silent with the phone pressed to his ear.

"Oh, I know that and I'm glad of it. You can have them. So they, too, would be tried in Washington. Well, anyway, when are we going to see you again down here?"

Eddie laughed. "Not until we catch the guys, huh? And all this time I thought it was your job. It is the reason they pay you the big bucks, isn't it?"

Eddie laughed again. "OK, stay in touch."

Putting the phone down, he repeated to Mike what Mack had just told him.

"So they're gonna execute the guy sometime in the next couple of days? Boy, that is fast. I've never heard of anything like that before; usually it takes months if not years. But, I guess it is wartime."

"All I can say is if that doesn't give any German agents operating around here second thoughts, I don't know what will."

"You're right about that," Mike replied thoughtfully. "On the other hand, if they're going to execute someone for even thinking about committing sabotage, then that person might just as well go through with it. After all, they can only execute you once."

"You might have a point there, Mike. I hadn't really thought of it that way. I was thinking that if a potential saboteur read the article he might have second thoughts about going through with his operation. If I were in their situation I'm certain I would."

Karl's first reaction upon reading the article might not have been to have second thoughts but he was definitely stunned. He felt a sudden shiver steadily work its way from the base of his spine to the nape of his neck. It was only by chance he had even seen the article. Anne had been in the process of throwing out several days' worth of old newspapers when, spotting Karl in the yard, she asked if he'd like to go through them first. He replied he would and lugged them back to his apartment. Unfortunately, because he had been busy, he hadn't gotten around to reading them until two more days had passed.

The day he spotted the article he had spent repairing shingles on the barn roof. The weather had been perfect for it---sunny but with an east wind off the water that kept temperatures in the sixties. By mid-afternoon, however, he had had enough and decided to call it quits; he wanted to shower and relax a bit before heading off to work at the shipyard. Grabbing a beer from the icebox, he sat down at the kitchen table and casually began sifting through the pile of newspapers Anne had given him, generally reading only those articles covering the war. It was then that his eye caught the headline appearing in the Boston *Globe*, the very same headline Mike Bradford had noticed and brought to Eddie's attention. Karl read the article accompanying the headline quickly, then reread it several more times. He couldn't believe it; the FBI had caught Oberg and was now planning to execute him. How could they have picked them up so soon? They must have done something stupid, he decided, and a good reminder to be even more careful.

For what seemed like ages he sat there staring blindly at the newspaper article, his mind swirling with every conceivable emotion. Gradually, though, he began to regain control of himself and to think rationally again. What, he wondered, might Oberg have told them? Is it possible he might have given up everything he knew in a desperate attempt to save his own life? If he had it obviously didn't work since they were going to execute him. But, even assuming he talked, how much did he really know, certainly not anyone's real name, other than his own. Neither could he have revealed the locations of where other agents were to be dropped off, though it probably wouldn't be too difficult to figure it out. The most Oberg could probably have done, Karl reasoned, was to have given the FBI physical descriptions of everyone as well as having provided them with details of their operational procedures, neither of which should be sufficient to lead the FBI directly to him or to the other agents.

He was thankful he had to go to work for he hoped it would take his mind off Oberg's execution. But, it didn't; he couldn't help wondering what Oberg was thinking facing the electric chair. Admittedly, he had never really liked the guy; he was too dedicated a Nazi for him. Still, he found it impossible to concentrate on his work imagining what it would be like to die by electrocution. Even Tom O'Malley noticed he appeared distracted and Tom was not the most perceptive person, generally preferring to wallow in his own personal problems. Finally, Karl gave up and left the yard early, explaining that he wasn't feeling very well. There was more truth to that statement than he was prepared to admit.

The ride home had a momentary calming effect on him. The east wind that had kept the day so cool had disappeared and now the night was blanketed with a soft velvety warmth. Through the branches overhead, Karl could glimpse the moon, which nearly full provided him with sufficient light to actually see where he was going. Somewhere off in the distance an owl softly hooted, but otherwise the only sound was the crunch of bicycle tires on the gravel road.

Pedaling into the yard Karl could see that Anne was still awake by the thin rim of light visible around the edges of the blackout curtain. Recently, she had been waiting up for him and he had been spending the night with her. On this night he couldn't do it; he had far too much on his mind. He would tell her tomorrow that he had been too sick to stop by. He did come home early and he was sure she would hear him. But for now he needed time to think---to make sure he was still safe, that his cover was still in place, and that he had no reason to make a run for it. It was going to be a long night without much sleep, he was sure. Yet, strangely, he fell asleep fairly quickly. For all his worries, he was simply too physically exhausted after a long day working in the fresh air to let them get to him. Even the realization that his chances of surviving this operation were getting less by the day was pushed aside for a few hours.

Chapter Twenty-Five

Anne was sitting in bed reading when Karl returned. Glancing at the clock she was surprised to see the time; he was early. Something must be wrong. Slipping out of bed she padded over to the window and looked out in the direction of the barn. It was still too dark to see anything clearly but she was able to make out the sound of his footsteps as he climbed the stairs leading to his apartment. Curious, she thought, wandering back to her bed and getting under the covers. She returned to her reading but found she couldn't concentrate on it. Putting her book aside, she sat staring blankly at the far wall. She continued to hope that at any moment she'd hear Karl come back down the stairs and make his way across the yard to her house. But as the minutes ticked by it became increasingly evident to her that on this night he wasn't coming. Disappointed, she reached over and turned off the light.

Anne had hoped she'd be able to fall asleep quickly, but she remained wide-awake, tossing and turning for what seemed like forever. Finally, out of desperation she swung out of bed and padded over to the window. She looked over at his apartment thinking perhaps he was sick, but there was no light on. If there had been, she wondered if she would have gone to him. Feeling suddenly alone, she flung herself back in bed, burying her head under the sheets.

It proved a very long night and she was relieved when the first light of dawn began stealing through her windows. Unfortunately, the lack of sleep had taken its toll; she felt completely exhausted. All she could do was lie there in a state of semi-consciousness, until at long last she summoned up the strength to drag herself out of bed. Making her way to the bathroom, she stood before the sink and looked into the mirror. She shuddered at the sight of the face staring back at her. Her eyes were puffy and bloodshot, her hair a mess. Grabbing a hairbrush, she tried to make herself look a bit more presentable but it didn't work. Her head, she noticed, was beginning to ache. Maybe she should take a couple of aspirin; a shower, she decided, would probably be better for if nothing else it would give her something to do.

It was nearly ten-thirty before she heard the door to Karl's apartment slam and rushing to the window she watched as he came down the stairs and headed towards her back door. Curiously, he appeared as tired and drawn as she did.

"Karl," she cried, rushing out onto the screened porch. "Are you all right?"

"It was a tough night," he explained. "Wasn't feeling well and didn't get much sleep. Thankfully, I feel a little better this morning."

"Would you like me to call a doctor? I know Doctor Manning would be more than willing to come out if I asked." She was genuinely worried; she had never seen him this way. He always looked so physically fit it was difficult to think of him ever getting sick.

"No, thanks, that won't be necessary. I could use a good cup of coffee though, before I get out and do some work. But, I don't think I'll go up on the barn roof today; I suspect it's going to be too hot for that."

"You're not going to do anything today but take it easy. There's nothing pressing that needs doing. And besides, you've been working far too hard," she chided him in a motherly tone, but then softened her words. "You work all day around this place. Then you go to work at the shipyard, and often spend your nights with me." Smiling, she added, "And I know you don't get much sleep on those nights." She wondered how he'd react to her last remark but was relieved to see a slight smile cross his face.

"You may be right," he assured her. "I'm sure I'll be fine by tomorrow."

Over the course of the next several days Karl settled into a state of nervous calm. Though he could not blot the thought of Oberg's execution from his mind, he was relieved by the gradual realization that he was not a suspect; he couldn't be. If the FBI had any reason to believe he was a German agent, any reason whatsoever, they would have arrested him by now. They wouldn't even wait until they had evidence. After all, Oberg was not about to be executed for anything he had actually done, but for something he had only intended to do. Thus, if the FBI even thought he was planning to do something, they'd have arrested him by now and would be making preparations for his own execution. Still, the very thought of the electric chair was not an especially comforting one and it did little to relieve the growing doubts he was having about the mission. He could only be thankful that the two-month moratorium on commencing the operation still had another two weeks to run. But, he wasn't kidding himself; he knew it was just an excuse. Berlin would not hold it against him if he decided to commence his activities early, not with the way the war appeared to be going.

In the meantime Karl continually checked to make certain the explosives he had smuggled into the shipyard remained securely hidden. He had worked out a rough plan as to where he would set the devices for maximum effect. He was certain the damage to the yard would be considerable. Strangely, when he was at work he found himself feeling very confident about the operation. He suspected it had something to do with comments of his co-workers; they seemed completely unable to separate Germans from Nazis. It never occurred to them that someone could be a German patriot without being a Nazi. It was a distinction that was very important to him, though when he took the time to actually think about it, he could understand why it would be an irrelevant distinction to most Americans. What difference was it to them whether a loved one was killed by a Nazi or a German patriot, was he any less dead? Karl decided it was something worth remembering.

He and Anne had resumed their pattern of spending nights together. And if he were not always as attentive as he had been previously, she seemed quite prepared to accept his excuse that he was not one hundred percent healthy yet. She seemed perfectly content with their relationship. For some odd reason, the war seemed not to affect her at all; she seldom mentioned it and to the best of Karl's knowledge chose not to follow its progress through the newspapers or on the radio. She never even complained about its little inconveniences, unlike many of her friends. Only in relation to her son was the war acknowledged as a worry but in front of Karl she seldom, if ever, mentioned her son.

It was about this time that Anne and Karl's relationship entered a new phase though neither chose to acknowledge it. Anne, who heretofore had left Karl largely to himself during the day, now began the habit of visiting him as he worked about the place. Much of the time she would do nothing more than sit watching him, admiring his strength and seemingly endless supply of energy. On one occasion she had brought along her camera and tried surreptitiously to photograph him. But, when he caught her doing so he became so angry with her she stopped after managing to take only a single photo. Then, there were other times when he'd halt what he was doing and drop down beside her. The two of them would sit quietly staring out at the broad expanse of the salt-marsh spread before them, holding hands, occasionally exchanging a brief kiss, until one or the other would notice it was time for Karl to leave for work. At such times Anne always felt a little sad and a little guilty. There was a war going on, and yet for her, life could hardly have become more idyllic. She knew this couldn't continue forever. There had to be a day of reckoning, she decided, and she dreaded even the thought of it.

On the final Friday of the month Anne unexpectedly announced she was going up town to fetch something. She was acting suspiciously and when he had inquired if she'd like him to drive, she had politely declined. Left alone, and with nothing better to do, Karl grabbed an old .22 caliber rifle that must have once belonged to her son and headed down the path in the direction of the garden. Perhaps, he thought to himself, he might just get one of the woodchucks that had been raising such havoc with Anne's, actually his, vegetables. Creeping up behind a small hillock, Karl slowly raised his head and gazed down over the garden. There amidst the rows of carrots were two tiny woodchucks contentedly nibbling on the soft green stems. As he slowly raised the rifle to take aim, he was suddenly struck by the ridiculousness of the whole scene. Here he was, a highly trained German agent, about to defend an American victory garden against woodchucks. What would his superiors in the Abwehr think if they could see him now? Worse, what would his friends serving on the Eastern Front think? He hesitated for a few seconds, then, lowered the rifle. Letting out a sudden yell, he watched without emotion as the woodchucks quickly scampered away.

As he stood there, staring at the now empty garden, he heard an automobile driving into the yard. It was followed almost immediately by the sound of a door slamming, then, Anne's voice calling out to him. As he started back up the path towards the house he was surprised to see a light tan pup racing excitedly towards him. Before he could even utter a word the pup began jumping all over him.

"Easy boy," commanded Karl with a big grin on his face. "Take it easy, now."

"Its not a boy, its a girl and her name is Honey," explained Anne strolling down the path. "You said I should have a dog around here; isn't she sweet?"

"When I said you needed a dog around here this was not exactly what I had in mind. I meant a dog for protection, though I guess Honey will grow larger in time. But, somehow I just can't picture Honey frightening away any would-be intruders."

"What would I need a dog like that for anyway? I want one that will make a good companion and Honey will definitely be that."

"Well for one you live alone down here. There's not another house in shouting distance. And there's a war on in case you didn't notice."

"I don't see what the war has to do with it and in case you didn't notice, to use your words, I don't live alone. There is a man living here who makes me feel perfectly safe." She pretended to appear angry.

"But I may not always be here," he replied. Almost instantly he detected the hurt look in her eyes and he regretted his choice of words.

"Is there something you haven't told me about?" Her voice had a coldness to it he had never heard before.

"Look, I didn't mean it the way it came out," Karl replied, trying in vain to reassure her. "I simply meant I would not necessarily be around if something were to happen. I am at the shipyard every evening after all and that's probably the time when you most need protection."

But the damage had been done, at least for the moment. He had inadvertently given voice to her greatest fear--that there might not, in fact, be a future for them to share.

Before he could say more Anne grabbed a reluctant Honey by the collar and began dragging her back up the path. Honey did her best to free herself and return to Karl but Anne was not about to put up with any additional displays of disloyalty and certainly not from a dog.

Later in the day as Karl was preparing to head out to work on his bicycle, Anne came out of the house looking very upset. She informed him she would be leaving for Boston first thing in the morning and would he be willing to look after Honey while she was gone; it would only be for a couple of days. Karl couldn't tell from her demeanor whether she had planned this visit some time before and had simply forgotten to tell him about it or whether it was her way of punishing him for raising the delicate issue of their future. Either way, he decided, he had enough on his mind for the moment. Was there no part of his life free of complications, he wondered?

Certainly his work at the shipyard was generating its own set of problems. Ironically, he was now recognized as one of the most highly skilled craftsmen at the yard and had been commended on several occasions by the quality control officials for the care and precision of his work. The problem, of course, was that the LCTs upon which he labored with such pride were destined for use against his own countrymen. Not surprisingly this caused him a considerable amount of guilt and uneasiness. He wondered what Canaris and the rest of the Abwehr leadership would think of him. No doubt some would praise him for building such an impregnable cover story. Who would ever suspect that one of the shipyard's most skilled welders was actually a German agent. But most Nazi leaders would probably rightly view his activities as traitorous. He was sent to America to weaken its military response, not to contribute to its strengthening.

Unlike most Friday evenings this one seemed to drag by ever so slowly. He found it impossible to focus on his work. If he were not worrying about his mission, he was thinking about Anne and her childish reaction to his admittedly poorly phrased remark. And, then, to top it all off, Tom O'Malley had arrived more inebriated and belligerent than usual, and after an angry exchange, he had stumbled off in search of other likeminded drinkers. No wonder he trained me so well, thought Karl disgustedly, he expects me to do all his work for him. Well, screw that!

The ride home was a chilly one, though as if to compensate the moon was shining down brightly enough to illuminate his way. With

Anne in Boston he had already decided to attend the launching of one of the larger sub-chasers this weekend; they could only be held at the time of the monthly neap tides since the waterways connecting the yard to the ocean were so shallow. Since launchings were held at night few people attended other than some of the workers. However, rumor had it that the owner's wife was going to christen the ship and he was curious to see her. She was a member of the Crane family and apparently it had been some of her money that had helped underwrite the shipyard. Of course, there might also be a contingent of War Department officials who would journey down from Boston for the occasion and one never knew what nugget of intelligence might be gleaned from any comments they might make.

As he had more-or-less expected, Anne's house was completely dark; she had said she was leaving very early in the morning. He had to admit, he really didn't understand women, or at least, American women. Maybe it was cultural, or then again, maybe it had something to do with his mother. No one could ever accuse him of having a normal upbringing. But, would that really explain how a person could go from being the object of a person's affections one moment to being, what was the American expression, "in the doghouse," the next? And all of this had happened simply because he hadn't chosen his words properly? Women and men were so different.

His apartment was chilly; he had left the windows open and now a cool East wind was pouring in. Closing them, he thought briefly about checking the icebox for something to eat, then, rejected the idea. If anything he was feeling tired so sprawling across the bed he fell instantly asleep. At some point during the night he thought he heard the rumble of thunder or was he dreaming; later it was the sound of sirens, though none of this quite registered in his consciousness. It was not until he heard a pounding on his door that he actually woke up and to his surprise found that it was not only daylight but that he was still in his work-clothes from the night before.

There was another round of pounding and this time he heard Anne's voice excitedly calling to him.

"Karl, Karl, are you in there. Open up, please."

He was fully awake now and raced to the door. Throwing it wide he saw an obviously agitated Anne standing there bare-footed and with only a light summer robe hurriedly thrown over short nightgown.

"Karl, I just received a call from Jan Cunningham saying there was a huge fire at the shipyard last night and much of it has been destroyed. Apparently there were some people killed, too. They have no idea what caused it."

Chapter Twenty-Six

The phone woke him with a start; phone calls in the middle of the night did that to him since they almost always brought bad news. He glanced quickly at the clock; the luminous hands indicated it was four-seventeen.

Grasping the receiver, he mumbled, "Sawaski, here."

"Eddie, its me, Smitty. You'd better get down here right away. I've just received a call from one of the security guards at Robinson's Shipyard. There's been an explosion of some kind down there and much of the shipyard was destroyed by the blast. He also reported that a number of people had been injured. That was all the information he could give me at this time."

Eddie was wide-awake now.

"OK, Smitty, you'd better call Mike Bradford and tell him to meet me at the station in fifteen minutes. I'm on my way."

Oh, God, tell me this isn't what I think it is, Eddie murmured slipping into his uniform, not here, not in this town. But, it wasn't as if they hadn't been given plenty of warning that something like this might happen.

Twenty minutes later he was at the police station. With relief he saw Mike was already there.

"Mike, you stay here and handle any calls that come in; I'm sure there'll be plenty. I'm going to take Smitty and head down to the shipyard. Oh, yes, you better call Mack and tell him what's happened. I know it's the middle of the night but he'll want to know. Make sure, however, that you explain we have no reason at this time to suspect it's anything but an accident. Have you got that? The last thing we need is to start some kind of panic."

"I've gotcha, boss, but what do you really think caused the explosion?" Mike asked quizzically.

"Have you ever been down there?" Eddie replied. "There are fuel tanks and canisters of compressed oxygen and other gases all over the place. Any one or several of those things could have exploded. To be perfectly honest, it's a wonder there hasn't been an accident before this."

Mike didn't exactly appear convinced; truthfully, Eddie wasn't either.

"Anyway, we'd better get going. I'll keep you posted, Mike. Come on, let's go Smitty."

They made good time getting to the shipyard since at that hour of the morning there was little traffic on the road. This situation changed dramatically, however, once they turned onto the narrow dirt road leading to the shipyard. Both shoulders were lined with cars and trucks of every make and model. Most, Eddie guessed, belonged to volunteer firemen or shipyard workers who had come down to assist in any way they could. Fortunately, there appeared to be just enough room for the ambulances to squeeze through although he was certain no fire trucks could now make it in.

Driving as close to the main gate as he deemed prudent, Eddie pulled the cruiser into a tiny space between two cars and, then, he and Smitty raced the remainder of the way on foot. The scene that greeted them as they entered the yard was one of absolute chaos. There were fire trucks everywhere as well as miles of heavy canvas hoses running in all directions. Scores of men were rushing about shouting orders to one another, searching for survivors or dousing still smoldering embers. But it was the shipyard itself, or at least what remained of it, that contributed the most surrealistic quality to the scene. Half of the yard had literally disappeared. What had once been construction sheds and machine shops were now nothing more than black, smoking ruins. No exploding oxygen tanks had done this, Eddie quickly concluded. All he could think of was Mack's description of the explosives brought ashore in Virginia by the German agents---blocks of dynamite painted black to look like lumps of coal. Could German agents have penetrated the shipyard and planted their innocuous-looking lumps of coal here?

Glancing around he spotted Bill Peterson, the Ipswich fire chief, standing next to one of the pumpers, a bullhorn in hand.

"Bill," shouted Eddie, walking over in his direction. "Any idea how all this happened?"

"Hey, Eddie, some mess, huh?" replied the chief. "No, it's going to be awhile before we figure that out. I'm just amazed at the destruction. We know something caused a huge explosion, or actually several explosions, but we have no idea at this moment exactly what it was; it could have been almost anything."

"Could dynamite have caused this much damage?" Eddie asked. He was suddenly embarrassed by his ignorance of explosives, though until now he had never had reason to know anything about them.

"I suppose, though we'll have to wait for the arson investigators before we know anything for sure. But why would there be dynamite here at the shipyard?" The chief was eyeing Eddie curiously.

"Probably because it's the only kind of explosive I've ever even heard of," he replied, pleased with his answer. Changing to a safer subject, he asked, "How many bodies have you found?"

"Only two so far though there are quite a few injured, some seriously. But, it could have been a lot worse if the blast had not occurred as the late shift was ending. We were really lucky on that at any rate."

"So, have the two bodies been identified?"

"One of them has been positively identified as Brian Sullivan from Newburyport; he works here as a security guard. He was probably killed by the blast since his body was in such good condition. Sorry to say it appears the other body is that of Tom O'Malley. We're not a hundred percent positive yet because the body was so badly charred but he's unaccounted for. Of course, if I had a dollar for every night he's disappeared since his wife died I'd be a very rich man. As you know better than most, Tom has become a very heavy drinker and a heavy smoker so it's entirely possible he could have started this fire accidentally. It was Friday night after all and it's common knowledge that some of the guys bring bottles to work with them. I can only hope Tom was unconscious when the place went up in flames."

"So, you think the fire was an honest-to-goodness accident, then?" exclaimed Eddie.

"I'm just guessing, Eddie, really. As I said, I won't know anything definite until the arson guys have had a chance to poke around here. Even then, you know, we may not be able to tell anything; it does happen from time to time, though not often, I admit."

"But what is it that makes you think it might have been an accident?" Eddie was pressing him now.

"Well, for one thing, if it were not an accident it would mean someone set it intentionally and that would be sabotage. I just can't believe anyone in this area would do such a thing. But there is something else--the location and position of Tom O'Malley's body, if in fact it is Tom. He was found in what would have been one of the construction sheds and he was the only worker still here. Tom may have been a drunk but he wasn't a saboteur. I'd bet my last cent on that."

"Is it possible to tell how he died?"

"No. It'll take an autopsy to determine that. Even then it may be difficult since the body was so badly burned. But what are you thinking?"

"Thinking? I'm just doing my job," responded Eddie grinning. "And I think I'd better let you get back to yours. Thanks for your help."

Eddie wasn't sure what more he could do at the moment but his suspicions had been sufficiently aroused that he wanted to talk to Mack about it first thing in the morning. He also suspected that Mack would be bringing his own people into the investigation.

Eddie couldn't have been more right. No sooner had he arrived at the station the next morning than Mack arrived with a team of FBI arson investigators. In fact, Mack had been placed in charge of the entire investigation; it was officially a federal case now, which was fine with Eddie. Though he had no direct evidence to support his conclusions, he was convinced the fire had been deliberately set and if so, it had to be by German agents.

It was the first thing he asked Mack. "So what do you think, Mack, could it have been?"

"A little too soon to tell, Eddie, but if they did, my men will find out; they're the best. I understand there were several large explosions that can't be easily explained by the fire department. We'll certainly want to interview some of the less seriously injured to try to figure out exactly what happened. In the meantime I've had roadblocks set up on all major roads leading out of the area and we've assigned agents to every train and bus station as well. On the other hand, it could have been a legitimate accident; we do have them, you know. It's just in wartime every accident takes on a sinister cast. Anyway, let's get going. The sooner my colleagues here get to work, the sooner we'll have some answers."

Once the FBI agents had left the office, Eddie suddenly found himself with little to do. Mack was now in charge of the investigation and Eddie had done his part by assigning two officers to handle traffic and keep people away from the site of the fire so the arson investigators could do their jobs. He wandered over to the coffeepot and began to pour himself a cup when it occurred to him that he hadn't eaten anything that morning.

"Mike, since there's not much going on here for the moment, I think I'll go get some breakfast at the Atlas. Do you want me to bring you anything?"

"A pack of Camels." As usual he hadn't even looked up from his newspaper. It was a habit that really annoyed Eddie, but he suspected that if he actually complained to Mike about it, he'd probably just up and quit, so he let it go.

"OK, I'll be back in about an hour. You know where to reach me."

Eddie stepped out into a beautiful summer day, though one that held the promise of being hot and humid. The sky had a thin veil of overcast that did little to reduce the sun's glare and the only air movement Eddie experienced was when he crossed the stone bridge spanning the Ipswich River. He was already sweating by the time he reached the Atlas and as he pushed open the door the restaurant's coolness came as a welcome relief.

"Hey, Johnny, what's your breakfast special this morning?" It was a greeting more than a question.

"Eddie, you really need to work on your conversational skills. You ask the same thing every day. Your questions actually change less than my specials."

Johnny was already pouring Eddie a cup of coffee.

"OK then, here's a new question for you, what's happening to your coffee? I swear it tastes worse than what I make at the office."

"I've got a news flash for you, Eddie, there's a war on and the government is rationing certain food items; I can't get decent coffee anymore, or sugar or meat or most anything else."

Johnny was one of the few people who could tease Eddie about the war; they had been friends for years. Most people in town knew only too well that Eddie had lost his only brother in the war and politely stayed away from the subject; not Johnny. Before Eddie could respond, the door opened and Bob Wallace came strolling in; he took the seat next to Eddie.

"Coffee, Johnny," he ordered. "What are you doing here, Eddie, I thought you'd be down at the shipyard. I hear they had quite a fire down there last night."

"I was down there much of last night, but it's not my problem now; the Feds are in charge of the investigation. They're down there as we speak."

"What are they doing?" asked Johnny curiously.

"They're trying to figure out what started it, then, they'll have to figure out who started it. As you probably know, since the next secret in this town will be the first, there were apparently several large explosions and a couple guys were killed, including Tom O'Malley."

"I hadn't heard about Tom," Wallace answered with surprise. "So, he was killed in the explosion? That's horrible. I didn't know him that well but he always seemed like a nice guy."

Johnny brought over his breakfast and placed it before him, refilling his cup at the same time. "So, is there some question about whether this was an accident? I mean, we've all heard that one of the Coast Guardsmen stationed down there has been missing for several weeks. Is there any connection?"

"That's one of the things the FBI is looking into," Eddie replied, trying vainly to remain non-committal.

"Well, speaking of the FBI, I heard they had the beach staked out looking for a couple German agents," Wallace continued.

"Is that right, Eddie?" Johnny asked eagerly.

Eddie laughed. "I really can't believe you guys. You know as much about this as I do. The FBI passes information along to me and they tell me not to say a word about it. So, I do as they ask and then I find out you guys know everything anyway. So what's the point of being police chief in this town?"

"What's really going on Eddie? Come on, you're not telling us everything," Johnny pleaded.

"There's nothing to tell really. You may have read in the papers that a German agent was executed recently down in Washington. The FBI arrested him nosing around the Norfolk Naval Base; a second guy with him was shot when he attempted to escape. Anyway the FBI is simply looking into this fire to make sure it wasn't sabotage."

"You mean, the FBI thinks that German spies may be operating around here?"

"Its just something they have to check out." Eddie didn't say he thought there was a good chance it was sabotage. "It could also have been an accident. They do happen you know. And to be honest we've found absolutely nothing to suggest there are enemy agents working around here."

"Maybe there's only one guy. I mean, there are so many new faces in town it could be somebody we see all the time," Johnny offered.

"It's entirely possible," replied Eddie, for the moment more interested in his breakfast than the conversation at hand.

"Even I picked up a stranger one morning several weeks ago coming up Argilla Road. I thought it a little strange at the time to see someone walking along at that hour but he said he had come up from Essex. I had no reason not to believe him. In fact, I dropped him off right here at the corner so he could get some breakfast. Do you remember him, Johnny?"

Eddie was listening intently now.

"Do you remember the guy, Johnny?" Eddie asked.

"I see so many strangers in here these days. But come to think of it I do remember a guy who gave me a dollar tip for breakfast; I returned most of it. He was also really hungry, if that was the same guy."

"Did either of you get his name?" Eddie was getting excited now, though he realized it might be nothing.

Johnny shook his head.

"He introduced himself," said Wallace. "But I can't remember what he said his name was. I'm sure if I heard it I would recognize it."

"Describe the guy then." By this time Eddie had lost all interest in eating; the conversation was becoming far too informative.

"Rugged-looking guy, close-cropped brown hair and big hands, the biggest, I think, I've ever seen. And he was carrying a small duffel bag."

"Yeah, that fits," said Johnny. "And I remember now that he told me he was from out-of-town. Actually, I knew it from his accent. Chicago is where he said he was from, I'm sure of it."

"Stoner," Eddie muttered out loud.

"Yes, that was it," responded Wallace. "I think it was Karl Stoner."

Eddie slammed some change on the counter and headed for the door. "I knew you guys would turn out to be useful for something one day. Now don't run off anywhere too far because I might need to talk to you again before the day is over."

Once out on the sidewalk he started running back towards the station. Too late he remembered Mike's cigarettes. By the time he reached the station he was breathing hard but there wasn't any time to waste. He had to get to Anne's house. As for Mack, he'd just have to let Mike try to reach him.

Rushing into the station Eddie was dismayed to learn the cruiser was out. He explained to Mike what he intended to do.

"Let me call them back," Mike suggested. "They only left a few minutes ago. They're on the way down to Little Neck to investigate a possible burglary at one of the summer homes down there."

"No, there's not time. I'll take my own car and when Smitty gets back you can send him down, if you haven't heard from me."

"You sure you don't want to wait?"

Mike knew he was wasting his time for it was obvious Eddie had already made up his mind.

"No, I'm on my way. If my suspicions are correct, there isn't a moment to lose."

Eddie's battered '38 Plymouth was parked just outside the door. Jumping in, he turned the ignition, slammed the car into gear, and headed quickly down Elm Street to County Road, wondering all the while if he completely understood what he was doing. He didn't have a single piece of evidence to link Stoner to the fire. And, it was certainly well within the realm of possibility that Tom O'Malley had accidentally started the thing. Still, he couldn't get the thought of those blocks of dynamite painted to look like coal out of his head. He was certain they were the cause of the explosions in the same way he was certain Stoner was not whom he claimed to be. His dislike of the man went far beyond his annoyance with the man's living at Anne's place. Something just wasn't right.

Chapter Twenty-Seven

Unfortunately, for Anne she misinterpreted Karl's confusion, thinking he had simply not understood what she had said, so she began to repeat her story about the fire; he cut her off savagely.

"I heard you, there's been a fire at the shipyard. What I need to know is how it happened." He spoke to her so sharply that it came out less a question than an order.

"Tell me,' he continued, becoming even more agitated now, "was it some kind of an accident?"

Karl was having trouble breathing; his heart was pounding wildly. He felt a wave of panic slowly begin to take hold of him. For just a second he thought of his father cowering in that trench; he wondered if he had felt panic-stricken or whether even in the face of certain death he had been able to retain his composure. Surprisingly this thought had a calming effect upon Karl and to his relief he felt his panic begin to subside.

"I have no idea what happened," Anne wailed. "All I know is that there was this terrible fire at the shipyard and people were killed."

If he noticed how stung she had been by his angry reaction to the news, he didn't let on and he certainly didn't apologize for it. His mind at the moment was completely absorbed with the question of how the fire had started. Frantically, he sifted back through the events of the previous evening in the vain hope of remembering something that might provide an explanation for what happened. There was his argument with Tom O'Malley. Karl had gotten upset with him not so much for arriving late to work as for arriving so drunk he was totally incapable of doing anything. Tom had staggered off angrily and Karl had not seen him again for the rest of the shift. So, it was entirely possible that Tom may have had something to do with the fire. He was drunk and though he hadn't been smoking at that moment, he almost certainly would have been at some point in the evening.

"Damn it," Karl exclaimed, only then realizing that Anne was still standing there. In fact, she had apparently been saying something to him but he had been so wrapped up in his own thoughts he had not heard a thing she had said. Now, suddenly, he became conscious of her words.

"Do you want to drive down to the shipyard to see what's happened?" she asked timidly, anticipating that he might begin shouting at her again.

For a second he actually thought he might like to see for himself what had happened before it occurred to him just how dangerous it would be if he were seen. Admittedly, it would be a natural enough reaction; many, if not most, of his co-workers were probably already down there. Under normal circumstances it would actually be strange for him not to show up but, then again, these were anything but normal times. The police and FBI would be swarming all over the place, and since both had questioned him previously, they would almost certainly want to question him again if they saw him there. The smartest thing he could do, he decided, was to begin figuring out how he was going to get away from here. It would only be a matter of time before the FBI found some evidence of the explosives he had hidden at the shipyard. Ironically, it was the perfect operation.

The fire had probably started accidentally, but he suspected strongly that it was his explosives that had caused most of the destruction. And, he even had Anne for an alibi, an alibi that should hold up at least long enough for him to get away safely. The more he thought about it, however, the more concerned he became. The authorities could be on their way to arrest him at this very moment, not even waiting until they had gathered sufficient evidence. Every second he stood there was costing him valuable time; he had to leave immediately. What an idiot he had been not to have yet devised an escape plan for the day he knew would inevitably arrive.

Amidst these thoughts Anne's face came into focus and he couldn't help noticing her worried expression. She had clearly sensed something was wrong by his indignant response to hearing about the fire. At the same time, Karl remained confident that she had no idea why he had reacted so.

"What is it, Karl, tell me?" she implored

He didn't know what to say so instead he stared at her for what must have seemed like an eternity. She was visibly nervous, clearly unsure what to expect next.

"I have to leave and I have to leave quickly," he whispered finally, taking her by the arms. "I truly wish I didn't have to but the fire at the shipyard leaves me no choice."

Now, it was her turn to be confused. For a moment Karl thought she was going to cry but she unexpectedly found some inner source of strength and regained her composure.

"Did you have anything to do with the fire?" Anne asked, more curious than shocked.

"No, I didn't; that's why I was so surprised when you told me about it. Unfortunately, there's a good chance they may think I did, just something that happened down there," he lied. "Anyway, it would probably be best if I left right away before they come looking for me."

"But, if you had nothing to do with it, running away will just make you look guilty. Please stay, you don't have to worry, my father knows every lawyer in Massachusetts. More importantly, he knows every good lawyer."

"If only it were that simple," he sighed wearily. She had that vulnerable look that he always found so irresistible and now there were tears in her eyes.

"Whatever it is we'll fight it together. I love you, Karl, and now that I've found you, I don't want to lose you." The words came tumbling out of her mouth almost as quickly as the tears began rolling down her cheeks.

In all their time together, through all of their lovemaking, they had always been too uncertain of the other person's feelings to say, "I love you." How ironic, Karl thought, that on the last day they might ever be together they were finally expressing their love for one another. It wouldn't have changed anything, of course, sooner or later it would have ended this way; it's just that it happened so unexpectedly.

"This is one battle all the lawyers in Boston couldn't win," Karl replied, gently wiping away a tear that had paused part way down her cheek. "I just wish I could tell you more but it would be too dangerous for us both if I did. I will tell you this, however, and I mean it honestly, I've never loved a woman more than I love you."

Karl took her trembling body in his arms and there they stood, holding each other tightly, desperately, neither wanting to let go. They said nothing; the time for words was well past. And still they clung to one another. Finally, Karl released her and stepped back.

"I need some time to myself. Don't worry I won't leave without saying goodbye."

Mute with grief, Anne turned and walked slowly down the steps. At the bottom she stopped and looked back. She had somehow managed to stop her crying, though probably only until she reached her house.

"Don't worry, really, I'll see you in a little while," he repeated, but he wasn't sure either of them believed it.

Closing the door, Karl went quickly into the bedroom where he lifted the mattress and drew out a brown paper bag, inside of which was his 9-mm Pistolen. Returning to the kitchen he sat down at the table and removed it carefully from its oilcloth covering. Methodically, he disassembled the gun, then, cleaned and oiled each piece to rid it of any accumulated salt or sand particles. He did the same with each of the eight-clip magazines. When he had finished, he reassembled the Pistolen and carefully reloaded each magazine. He slammed one of the magazines into the handle of the gun, satisfied that if it became necessary, the Pistolen would operate properly.

He was still not certain that he was even a suspect yet, or that he'd ever been one; on the other hand, he couldn't afford the risk that he might be. From now on he planned to operate on a worst-case scenario basis, which meant working on the assumption that he was a suspect and that they'd be coming after him fairly soon. It might take awhile before the FBI was able to detect whatever evidence remained of the explosives he had hidden at the shipyard but sooner or later they'd do it and immediately begin the search for the saboteurs. The local police chief was, of course, another matter. Karl had a feeling he'd be nosing around on his own and might very well already have him on a list of possible suspects. That fight with those two recruits was coming back to haunt him though there wasn't much he could do about it now except to get out of town as soon as possible.

The big question before him now was, of course, how to get away? He was certain the authorities would have the train stations and bus terminals under surveillance just as a precaution. He momentarily considered accompanying Anne to Boston when she went to visit her parents; a man and woman traveling together would arouse less suspicion than a single man, especially when the woman had Anne's credentials. Unfortunately, if they were stopped, Anne would almost certainly be arrested as an accomplice. If he could possibly avoid it, he did not want to involve Anne any further; she was probably in enough trouble as it was. One more irony about this operation, he sighed, putting her wellbeing ahead of his own.

He understood almost intuitively that his only chance of getting away safely was to transmit a message to Abwehr headquarters in Berlin asking to be rescued. It might work if the FBI or the local police didn't come looking for him immediately. Regrettably, even if Canaris were to send a U-boat for him, it would probably take at least several days for it to arrive off the beach. But, did he have that much time? It was a long shot, he knew, but it was better than any alternative he could think of at the moment. Of course, if he were going to send such a message he would have to do it soon, probably as early as tonight. First, he needed to retrieve to the transmitter. That would only be the beginning, however, for once he sent the message he would have to be prepared to hide out somewhere at the beach for whatever time it took for the U-boat to reach him. Unfortunately, with the Coast Guard continually patrolling the area, hiding out there would be very dangerous. Still, if there were a U-boat fairly close to the New England coast, the plan just might work. In the meantime he would have to come up with something to throw the FBI, or especially that local police chief, off the scent.

As he was finalizing his plans, he heard the screen door slam and a few seconds later the sound of Anne's car driving out of the yard. He had no idea whether she was actually on her way to Boston or just heading up town. Either way it was fortuitous. He would slip away while she was gone, which would avoid another tearful good-bye; that was probably the reason she had just left. It was definitely in his best interest that she did so because it would prevent her from knowing the direction he intended to take for his escape. What she didn't know, she couldn't reveal to the authorities if they chose to question her and Karl had no doubt they would eventually. And just to make sure she wouldn't spill anything of what she knew, he'd leave her a cryptic note suggesting he would be contacting her in Boston through her parents.

It took Karl only a few minutes to pack his duffel bag with the few food items he had on hand, his anorack and the extra clips for his Pistolen. The gun he stuck in the waistband of his pants so it would be easily accessible if ever he needed it. After writing a brief note to Anne, he took a hurried look around, then, strode quickly out the door. Though it was no longer of any consequence, Karl had carefully checked the apartment and was now fairly certain that when the FBI came to search the place, nothing incriminating would be found. He had transferred all the explosives he had brought from the beach to the shipyard where they had been destroyed. Proving he had anything to do with the explosives would be circumstantial at best. On the other hand, Oberg may very well have turned over the explosives he had brought with him to the FBI in which case they would quickly figure out where the explosives at the shipyard had come from. Inevitably, they would be traced back to him. The more he thought about it, the more he became convinced he had no alternative; he had to make a run for it.

Heading down the stairs, he tried to think where the best spot would be to leave the note for Anne. It should be somewhere not too obvious though clearly one where she would be certain to find it. After doing that, he would make his way down through the woods to the salt marsh, which he would need to cross without being spotted. He was pretty certain he could do it since the tide was out and he'd be able to use the channels and creeks for cover. For a short way he'd be visible to several of Anne's neighbors, if by chance they happened to look out one of their windows that faced in that direction; it was a risk he'd simply have to take.

As he started across the yard Karl was startled to hear an automobile coming rapidly up the driveway. It was odd because Anne never drove that fast, on the other hand, the only other person that typically came on Saturday was the Cushman baker who never came much before five o'clock since Anne was his final customer of the day. So, who could it be? He decided it might be best not to be seen but as he hurried back towards the barn, the car swung into the yard. He didn't immediately recognize the car but glancing at the driver he saw an all too familiar face; it was none other than the local police chief.

Even as he turned into Anne's driveway, Eddie remained uncertain as to how he was going to handle the situation. At this moment he had absolutely no grounds for arresting Karl Stoner; all he knew for sure was that he didn't want the guy getting out of town. Eddie decided he would first check in with Anne to be sure she was safe. This would also give him an opportunity to survey the situation and try to find out where Stoner was and what he was up to. At that point he better have a plan. In the meantime he'd just have to make it up as he went along.

Swinging into the yard Eddie slammed on his brakes and skidded to a halt. To his surprise he spotted Stoner coming down from his apartment. The expression on his face, as he turned to look squarely at Eddie, was also one of surprise. Eddie had no idea whom Karl was expecting to see, but clearly it had not been the police. Wherever Karl had been heading, he changed his mind instantly at the sight of Eddie's car and stopped dead in his tracks. He'd probably been expecting Anne, thought Eddie, having quickly determined her car was nowhere to be seen. Suddenly, he noticed the gun tucked in Karl's waistband but before he could open the door and order him to stop, Stoner had dropped the duffel bag he was carrying and raced around the side of the barn out of sight. Whatever concerns he had harbored earlier over how he would approach Stoner were now replaced with legitimate concerns over his own safety. All he could think of was the sorry condition of the two enlisted guys once Stoner had gotten through with them.

Eddie cautiously opened the car door and climbed out. Crouching behind the door for protection, he slowly withdrew his .38 from its holster. The thought that immediately came to mind was that he had never fired his revolver in anger. Worse still, he hadn't even been to the firing range in weeks and hadn't cleaned the gun in longer than that. For someone who had been professing disappointment that he was not fighting with General Eisenhower's forces in Europe, he thought wryly, he couldn't be less prepared to take on Stoner. His only hope was that Smitty was on his way down here at this very moment.

"Stoner," Eddie yelled. "I want to talk to you for a moment. Come back here. Now, please, don't do anything stupid."

There was no response; the only sound was that of a woodpecker hammering away at a nearby tree.

"Stoner, can you hear me? I just want to talk to you about the fire at the shipyard. You were working last night and I thought you might know what happened to Tom O'Malley?"

Eddie realized now he should have heeded Mike's advice and waited for Smitty. On the other hand, Stoner could be slipping away through the woods as he stood there. He decided to check first. Leaving the relative safety of his car, Eddie scooted over to the barn. He was vulnerable since Stoner could surprise him from any one of several directions. He was sure Stoner was not the kind of a person to run away from a fight.

Moving slowly to the open door Eddie glanced quickly inside the barn. Anne's pickup truck was there and behind it a door that appeared to open to the woods; the door was closed. Satisfied that Stoner wasn't there Eddie turned and edged backed towards the corner of the barn. He took a quick look around the corner; still no Stoner. He had just made up his mind to return to the car when Stoner stepped out of the barn, his gun leveled steadily at Eddie's chest. For just a second neither was certain what to do but then reflex and training took over. Unfortunately for Eddie, neither his reflexes nor his training were as good as Stoner's. Eddie had barely time to move before he heard Stoner's gun bark and a slug slammed into his shoulder joint, smashing bone and sending his cap and revolver flying. The pain momentarily took his breath away and all he could think of was trying to steady himself against the barn, but there was nothing to hold onto. Vainly trying to remain upright he turned towards Stoner just in time to catch two more rounds squarely in the chest. Their impact thrust him over sideways and mercifully he lost all consciousness as the back of his head struck the hard gravel driveway. He lay there motionless as a small cloud of dust kicked up by his fall settled slowly over his bloody and near lifeless body.

Chapter Twenty-Eight

Anne was so confused and hurt she didn't even try to stem the tears that were streaming freely down her face. Why had Karl become so upset over the news of the fire? And, why had he become so angry with her? She couldn't understand it, especially the anger he had directed towards her. It seemed almost as if he were blaming her in some way. And now, suddenly, he was leaving and without much of an explanation, though it was fairly obvious it had to do with the fire.

His entire reaction had been so unexpected. When she'd knocked on his door to tell him the news, she had been so certain he would ask her to drive him down to the shipyard. Instead, he declared he would immediately have to leave town while she was left standing at his door wondering if she'd ever see him again. Of course, she had only herself to blame in the sense she'd made a conscious effort not to think about where her relationship with Karl was heading. Had she done so even for a minute she might have foreseen that it would end like this; it was as inevitable as it was tragic.

As she wandered aimlessly about the house she kept coming back to what Karl had said to her; that he loved her as he had never loved another woman. But, if that were true, she reasoned, why hadn't he chosen to stay and at least attempt to solve whatever the problem was? Or, at the very least he could have suggested she go with him, though in all honesty she wouldn't have done that, and he probably knew it. So, now, all she was left with was the feeling of having been used. She began sobbing again, loudly enough that Honey came over to her side as if to reassure her everything would be all right.

Anne recognized that she was spoiled; everyone had always looked after her and taken care of her. That's what had made her husband's death so difficult; she had been forced to look after herself in a way she had never faced before. But, then, Karl had unexpectedly come along and he began to do those things she had always come to expect others to do. And, he loved her in a way she had never been loved before, and she didn't want it to end. Karl always seemed so strong and sure of himself, yet he was warm and understanding with her. That is, until this morning when for the first time she had gotten an unexpected glimpse of another side to Karl, one he had apparently kept hidden from her. In those few seconds after she had explained to him about the fire she was certain she had detected a sense of panic, or at least, fear. But why, she wondered? He'd insisted that he had nothing to do with the fire, and she tended to believe him. It was a fact that he'd been in the apartment when the fire broke out and he'd clearly been asleep when she gave him the news. So, what was this mention of some complication, of something that had occurred at the shipyard that left him no choice but to leave at once? He was holding something back and she was reminded of his comment from a few days earlier, the one about not always being there. Had he been suspected of something even back then?

Anne had again brought her sobbing under control though she couldn't stop pacing about the house, Honey by her side the whole time. She considered opening the liquor cabinet and pouring herself a stiff drink, but she knew she'd never get it down; the only thing she ever drank was wine and even then she typically only had a single glass. That wasn't going to help. Out of desperation she decided to get out of the house; the walls seemed to be closing in upon her. Throwing on the first clothes she could find, Anne hurried out to her car without the slightest idea of where she was going. It didn't really matter, what she needed was to get away from that house.

Heading the car in the direction of town, Anne stepped on the gas pedal and within seconds was exceeding the 25 mph speed limit. There was little traffic on the road and as she drove she found herself gradually beginning to relax. Her mind began to clear as well and for the first time since the incident at his apartment, Anne found herself worrying about Karl. He was clearly in some kind of trouble and had not wanted to involve her in it; perhaps that had been the reason for his unexpectedly rude behavior. And what had been her immediate response? She had let him send her away without a struggle, without demanding some kind of explanation. How could she have been so self-absorbed when clearly he was the one in some kind of trouble?

As she was pondering what to do she saw the sign for Northgate Road and quickly decided to take it. Evelyn, one of her best friends, lived at Northgate Farms and the thought occurred to her she might be someone with whom to share her concerns. By taking the turn, however, it meant she never saw Eddie racing in the direction of her house. It was a spur-of-the-moment decision but the consequences of it would prove serious. Had Eddie only seen Anne take the turn onto Northgate Road so many things would have turned out differently. Most probably he would have turned too and followed her, all the while feeling relieved she was safe. At the very least he would have continued on to Anne's house but now he would have waited for assistance before confronting Karl. But, not seeing her he raced blindly ahead, his only concern Anne's safety.

As for Anne, just as she was reaching the driveway leading into Northgate Farms she felt a strange and sudden chill. It was odd because the inside of the car was so warm. Frightened, she pulled the car over to the side of the road and sat there hoping the feeling would go away. In fact, it disappeared as quickly as it had come on, but she couldn't escape the feeling that something was wrong. Karl, she thought suddenly, it had to be Karl. She had to go back to the house immediately. Slamming the car into gear, Anne made a quick U-turn and headed back in the direction she had just come. She prayed he would still be there. If he weren't, there would be little she could do for she didn't have the slightest idea where he intended to go.

It took only about five minutes for her to reach the driveway and race up towards the house. As she drove into the yard she was forced to jam on her brakes to avoid running into the back of a car parked directly in the middle of her driveway. Whose car was it? And why was its door open like that? Suddenly, she remembered why she had come back. Karl, she exclaimed, jumping out of the car. It was only now that she noticed the body lying sprawled next to the barn. From the police uniform he was wearing she knew instantly it was not Karl. Just as quickly she could surmise the person was either already dead or, at a minimum, he had to be seriously hurt; there was blood everywhere. Anne had never seen so much blood in her life; it was even on the side of the barn. Staring down at the shattered form, she was shocked to see it was the town's police chief, Eddie Sawaski. His normally full, reddish face was ashen white and made only more macabre by the thin film of dust that covered it. For a moment she thought she was going to faint but after forcing herself to take several deep breaths Anne was able to steady herself. Kneeling down next to him she tried to determine if he were still alive. He didn't seem to have a pulse though she wasn't certain she even knew how to find it. But, just then she detected what appeared to be a slight movement in his chest; there it was again, he was alive and breathing if ever so faintly. Her sense of relief was only momentary, however, as the realization struck her that his life might very well be resting in her trembling hands. What should she do? She had to get help. Straightening up, Anne raced for the kitchen and the telephone. For the moment all thoughts of Karl had been erased from her mind.

"Operator, operator, this is an emergency," she screamed into the receiver. "This is Anne Westbrook and I need a doctor down here at my house on Argilla Road. The police chief, Eddie Sawaski, has been shot and there's blood everywhere. If somebody doesn't get down here right away he may bleed to death."

The operator did her best to calm Anne, then, asked her to repeat everything slowly to be certain she had the information right. Once she had the necessary information, she asked Anne to go back and do whatever she could do to keep Eddie from moving; she promised to get help down there immediately.

Putting down the receiver Anne began to feel frightened again.

"Get a grip on yourself, get a grip," she whispered to herself.

She wasn't certain she'd be capable of doing much but just in case she grabbed a couple of clean towels from the closet; if nothing else, she decided, she could at least try to stem his bleeding. As she stepped out onto the screened porch she heard a vehicle of some kind coming up the driveway. It couldn't be the doctor yet, there hadn't been time enough, but right now, she'd be thankful for anyone. A car skidded to a stop just behind her own; it was the Ipswich police cruiser. Almost immediately two patrolmen jumped out, the older of whom she recognized as Smitty; like everyone in town it was the only name she knew him by.

"Hurry," she yelled to them. "Over here by the barn. Your chief has been badly wounded."

It was Smitty who reached Eddie first. Kneeling down beside him, he exclaimed to no one in particular, "Oh, Jesus, he's in bad shape. I can't even tell if he's still alive."

"He was a few minutes ago," replied Anne in tears, her self-control beginning to slip now that help had arrived. "I've already called for a doctor; he should be here in a few minutes. I was about to use these towels to try to stop the bleeding."

"Here, give them to me," he growled. Carefully, he began to peel Eddie's shirt away from his chest. "My God, how many times did that son-of-a-bitch shoot him. I can see one, two, and maybe a third wound up here near his shoulder. Whoever did this was not fooling around." He placed the towels over the wounds and gently applied the necessary pressure to hopefully slow the flow of blood.

The second officer, who by this time had identified himself as John Leclair, took Anne aside.

"Were you here when this happened?" he asked.

"No, I wasn't. I had driven down the street...to see...a friend and when I returned I found him lying there like this?"

"Do you possibly have any idea who might have done this?"

Anne knew this question was coming and she dreaded having to answer it. She couldn't believe Karl would have done this but who else could it have been. Before she could formulate an answer, however, the patrolman himself brought up Karl's name.

"We were told to come down here to provide back-up for Eddie. Apparently, he was going to talk to some guy named Stoner about the fire at the shipyard. Is there someone named Stoner who lives here, and if so, do you know where he is now?"

"There is a Karl Stoner who lives here and he does work at the shipyard. He helps around the place in exchange for a place to stay. He lives right up there over the garage." She pointed to the apartment almost reluctantly. She still couldn't believe Karl could have done a thing like this; he was so gentle, so loving with her. And for the moment, at least, she was not going to say anything about their relationship.

"Christ, if he's up there at this moment we're sitting ducks, though

I'm pretty certain he wouldn't hang around here after what he's done to Eddie. You'd better get behind the car there just in case. Tell me, is there a back way out of the apartment?"

"No, those stairs lead to the only entrance. But, I'm pretty sure you're right; he's not up there now."

Anne couldn't help but wonder where Karl was though. Could he, too, have been shot? Maybe some of the blood was his. Before she could think about it further Smitty spoke up.

"For Christ's sake, John, of course he's not up there. Do you think if this guy Stoner shot Eddie like this he'd just go back to his room, light up a cigarette and wait for us to arrive? Of course not, he wouldn't be that stupid. He could probably guess what we'd do to him. By the way, call the station and tell them what's been going on here. I don't know if the FBI will be getting involved in this or not, but I suspect they will."

"OK, Smitty," replied Leclair, a little crestfallen. He had the look of a kid who had just been reprimanded by a teacher.

At that moment the sound of a car could be heard coming up the driveway. Suddenly, a gray Oldsmobile, looking more like a hearse than an ambulance, screeched to a halt just behind the cruiser. Two men climbed out and walked over towards them.

"Help at last," said Smitty wearily. "I've done all I can do for him. He's lost a ton of blood." Glancing up at the window, he added. "As soon as we get Eddie in that ambulance we'll go take a look around. Eddie's our main concern right now. I realize every minute we wait to begin looking for the guy means he gets that much further away but the FBI will get him, they have the manpower that we don't."

While the driver of the ambulance was examining Eddie, the second man pulled a stretcher from the back of the ambulance. Little was said as they placed Eddie on the stretcher; everyone was well aware that time was of the essence. It took only a couple more minutes to slide Eddie into the ambulance and make ready for the dash to the hospital.

As the driver climbed into the ambulance he spoke aloud what everyone was already thinking. "Let's just hope we get him to Cable Hospital in time." With that he revved the engine and headed slowly down the driveway. A moment later the wail of the siren broke the morning's stillness as the ambulance raced up town in a desperate attempt to save Eddie's life.

Karl was not so far from Anne's house that he could miss the sound of the ambulance's siren. He was about half way to his most immediate destination, Hog Island, but it was not an easy trek if one wished not to be seen. The straight-line distance between Anne's house and the island was only a mile and a half; Karl, however, had chosen to follow the meandering course of the Castle Neck River. Since it was low tide the channel's high banks provided effective cover from the prying eyes of Argilla Road residents, not to mention the police, but it also meant he had to trudge through nearly knee-deep mud. The rising tide would soon obscure his tracks, which is why he walked as close as possible to the water's edge. It wasn't until shortly after noon that he finally reached the relative safety of the woods that skirted the slopes of Hog Island.

The island could not have been more than a square mile in area although it appeared much larger because of the perfectly flat marshland that surrounded it. Since Colonial times its well-rounded slopes had been used for grazing livestock and most of the original hardwoods that had once covered nearly the entire island had been systematically cut down. It was not, in fact, until the Crane family had purchased the island that the hardwoods had been allowed to grow back. The Cranes did maintain a farm on the island for raising sheep, still nearly half the island was now woodland and it was for this reason Karl had chosen to hide out here.

About halfway up the steep northwest-facing slope of the island, Karl settled himself at the base of a large oak tree. The spot gave him a commanding view of the marsh he had just crossed while at the same time he would be largely invisible to anyone coming from that direction. He planned to remain in that location until dusk when he would depart for the beach. There was no need of getting there any sooner since he wanted to send his message at night when the chances of it being picked up in Berlin were greater. For the moment, though, there was nothing for him to do but wait.

Throughout the course of the long, hot afternoon Karl stared out across the marsh unable to detect any sign of movement. This did not mean, of course, they were not out searching for him. From where he sat he could see cars moving along Argilla Road in the direction of the beach though it was impossible at that distance to make out whether they were civilian, police or military.

Sometime during the afternoon a light plane flew over the island and for about an hour continued to circle the area. It was clearly looking for something or somebody and he suspected it was himself. As he was watching the plane, he suddenly heard a shout. It was not close but it definitely came from the island. He held his breath and strained to detect any further sounds. Nothing. Gradually he began to relax; it must have been someone at the farm. By this time the aircraft had disappeared though he assumed it would be back tomorrow. Now the only thing left to disturb the afternoon's stillness was the shrieking of seagulls as they followed the in-rushing tide up the Castle Neck River.

Karl had hoped to catch a few minutes sleep, but first the search plane, then the sound of voices somewhere on the island, and for the past hour or so a seemingly coordinated attack by a combination of deer flies and greenheads, all conspired to make that impossible. Instead, he found himself thinking about Anne and how he had obviously hurt her feelings earlier today. It pained him to think of it for he had, in fact, fallen deeply in love with her. But, he had had to do something to protect her, although he wasn't certain he had actually done so. In time they'd find out about her affair with him and one way or another she'd be forced to suffer for it. Still, he couldn't help picturing her lying naked on the bed, the sheets strewn about from their vigorous lovemaking. He would gently trace the length of her spine with his finger; she would moan softly, turning her head in order to offer him her lips. They would kiss long and hard. It all seemed so real that he could almost detect the faint, sweet smell of her shampoo. But he couldn't keep it up; he was torturing himself. He had to stop thinking about her.

Unfortunately, whenever he was able to free his mind of Anne, the image of the dead police chief rushed in to fill the void. He felt vaguely uneasy about having killed him and he wasn't certain why. The man had clearly come to arrest him and if he were convicted, which unquestionably he would be, he'd die in the electric chair just like Oberg. So, he really had no alternative. And, anyway, their two countries were at war and he was basically on a military mission. Killing and being killed was what war was all about; he had only done what was necessary, he assured himself.

Karl had lost all track of the time when he noticed it was beginning to get dark. A quick glance at his watch showed it was nearly eight-fifteen. He had to be on his way. This would probably be the only chance he'd have of contacting Berlin and arranging for an escape. The odds for success were not great but the risks involved in remaining here presented him with little choice. As he stood up he suddenly remembered the note he had written to Anne; its intent was to have her think he would soon be contacting her both to give her hope as well as misleading the police. He was, of course, misleading them both. But, what had he done with it? A quick check of his pockets revealed nothing. He must have dropped it somewhere in his haste to get away after shooting the police chief. At any rate, he had not been able to leave it in her house as he had planned. He could only hope that Anne would be the one to find it and not the police, though it probably didn't matter now. Cursing his carelessness, he headed out in the direction of the beach.

Chapter Twenty-Nine

While Leclair was in the car radioing his report back to the police station, Smitty took the opportunity to gather up Eddie's cap and revolver, taking note of their location in relation to where they had found Eddie's body. The gun, he quickly determined, had not been fired. So, Smitty concluded angrily, Eddie had to have been taken by surprise; he hadn't even gotten off a single round. Thus, whoever did this was out there unhurt and fully capable of doing to others what he had just done to Eddie.

Just then Leclair stepped out of the police car. Glancing over, Smitty was puzzled to see a big grin on his face.

"What are you smiling at for Christ's sake? Nothing funny has happened around here," he snapped.

"It's you," Leclair exclaimed, acting like a kid who had just learned a secret and now desperately wanted to tell everybody about it.

"What do you mean it's me? Have you suddenly gone crazy?"

"Mike just said that as senior officer you're the acting chief till Eddie gets better."

"And you find that funny? I could care less about being acting chief; all I want is for Eddie to get better. And I want to find the guy who did it. Of course, it's not going to be easy if I have to work with idiots like you."

Leclair tried his best to stop smiling without much success. As the youngest and newest member of the police department he had to put up with a great deal of good-natured kidding from his colleagues. To his credit he saw it for what it was--a kind of initiation into the police fraternity. There was no question that Smitty was harder on him than the others, but Leclair had worked with him long enough to recognize that Smitty was a good cop. It was just his sense of humor could on occasion be a little mean. Leclair also suspected that at the moment Smitty was probably feeling a little scared.

"All right, Leclair, since you seem to find something amusing about my being acting chief, let me issue you my first humorous order--check out the house while I look around up in his apartment. And, whatever you do, please be careful; the guy who gunned down Eddie could still be hiding around here someplace and we can't afford to lose another officer right now, even you. Do you understand?"

"Don't worry, I can take care of myself," Leclair replied, all business now. However, Smitty noticed by the way he approached the house that he was clearly anxious about what he might find there. He had drawn his revolver and as he stepped onto the porch he suddenly froze.

"Smitty," he whispered loudly. "I hear something moving in the house."

Before Smitty could respond, Anne pushed by him and entered the house. "It's only, Honey, my dog. Let me put a leash on her and bring her outside."

A second later Honey came bounding out the screened door pulling Anne along behind her. Leclair was so visibly relieved at the sight of the dog that it was Smitty who now couldn't stop himself from laughing.

"Well done, Leclair," Smitty exclaimed, trying his best to keep a straight face. "Thank God you didn't shoot the poor thing."

The incident helped break the tension that had been gripping everyone. Smitty waited until Leclair disappeared into the house before climbing the stairs to Stoner's apartment. He entered cautiously though it had long become obvious that no one was there. Quite a nice place, thought Smitty, wandering into the bedroom; this guy lives better than I do. A quick check turned up nothing unusual. He was very careful not to touch anything for he knew the FBI would have a fit if they came in and found his fingerprints all over the place. Completing his search, he closed the door to the apartment and stepped out onto the landing. He scanned the marsh for any sign of movement, but the sun made it nearly impossible to see much. Still, what he could see was impressive. Hell, he wouldn't mind living here himself.

Coming down the stairs Smitty noticed a slip of paper on the ground directly below him. It couldn't be missed if for no other reason than the yard was so well maintained. Picking it up, he saw immediately that it was a note of some kind. He read it quickly, then to be absolutely certain he understood the meaning of what was written there, read it a second time. Satisfied, he went directly to the car and radioed the station.

"Mike, this is Smitty. If there's any way you can get in touch with Mack McCarthy, I think you should do it. There's a good chance this Stoner character may be heading for Boston. And, oh, there's one more thing. I'm planning to bring Anne Westbrook in for questioning. I'm not actually going to arrest her or anything like that but I'm curious as to what her reaction will be to my request. I'm doing it on the basis of some evidence I've just this minute come across and since I guess technically this is his case, I think it would be a good idea if Mack were there when I bring her in. I'm just not sure what the jurisdictional boundaries are yet and I'd rather not step on any toes if I can avoid it."

Climbing out of the car he saw that Leclair had come out of the house and was talking with Anne.

"Nothing. I checked every room in the house," said Leclair seeing Smitty heading his way. Smitty nodded, then turned to Anne.

"Mrs. Westbrook," he said, "I wonder if you'd mind coming down to the police station to answer a few questions. You know, about Eddie and anything else you might have seen."

Anne looked at him with surprise. "I don't understand, why can't I just answer any questions you have right here? I'm not under arrest or anything like that am I?"

"Oh, no," responded Smitty quickly, perhaps a bit too quickly. "It's just routine in these matters."

He didn't want to let on about the note he had found, at least, not yet, but he was groping to come up with an explanation that wouldn't frighten her. "My problem is I'm not exactly sure who's in charge of this case, the FBI or ourselves so it would be a lot easier for everyone concerned if you'd just come down to the police station."

"As long as you give me your word you're not arresting me for anything, I'll come with you. However, if you don't mind I'm going to make a call to our family lawyer."

219

Smitty nodded, concluding it was probably a smart move; things were suddenly not looking good for her.

"Oh, and one more thing, Mrs. Westbrook. Would you by any chance have a photo of this Stoner character?" His question appeared to catch her by surprise and she didn't answer immediately. She seemed to be mulling something over.

"Yes, as a matter of fact I think I do have one. I can get it right now if you'd like?"

"No, that's all right. Just be sure to bring it with you when you come down to the station." Smitty had not really expected she'd have a photo of Stoner. Now, suddenly, he was very curious why she did.

Mack was elated. It was the first real evidence found that indicated the fire at the shipyard might not have started accidentally. And it had taken less than two hours to come up with it. Sifting through the charred ruins of what had formerly been a construction shed, arson investigators discovered the remains of what appeared to be three pen-and-pencil sets. Now, were it not for the fact that identical pen-and-pencil sets had been included among the materials brought ashore by the German agents arrested near Norfolk, investigators might never have been able to identify them as incendiary devices.

In fact, Mack had been in the very process of examining one of the sets when he noticed one of the Ipswich police officers, who had been assigned traffic duty outside the main gate, hurrying in his direction. From his manner it was clear he had something urgent to report.

"Are you Field Agent McCarthy?" the officer inquired; he was almost out of breath.

"I am; what can I do for you?" Mack responded, wondering what the officer had to report.

"I just received word from back at the station that the chief, Eddie Sawaski, has been shot and is being transported to Cable Hospital by ambulance at this very moment. He's in pretty bad shape; he's lost a lot of blood and they're not sure he's going to make it. Anyway, they wanted me to tell you he had gone down to an Anne Westbrook's house on Argilla Road to have a talk with this guy named Karl Stoner. The next thing they knew a call came from this same Anne Westbrook reporting that Eddie had been shot. They're trying to determine Stoner's whereabouts right now."

Mack didn't respond immediately; he was desperately trying to recall what exactly Eddie had said about Stoner. Clearly, Eddie's instincts about the guy had been correct from the beginning. But why had he gone to confront Stoner on his own, without backup of some kind? It didn't make sense. Eddie was not ordinarily a risk-taker.

"So, Officer, was this Karl Stoner living at Mrs. Westbrook's place?"

"Yeah, I think someone said he was living in an apartment over the barn."

"Well, that makes a few things clearer, including why he rushed down there. I guess, though, I should take a run up to the hospital and see how he's doing. Everything's pretty much under control down here. And thanks."

"No problem," the young man replied, turning smartly and heading back in the direction of the main gate.

Mack stood there thinking for a moment. Things were suddenly beginning to fall into place and this Stoner character, or whatever his real name was, had clearly become their prime suspect. It was probably time to call his superiors and have them draw up an arrest warrant; they might also want to check out the electric chair while they were at it to make sure it was working.

The Benjamin Stickney Cable Memorial Hospital was an attractive brick structure located at the intersection of Essex and County Roads. It was a relatively new facility, having been built only a few years before, thanks to the generosity of the Crane family. A friend of the Cranes' visiting their summer estate had been involved in a serious auto accident and had died on his way to the hospital, the nearest of which at that time was twelve miles away in Beverly; the Cranes had put up the money to have this hospital built in their friend's memory.

Entering the hospital's front door, Mack went straight to the reception desk where an older woman greeted him warmly.

"I'm here to see the police officer, Eddie Sawaski, who was brought in here about an hour ago." He said this with what he thought was his best smile but she was quite unmoved.

"I'm sorry," she replied without a trace of emotion. "They've just brought him up from the emergency room. No one will be allowed in to see him until tomorrow at the earliest, and maybe not even then. He's in very serious condition."

He thought about trying to reason with her; she was obviously a sweet grandmotherly type and given a few minutes he could probably prevail on her to let him in, only he didn't have that much time. He chose the classic FBI approach. Flashing his credentials, he whispered, "Ma'am, I'm with the Federal Bureau of Investigation and I must see Officer Sawaski, even if it's only for a second or two."

Now that had the desired effect.

"Well, why didn't you just say so to begin with," she replied, addressing him like she would a grammar school student. "He's in Room 105. It's around the corner and down the hall to your left, but that badge won't do you much good this time. There's no way the nurse will let you in."

"Thank you, ma'am," Mack answered, uncertain why he had even bothered to come. He certainly wasn't going to be able to question him about what happened; he just wanted to see for himself that Eddie was still alive and stood some chance, however slight, of recovering.

Swinging around the corner, Mack walked briskly down the hallway, his footsteps echoing off the walls. He was amazed how still it was. The only sign of life was a custodian up ahead noiselessly mopping the linoleum tiles; there was a strong smell of disinfectant in the air. The first two rooms on the left were empty, their doors standing wide open. Not so the door to Room 105. Stopping before it, Mack hesitated, then gently turned the handle and pushed. He was surprised by the brightness of the room after the dimness of the hallway.

Eddie was lying motionless; he could have been dead for all Mack could tell. His face had a ghostly pallor to it, not unlike the sheets that covered him. There were tubes protruding from various parts of his body, an oxygen mask covered his nose and mouth, and all Mack could think of was how small he looked. A nurse was standing next to him checking on an IV tube that ran into his arm. Behind her sat a tiny woman whom he guessed was Eddie's mother. How could she have gotten here so fast, he wondered? The nurse looked up as he entered.

"You're not to be in here; he's heavily sedated and probably won't be awake for hours." Her expression suggested she meant what she said. "Not even close family are supposed to be in here at the moment though we made an exception for his mother. She's already lost one son in this war."

"I'm not staying, I just wanted to check up on him. Is he going to pull through?" Mack looked over at Eddie's mother but she seemed not to have heard him. She had the same stoic expression Mack had seen on the faces of so many European immigrants. Like his parents, they had endured so much hardship and suffering just to get here and, then, to have this kind of thing happen.

"All I can tell you at this time is that his condition is serious but stable. If we can just get him through the next twenty-four hours, he may have a chance."

"Is there anything I can do..... Miss Sweeney, is it?" Mack was reading her nametag from across the room. "You know, donate blood, anything like that?"

She studied Mack for a moment with that weary look that all nurses develop over time. "If you're a religious man, and I suspect you are, he certainly could use your prayers."

Mack nodded. Though she appeared serious about what she had said, he also knew she was politely asking him to leave. As he turned for the door, he chanced a final look at Eddie's mother. No movement, no change in expression, not even an acknowledgment he had stopped by to see her son. She had probably been praying since she arrived, he concluded.

Passing the reception desk, he was startled to hear the older woman call out his name.

"Mr. McCarthy, a telephone call came in for you while you were down the hall. An Officer Smith asked if you could stop by the police station. He said it was very important.

Another big smile, another "Thank you, ma'am," and he was out the door.

It took Mack no more than five minutes to reach the police station, just enough time to bring to his attention the fact he had not eaten a thing since early that morning. Had Smitty not said that whatever he wanted to talk about was important, he would have driven into town and had some lunch. Oh well, he could well afford to miss a meal; the suit he was wearing was only a month or two old and yet it was already beginning to feel just a little tight around the waist. How could that be happening? He didn't eat nearly as much as he used to but he was gaining weight all the same. His metabolism was shot. What was he going to weigh in a few years? He had already decided getting older was not all it was cracked up to be.

Pulling into an empty parking space directly in front of the police station, he began wondering what Smitty could have found that was so important, or at least, that he considered so important. Whatever it was he hoped it would help shed some light on the events of the past twenty-four hours. It'd be even better if it provided some clue as to where this Stoner guy might have gone.

There were three police officers in the room as he entered; they all greeted him warmly. He had been in and out of the station so much recently he was beginning to feel like a member of the force himself. It wasn't such a bad feeling; they were a good bunch of guys.

"So, Smitty, what have you got that's so important I'm having to miss my lunch," Mack asked with a big grin.

Smitty handed him the note. "I found this at Anne Westbrook's place not far from where Eddie had been shot. It was clearly written to Anne and it appears to have been written by Karl Stoner. I'm not sure what it was doing on the ground; I can only assume this Stoner guy must have dropped it when Eddie suddenly showed up. "

Mack examined the note carefully, reading and re-reading the hurriedly scrawled words as if they might be some kind of code.

Anne,
Will try to contact you through your parents in Boston.
K

"So, it looks like our Mrs. Westbrook may be involved in this after all. The note would seem to suggest she and Stoner might be planning to rendezvous in Boston after the heat dies down a little. Is that the way you interpret this, Smitty?"

"That's certainly the way it looks. Though we should remember that Stoner wrote the note, not Mrs. Westbrook. She's probably never seen it."

"On the other hand," continued Mack, playing the devil's advocate, "it may have been Mrs. Westbrook who accidentally dropped the note."

"I hadn't thought of that but I guess it's possible," Smitty admitted. "But the real question is whether the note was dropped accidentally or on purpose."

"Why do you say that?" Mack was impressed by Smitty's line of reasoning. It was easy to see why people considered him such a good cop.

"It just might have been dropped there so we'd find it and go looking for Stoner in Boston when, in fact, he was heading in another direction. Anyway, we can at least question Mrs. Westbrook about it since I've asked her to come here this afternoon. She'll be bringing her lawyer; people like her never seem to go anywhere without a lawyer. She's also bringing a picture of Stoner, she said she had."

"Does she by any chance know you found the note," Mack asked.

"No, she doesn't," Smitty replied. "Or at least I didn't tell her I did so, it'll be interesting to see how she reacts when she discovers we have it."

"Good work, Smitty. Perhaps, I should just get out of the way and let you handle this case," Mack said with a chuckle. "Unfortunately, all you guys can charge him with is attempted murder, if he's the one who actually did it. Needless to say, the federal charges take precedence. And since those charges will probably be espionage or sabotage, he'll get the electric chair if he's found guilty and that won't leave much for you guys."

"Fine by me," replied Smitty grimly.

"Now, why don't you guys fill me in on this Mrs. Westbrook before she gets in here. I met her once, you know. Eddie took me by there. I suspect he has a thing for this woman and that's probably why he raced down there without waiting for backup. He'll be crushed if it turns out that our Mrs. Westbrook is involved in this thing."

Chapter Thirty

In all the years she had lived in Ipswich Anne had never been inside the police station. For that matter, no Westbrook had ever been inside any police station, or at least that's what she remembered her father once saying for some undoubtedly inane reason. Such places, he had remarked disdainfully, were only for drunkards and common criminals. Now, here she was entering the police station with a lawyer she had never even met before today. And, if that were not enough, Anne was certain she and her lawyer made for a most unlikely-looking couple, judging from the number of smirks they received from bystanders as they walked into the police station from his car.

Dominic Petrocelli, to be sure, was no Boston Brahmin. He was short, swarthy, and wore the expression of someone who was in constant pain; as a point of fact, he was. He had a wooden leg, having lost his own as a young boy betting his friends he could remain on the streetcar tracks until the very last moment before leaping away from the on-coming train. Dominic had lost the bet along with one of his legs. At some point during the months of convalescence that followed, he made a promise to himself that he would not lose at anything again. At least in terms of his legal career he had kept that promise; he had become a highly successful, and sometimes ruthless, courtroom lawyer.

Dominic was the son of Italian immigrants who, because of his disability, had encouraged him to pursue his education. He had attended Northeastern University, graduating in only three years with a degree in business administration. But, after a year or two of trying his hand at various jobs he decided that business was simply not exciting enough for him so he entered Boston University's law school. Once again he would graduate near the top of his class, making Law Review in the process.

One of the many lessons Dominic learned during his years in law school was that poor people were not the only ones who needed lawyers, the wealthy did, too, and what's more they were willing to pay better for them. However, he also found there were conditions that went along with their business--they wanted results and just as importantly they wanted discretion. Dominic gave them both, and once he had successfully demonstrated these qualities, his law firm grew quickly. In time, he even moved his firm to the North Shore where he could better serve many of his wealthiest clients. And so it was, when he received a telephone call from the Westbrook family lawyer, Charles Sumner Barrett, III--Groton, Harvard, and Harvard Law--Dominic Petrocelli knew exactly what was expected of him. He dropped everything and drove straight to Anne's house.

As Anne entered the police station with her lawyer a heated conversation was underway between three uniformed officers and, judging from the abruptness with which it was terminated, it was obviously about them, or more correctly, about her. Glancing over at the three, Anne was relieved to recognize them all-- Officers Smith and Leclair, both of whom had been at her house earlier, and Officer Bradford, whom she had often seen around town. It was then she noticed a fourth man, sitting huddled over a telephone, his back to her. He appeared to be taking notes on what was being said. After a few moments, he placed the receiver down and stood up. When he turned to face her she was surprised to see the FBI agent who had stopped by her house with Eddie Sawaski. Though he nodded to her and smiled, his presence had an unnerving effect on her; this was clearly not a social visit. To this point the fear she had experienced had been for others, first Karl, and then, when she had found him lying in a pool of his own blood, Eddie. But now, suddenly, she began to feel afraid for herself. What was she mixed up in? And, what did they want from her? For just a moment she felt as if she were about to faint and had to place her hands on the reception counter to steady herself. She could only hope no one noticed.

As Anne stood there, her lawyer introduced himself to everyone. For all her nervousness Anne couldn't help but be impressed with the way he handled himself, especially his ability to immediately put people at ease. It seemed almost as if he were drawing attention to himself in order to take some of the pressure off her. She knew it was only temporary but it did buy her time to calm herself. The small talk suddenly ceased and she could tell by the FBI agent's body language that the serious business was about to begin.

"Mrs. Westbrook, I wonder if you and Mr. Petrocelli would join Officer Smith and myself in the back conference room to answer a few questions. It shouldn't take very long." He motioned them to follow him.

The conference room, as Mack had referred to it, appeared to her more like an interrogation room; it was a depressing-looking place. The walls were covered with cheap wood paneling, dark and scratched; the furniture was a table and several chairs, none of which seemed to match. The only light, other than that provided by a small window with frosted glass, came from a ceiling fixture. She felt her fear creeping back. Well, if she were about to be interrogated all she could think was "thank God" Dominic Petrocelli was there at her side.

Barely had they seated themselves across the table from one another when Mack spoke; there was no mistaking the seriousness of his tone.

"Mrs. Westbrook, I understand from Officer Smith that you were to bring a photo of Karl Stoner with you when you came here this afternoon. If so, may I see it, please? To the best of my knowledge I've never seen the man."

As she drew the photo from her pocketbook Dominic reached over and took it from her. As he studied it, she noticed a troubled expression cross his face. Leaning over he whispered, "I suggest you find another photo; this could be somewhat incriminating."

She looked again at the photo. The camera lens had caught Karl with a grim expression on his face. He was standing next to a pile of wood, stripped to the waist, an ax held casually in his hand. She remembered his unease when she took the picture and she suddenly understood why. Even without the smile it would have been impossible to miss the sense of intimacy in the scene. Her lawyer was correct; the photo would undoubtedly raise questions about their relationship. But so what, she had committed no crime, or had she? All she really understood was that she'd better cooperate or she might just end up spending the night in the building. She motioned for her lawyer to hand the photo to Mack.

Taking the photo, Mack turned to Smitty. "Is this the guy?"

"That's him," responded Smitty, "although to be honest I've seen him in person only once and that was when we interviewed him at the Hayes Hotel after the fight. But, that's him, all right; I'd recognize that arrogant look of his anywhere."

Mack sat silently staring at the photo for several minutes as if committing the face to memory. At one point Anne thought she even detected a slight smile, though she couldn't be certain. Finally, Mack looked directly at her.

"Mrs. Westbrook, why don't you tell us everything you know about our Mr. Stoner here, and when I say everything, I mean just that, everything."

Again the slight smile, this time she was sure, but there was no warmth to it. As she was about to respond, Petrocelli spoke up.

"Now, if I may, let me ask just one more time for the record, is Mrs. Westbrook being accused of any wrong-doing? If that is the case I want to hear the charges before deciding whether she should answer any of your questions." There was a business-like tone to his voice now and he stared directly at Mack McCarthy.

"She is not under arrest, if that's what you're asking," responded Mack, without a trace of his usual grin, "at least not for now. And if she cooperates fully there should be no reason for doing so later. But whether wittingly or otherwise she is involved in a potentially serious situation here. Maybe I'd better explain so you'll understand just how serious the situation is. A few days ago a man by the name of Kurt Oberg was executed in Washington, DC; you may have read about it since it was in all the newspapers. He was a German spy who, along with another man killed while resisting arrest, was brought to this country by submarine to commit sabotage against American military and industrial facilities. Before Oberg was executed, however, he revealed that several other agents had been sent here as part of a larger operation. A massive manhunt is underway at this very moment to find those agents."

"This is all very interesting, Mr. McCarthy, but what does it have to do with Mrs. Westbrook?" Anne's lawyer interjected.

"If you'll permit me, Mr. Petrocelli, I was about to get to that. We have good reason to believe that Karl Stoner is one of the German agents for whom we have been searching."

"No, you're wrong," Anne gasped. She should have remained silent but she couldn't help herself. "I know Karl too well to believe he could ever be a German spy. He's kind and gentle; you don't know the man, you're wrong I tell you."

"Kind and gentle?" Mack looked like he would explode but somehow managed to maintain his composure. "Mrs. Westbrook, if our suspicions are correct, and there's every reason to believe they are, then your Mr. Stoner is a ruthless killer. It's almost certain he's responsible for the death of the young Coast Guardsman at the beach, two more men in the fire at the shipyard, and if it hadn't been for your own quick action, he would have added a fourth to the list, one Eddie Sawaski."

Anne could not have responded had she wanted to; her vocal chords were virtually paralyzed. Neither was her lawyer any help. For the first time he, too, was at a loss for words. Only Mack seemed capable of speech at that moment.

"On the assumption, then, that you knew nothing of this side of Stoner's personality, what did you know of him?" Mack inquired.

Anne struggled to gain control over her emotions. When she finally spoke it was barely a whisper.

"I guess I didn't really know him as well as I thought I did. He was very quiet and, to be honest, when the two of us were together, I was probably the one who did most of the talking. I do remember he told me he was from Chicago and had left for personal reasons; he was looking for work or, at least, that's what he said."

"Didn't you find it strange he wasn't in the military like other men his age?"

"Yes, I did. I even asked him about it."

"And what did he say?"

"That the military had rejected him because of weak lungs, the result of having had tuberculosis when he was young boy."

"Yeah, that was the same story he gave us when we questioned him about the fight up at Depot Square," Smitty suddenly interjected. "Said he had taken up boxing to build up his strength. After the job he did on those two southern boys, it all seemed quite reasonable."

Mack was silent for a moment, then, continued his questioning.

231

"Did you know about that fight, Mrs. Westbrook, the one that sent a couple of recruits from Camp Agawam to the hospital for treatment?"

"He never said anything to me about it," Anne explained. "But not long ago one of my friends made mention of it in passing."

"What did you think when you heard about it?"

"To be honest, I didn't really think about it very much. It simply didn't register. Karl didn't seem to be that kind of person at all."

Another silence, though Mack never took his eyes off Anne.

"Let me ask you a very different kind of question. At any time did Mr. Stoner ever say anything that could be interpreted as anti-American? You know, criticisms of President Roosevelt's policies or things like that?"

It was the one time all day that Anne had to suppress a smile because her parents, not to mention, most of their friends, were very anti-Roosevelt; they were constantly criticizing everything he did, though not so publicly what with the war on.

"No," Anne replied. "He never said anything like that to me. I should point out, however, that we seldom discussed politics. I don't have much of an interest in the topic."

Anne's breathing had just begun to return to normal when she saw Mack pick up the photo of Karl and study it. As the seconds ticked by she felt her now familiar sense of dread was becoming even more intense. What was he thinking, she wondered? When finally he broke the spell by asking a question, it was anything but the one she expected.

"How well do you know Officer Sawaski, Mrs. Westbrook?"

So surprised was she by the question that she concluded she must have misunderstood him.

"Officer Sawaski?"

Mack smiled, though this time she had no idea what it meant.

"Yes, the police chief, the man you found lying bleeding in your driveway."

"I guess I've known him for years, though I can't really say I know him well. I mean we always speak whenever we meet on the street but that's about it." She was still confused by his question.

"Nothing more than that?" he persisted.

"No, nothing." She truly was becoming panicky by the direction the questioning was heading. Did he think she had something to do with

Eddie being shot? Mack's next question was probably inevitable but she was unprepared for it just the same.

"So, how would you describe your relationship with Mr. Stoner?"

The very thought of talking to these men about her affair with Karl made her angry and resentful. She had made a conscious point of never speaking to anyone about it, not even her best friends. It was too personal, too intimate. She had always worried that just mentioning it to another soul would some how compromise it. And now she was supposed to explain it to these strangers? Down deep, of course, she realized she had little choice. Just the thought of spending a single night in that jail was more than she could bear. So now the only question was how much should she tell? Yet somewhere in the back of her mind another question nagged at her. How much did she owe Karl anyway? After all, he was the one who had placed her in this horrible situation.

"Well, naturally, as time passed we became more friendly," she found herself saying.

"More friendly, huh?" Mack interjected; he was studying the photo again. "And how friendly was that, Mrs. Westbrook?"

"What is it that you're driving at?" Petrocelli protested. "Are you asking whether my client had an affair with Mr. Stoner? If so, ask it directly so she can deny it and we can get on with the questioning."

Anne was stunned. Her lawyer had unknowingly just set her up and she could tell by the expression on his face that Mack realized it.

"All right, Mr. Petrocelli, let's do it your way. Mrs. Westbrook, did you have an affair with Karl Stoner? Just a yes or no answer, please."

Anne felt like a rabbit suddenly flushed from its hiding place and she was sure the FBI agent had no intention of letting her slip away. Yes or no, that's what he said. And what had he explained earlier? Cooperate fully and there may be no reason to arrest you. Why couldn't they have left her this one thing she and Karl had secretly shared? What did it matter to them?

She suddenly realized all three of them were staring at her.

"Yes," she whispered her voice barely audible.

"I'm sorry, Mrs. Westbrook, I'm not sure I heard your answer. Would you repeat it and, please, speak more loudly."

You bastard, she thought, you heard my answer all right. You just want to rub my nose in it.

"Yes," she shouted. "Yes, yes, yes, I had an affair with Karl Stoner. Are you satisfied, now?" She didn't want to appear weak, not at this moment, but a wave of self-pity washed over her and she found herself close to tears.

Before Petrocelli could interject, Mack stood up and declared there'd be a fifteen-minute break. Although Anne did not actually see it, she was sure the FBI agent had a look of triumph of his face as he left the room, and she hated him for it.

With her admission of having had an affair with Karl, Anne assumed the worst was over, unfortunately, she was to be sadly mistaken. The note caught her totally by surprise; she had known nothing about it and could not provide a credible explanation for its existence. Even worse, she had no idea whether they even believed her. For the first time it struck home just how deeply implicated she was in Karl's crimes. Her lawyer realized this, too, and advised her to remain silent lest her answers be used to incriminate her. He brought up the issue of immunity, but Mack seemed to brush it aside by saying all she had to do was cooperate and everything would be all right.

But could Mack be trusted? She doubted it; she was beginning to doubt she could trust any man. Look what had happened with Karl. He had probably never loved her; he had simply used her to provide cover for his spying or whatever it was. How could she ever have let herself get involved in something like this, and with a man who in retrospect had been a complete stranger to her. Now, of course, she was quite prepared to admit how little she had really known about Karl. So, what was she to do? She had no choice but to cooperate with the FBI.

The interrogation continued unabated into the afternoon. In response to a question from Mack, she explained about going to Karl's apartment that morning to tell him of the fire and of his great surprise at hearing the news. Anne felt at least some faint relief from the fact they hadn't spent the night together. She hoped by saying she had gone to his apartment that this would somehow make her seem less involved.

"So what exactly did Stoner say to you when you told him of the fire?" Mack inquired.

"He didn't say anything for a few seconds; he seemed stunned. Then, he said something to the effect he couldn't believe it."

"He couldn't believe it," Mack repeated. "Then, what did he say?"

"He said he was going to have to leave."

"Did you ask him why it was necessary for him to leave?"

"Of course, I did" Anne responded, a hint of annoyance audible in her voice.

"So what did he say when you asked him?"

"That it was complicated. And when I asked if he had had anything to do with the fire, he said no. So, I replied, then why not stay and fight it, that I could get him a good lawyer."

"Now, let's assume for just a second that he was being truthful about not having anything to do with the fire, why did he run and, more importantly, why did he shoot Officer Sawaski? It just doesn't make sense."

"I honestly can't answer that, though I wish I could," Anne replied sadly. "He simply said that all the lawyers in Boston wouldn't be able to help him."

"And did you interpret his answers as implying at least some involvement in the fire?"

"It was all happening so quickly I honestly didn't have a chance to think."

Inevitably, Mack turned back to the note for which Anne continued to have no explanation, and no amount of questioning could draw one from her. Finally, he called a halt to the interrogation.

"Mrs. Westbrook, I do want to thank you for your cooperation today though we will undoubtedly have more questions for you in the future. Before you go, however, I would like to share some information we've uncovered about your Mr. Stoner. For one thing his real name is not Karl Stoner, it's Erich Stinnes, and he is not an American but a German national. Immigration records indicate he came to the United States in 1923 at the age of nine and remained here until early 1929 when he returned to Germany. That would explain his excellent command of English. During those five years he lived in Chicago with an aunt and uncle. The uncle worked for the Chicago *Tribune*, a right-wing newspaper owned by the infamous Colonel McCormick, who before the war, anyway, was well known for his anti-Semitic and pro-Nazi views. There was a time when the Bureau kept an eye on everyone who worked for him. Never found anything on him however. He died about a year ago but the aunt is still alive and agents have been questioning her for the past couple of days. Hopefully she'll be able to provide us additional information on our Mr. Stinnes."

A silence followed during which no one moved. Finally, Mack pushed back his chair and stood.

"You're free to go, Mrs. Westbrook."

Slowly Anne got up and made her way to the door. The revelations about Karl had been so unexpected; she felt slightly dazed. Mumbling her good-byes, she took Petrocelli's arm and walked out to the waiting car. They drove back to her house in silence. Anne had hoped to feel some relief, if for no other reason than she had nothing left to reveal. Instead, she found herself overcome by confusion and doubt. How could it be that she had awoken this morning secure in the knowledge Karl loved her, only to find out by evening that he was a German spy who had quite possibly used her affections as a cover for his activities. How quickly her life had been turned upside-down.

It was strange, she thought to herself, but for all distress he was causing her, she was finding it impossible to hate him. She couldn't even think of him as the enemy. Where was he, she wondered? And, what had really happened at the shipyard to make him fear for his life? Perhaps she wasn't being fair to him. Maybe he really did love her and somehow intended to contact her with an explanation for everything. Was there any chance the FBI could be mistaken, that just possibly they had him mixed up with someone else? If only she knew the truth; on the other hand, maybe right now it was better she didn't know it. The truth was proving to be very difficult to accept.

Anne saw her driveway up ahead and for the first time in her life she dreaded the thought of being in that house. No longer did it seem like a warm and secure refuge from the outside world for it was now filled with tragic and painful memories.

While all this was taking place, Karl was barely two miles from Anne's house making final preparations for his dangerous trip to the beach. He would travel lightly since among other things he would have to swim the Castle Neck River at high tide. His plan was to recover the transmitter lying buried in the dunes, broadcast a message for help, and return to his hiding place on Hog Island until the arrival of the U-boat sent to rescue him. It sounded ever so simple but he was enough of a realist to know that the chances of a U-boat ever being sent were infinitely small. There was simply no other option.

Setting out across the marsh, Karl felt fairly certain that any search for him had ended with the coming of evening though almost certainly it would resume with the first light of dawn. That gave him several hours of darkness to complete his life-or-death mission; it was not much time if anything were to go wrong, however. Keeping low, he made his way through the waist-high marsh grass. It was blessedly mild with just the faintest overcast. He had to pick his way with care for the numerous channels that crisscrossed the marsh were now brimming with water.

By the time he reached the edge of the river, it was completely dark. Fortunately, he could still make out the white sand dunes of the beach on the other side of the river. Slipping noiselessly into the icy cold water, Karl was surprised by the strength of the current; it was lucky he was a strong swimmer. After about fifteen minutes of strenuous swimming he emerged onto the beach soaking wet and cold. And while he would have preferred to dry his clothes next to a warm driftwood fire, it was far too risky. Wet or not, he would have to push on. But, now he faced another obstacle, would he be able to locate the spot where the transmitter was buried since he was approaching the spot from the opposite direction. Furthermore he had only a tiny waterproof flashlight to provide any kind of illumination.

Cautiously he made his way through the dunes taking advantage of any clumps of vegetation or shrubbery to mask his movements. If there were patrols on the beach it was possible they might spot a figure moving across a white sandy background even on a night as dark as this. He was especially concerned about the swishing sound his wet clothes made as he walked. Amid the deathly silence of the dunes, the slightest noise seemed to carry for miles. Though in reality he doubted he'd run into anyone here, he stopped every few minutes to listen just to make certain. You never knew when you might stumble across a pair of lovers or even a lone fisherman. The fact there was a war raging in Europe was not going to completely change human nature.

Finally, about eleven o'clock, Karl slid down the side of a large dune to confront a grove of pitch pines that looked vaguely familiar, even in the darkness. It took but a few minutes of poking around to determine this was the spot where the transmitter was buried. Quickly, he uncovered it. The case it came in, which resembled an ordinary suitcase, was designed to be waterproof. He tested the batteries. In a few seconds a small red light began to glow; they were fine. He breathed an audible sigh of relief.

He had been thinking for hours about the message he would send. It had to be short and to the point if he did not want it traced back here to the beach. Basically, he would ask for a U-boat to come rescue him in exactly two days time. He would probably be unable to hold out much longer than that, yet it would require some time to get a U-boat to the area. He provided the coordinates, a rendezvous time, and the signal he would flash from shore. Now, he could only hope Canaris considered him a sufficiently important asset to ask Doenitz for help. If he did, the one great advantage was that Doenitz was in almost daily communication with the U-boats under his command.

Now, it was time to encode the message for transmission. The code he'd be using was allegedly "unbreakable," though he'd never completely believed it. Using his flashlight as much as he dared, Karl converted his message into what appeared to be an indecipherable mix of letters and numerals. In theory, only the person receiving the message in Berlin would be able to unscramble it. Once the note was properly encoded, the only thing left was to transmit it. This was the most dangerous part since he would have to leave the safety of the trees to find a less obstructed spot from which to send the signal.

Picking up the transmitter, Karl climbed a nearby sand dune on whose summit was a small hollow surrounded by foot-tall marsh grass. It was about as good a spot as he was going to find. He placed the transmitter on the seaward-facing side of the hollow, raised the aerial and turned the set on. In Morse code he tapped out his call sign to the Abwehr radio center in Berlin and waited. The seconds ticked by, then minutes; it seemed like hours. He was getting very anxious. Then, just as he was about to send another signal, he heard a faint acknowledgment from Berlin. His signal had been received. Taking a deep breath, he now transmitted his emergency message and waited once again. Another acknowledgment--message received. He felt a rush of excitement but there was no time now to sit and enjoy it. He had to get out of there and back to Hog Island. Someone, somewhere had almost certainly picked up his transmission.

In fact, someone did pick up Karl's transmission. That someone was Seaman First Class Stanley Keralios, who was monitoring radio traffic from the Navy's regional headquarters in Boston. It was a job Stanley loved, and he was good at it. It never ceased to amaze him how much traffic he found late at night as he scanned back and forth across the various frequencies--short-wave radio transmissions, submarine communications, just about everything imaginable. So, it came as no great surprise when he detected Karl's transmission. Instantly twirling his radio direction finder he attempted to determine its location. It was not easy since the transmission had been brief. Nevertheless, he was able to calculate that it originated from somewhere on the North Shore. It was a suspicious enough event that he logged it and scribbled a hasty note to remind him to tell his commanding officer about it first thing in the morning.

Chapter Thirty-One

Mack awoke early the next morning in order to go over yet again everything he had learned from Anne. She appeared honestly to have known little, if anything, of Stoner's mission, though for the moment it was in his best interest not to inform her of that. She might still possess information she was unaware she had that could turn out to be crucial at some point. And, if by chance she did, he wanted to be in a position to extract it from her somehow. But, more than the information, there was the very real possibility that Stoner might try to contact her. On just that chance he had ordered twenty-four hour surveillance on Anne's house; he was also having her telephone calls monitored. The possibility of Stoner contacting her served another very important purpose; it provided him with a credible explanation as to why he hadn't arrested Anne, if one of superiors chose to question him about it later on. Though barely twenty-four hours had elapsed since Stoner had vanished, Mack was beginning to feel frustrated that not a single trace of him had as yet been uncovered. Where had he gone? Could he actually have made it out of the area? It was entirely possible, he concluded, though he had placed agents along the most obvious routes out of town. Or was he still hiding out somewhere in Ipswich? That was an intriguing possibility, but if he were still in Ipswich, where was he? Had he been given the names of people in the area that might help him--Nazi sympathizers or maybe just loyal Germans? It seemed doubtful, if for no other reason than there were so few Germans in the Boston area compared to New York or Chicago. Of course, it would only take a couple of people. On the other hand, he fled Anne's place on foot so there was always the possibility he had found refuge in one of the empty houses or barns along Argilla Road. In fact, the more Mack thought about it, the more he became convinced that Karl was hiding out somewhere in the vicinity of Anne's house, but where? Clearly, there was only one way to find out and for that he needed a number of men and a map detailed enough to show every house and barn in the area.

By mid-morning Mack was back at the police station with several field agents sent down from the regional office in Boston. They were all standing around the reception counter drinking coffee while examining a large topographic map of the town provided by the Tax Assessor's office.

"No shortage of places to hide down there," Mack murmured, pointing to the area around the beach. "Look at all the woods and marshland. You could actually hide a small army in there."

"That's if they didn't surrender because of the deer flies and greenheads," Smitty laughed. "They're murder this time of year, which means if Stoner is hiding out there, he'll have to keep moving; he won't be able to just stay put."

"That's something worth remembering," nodded Mack. "Now, here's my plan, if you can call it that. Before I left Boston I called the Coast Guard commander for this district and he agreed to have the Coast Guard contingent at the beach do a complete search of the area that's called Castle Neck on the map here. He'll also assign an aircraft to be overhead in case they flush him from his hiding place. In the meantime we'll check all the houses and other structures along Argilla Road. Let's just see how big a job that will be."

After studying the map again for a few seconds one of the agents commented, "Doesn't look bad. There aren't that many houses along the road."

"No, there aren't," agreed Smitty. "But there is one thing you should remember. Most of the houses at the lower end of Argilla Road are summer residences. And, this summer, because of gasoline rationing and other wartime restrictions, many of their owners have chosen not to come down here so the houses are empty. Needless to say this makes them a perfect place to lay low."

"Good point, Smitty. And while we're on the subject are there other buildings, not shown on the map, that might also make good places to hide out?" Mack inquired.

"Not many, but there is a boathouse right here that belongs to the Crane family." He pointed to a small structure marked on the map. "And then there's a farm over here on Hog Island. I think during the summer there are people living there."

"What about all these little wooded islands scattered throughout the marsh? Could anyone hide out there?"

"It's possible if they had sufficient provisions; I wouldn't want to try living off the land in that area. On the other hand, I don't think anyone ever goes in there."

"Let's just suppose, then, our Mr. Stoner had hidden some supplies out there for just such an emergency. Could he keep out of sight for a while?"

"Sure," replied Smitty. "But how long do you think he'd try to stay there? The better question, of course, is why he'd go out there to begin with?"

"Unfortunately, I don't have an answer to either of those questions," Mack responded, obviously thinking about something else. "I suppose it's always possible someone intended to help him get out of there. I don't know who it might be or how it would be done but I've learned from experience never to rule anything out just because it doesn't appear at first glance to make sense. So, with that in mind let's just see if he's in there."

"What would you like me to do?" asked Smitty.

"I'd like to get out to this Hog Island and maybe some of these other wooded spots. What's the best way to do that?"

"That's easy," responded Smitty. "We have access to a motor boat so I can have someone run you out there."

"Great! I'll take Steve here with me, the rest of you divvy up the houses and go search them. If we don't find anything, we'll meet back here at 3:30 this afternoon. Any questions?"

There were none and, like a group of small boys hearing the recess bell, they headed eagerly for the door.

"Wait, just a minute more," Mack called out. "There is one additional thing I should pass on to you about our Mr. Stoner; it's information the Bureau has recently received from British intelligence. It's important that you don't underestimate this man. The first thing is that our man is one of the Abwehr's most decorated agents having been presented by Admiral Canaris himself with the Knights' Cross. He received this honor for having obtained the blueprints to one of our most heavily classified projects. Apparently, it's some kind of a device that allows bombardiers to hit targets with pinpoint accuracy; ironically, though the Germans now know all about the device, it's still so classified here the US government won't tell us anything about it. Anyway, I was told that when Nazi leaders first saw the blueprints they refused to believe they were real; they assumed that the US was intentionally sending them misinformation to confuse them. Later, I guess, after their engineers had gotten a thorough look at the documents, they were able to convince Berlin of their authenticity. Now, every new bomber that's being delivered to the German Luftwaffe has this device built into it."

"It's an interesting story, sir," commented one of the men. "But what does that have to do with our search for the guy?"

"What it means is the Abwehr will probably do everything possible to rescue this man. But there's more so let me finish. Our man, whose real name is Erich Stinnes, by the way, has not only received training in the use of explosives and light weapons but hand-to-hand combat as well. Remember that he sent two young army recruits who were foolish enough to pick a fight with him to the hospital. One was beaten so badly he's been sent home for rehabilitation. In addition, of course, we have every reason to believe he killed the young Coast Guardsman and nearly killed Eddie Sawaski, the local police chief here in Ipswich. So, as you can see, this guy Stoner, or Stinnes, is one very tough customer and it's not going to be an easy matter to find him. Even if we do, you can be assured he won't allow himself to be taken easily, not when facing the electric chair. So let's be very careful out there, please; this guy is armed and extremely dangerous."

Mack watched the men file out of the room in a more subdued manner this time. They were all business now and didn't say a word until they were outside. His comments about Stoner had obviously struck a note of caution with them.

At the same time as Mack was organizing his search party, the object of that search was trying without much luck to get some sleep. Karl had returned to his hideaway before dawn--muddy, wet and exhausted. It hadn't helped his spirits much that a heavy squall had passed through the area on his way back, though he understood that while it was soaking him it was also wiping away any evidence of his visit to the beach. Now, if only he could get some rest. He was definitely going to need it. The next two days would likely prove difficult since he was certain the FBI, and probably the military, would be out looking for him in force and he would have to remain alert.

Remaining alert, however, did not seem to pose any great problem at the moment; the adrenaline was still pumping and his mind would not stop churning for a second. It didn't seem possible that it was only this time yesterday that Anne was informing him of the fire at the shipyard. So much had happened in the past twenty-four hours. He wished he could have waited just a little longer before taking flight, of course, once that police chief had showed up it had become all but impossible to do so. There was no question it was the fire at the shipyard that had brought him racing down to Anne's. How ironic thought Karl that the very first thing they'd been taught was to be prepared for the unexpected. Their instructor, a veteran on the First World War, had made clear that how they handled such situations would probably determine the success or failure of their mission. It bothered Karl that when faced with the unexpected he had handled it so clumsily.

Too late to worry about that now, he decided. His more immediate concern was how to survive the next few days that would probably include more unforeseen events. It wasn't going to be easy, especially if they made the decision to systematically search this island. As the largest island out here it would certainly seem logical to do so. Karl wondered if they'd use dogs; that would make evading capture far more difficult. Thomas, he knew, would vouch for that. Then, of course, even if he were able to avoid detection he was still left with the uncertainty of whether Berlin would actually send a U-boat to rescue him. He knew there was no shortage of U-boats in the waters off New England but would Doenitz be willing to risk one for such a dangerous mission? He tried to imagine what he would do if he were in Doenitz's position. It would be a tough decision there was no doubt about that. Risk an entire U-boat crew to rescue one Abwehr agent? He wouldn't do it if he were Doenitz; thankfully he was not.

Thinking like this was beginning to depress him; he had to direct his mind elsewhere. He decided that if he were not going to be able to sleep, he might just as well check his food supply. It was something to do, though admittedly it wouldn't take long. All he had was what he had been able to grab from his apartment--two bottles of warm beer, one half empty box of crackers, the end of a loaf of bread, a hunk of cheese, and two slightly shriveled apples. It was probably sufficient to get him through the next couple of days. Of course, if the U-boat didn't come for him, he was in serious trouble. For that reason alone he couldn't stop wondering what Doenitz would do. Maybe if he drank one of the beers it would settle him down. He pried off the cap and took a deep swig. Too bad he hadn't brought more, he thought to himself.

It must have been nearly noon when he heard the drone of an airplane but he had trouble locating it because of the bright sunlight. Finally, he spotted it flying low over the beach. It appeared they were going to be much more serious about today's search. There were probably already men on the ground whose responsibility would be to scour every inch of the dune area; thank goodness for last night's rain shower. He was also beginning to feel just a little anxious about his last night's radio transmission. Had it lasted long enough for someone to get an exact fix on its point of origin? The length of the transmission certainly fell within the guidelines established by the Abwehr, but it was well known that the Americans were constantly coming up with new technologies to counter Germany's latest inventions.

As the day wore on, it became stifling under the trees. He would have preferred to strip down to his shorts but there were so many flies that delighted in attacking him that he didn't dare. His arms were already a mass of bites. After a while he was forced to move about just to avoid them, though whatever relief he experienced never lasted for long. He had to be very careful for there were people on the island and any quick movement could alert someone to his presence there. At that moment he detected the faint whine of an outboard motor approaching the island through a chorus of shrieking gulls. Now, who could that be, he wondered? If it was the FBI, it was about time. He decided to check.

Reaching down into his duffel, he pulled out the Pistolen. He inspected it to make certain there were still some rounds left in the clip, then slipped it into his waistband. Cautiously, he made his way through the woods in the direction of the farm. He had only walked a short distance when the woods abruptly ended in favor of a vast pasture, which extended up and over the crest of the hill that comprised the bulk of the island. As he stood there he could see two men trudging up the gravel road toward the farm; a third man remained back at the small pier with the boat. It was strange but one of the two men almost certainly looked familiar though at that distance he couldn't be certain. What was it about the man? Then, he remembered. Of course, it was the government agent who had visited Anne with the police chief. Small world, he decided, and a dangerous one, too. But, no dog, at least that was some consolation.

As he watched, the two men gained the top of the hill, then, disappeared out of sight. Now, he'd just have to wait and see what they did. It turned out to be a longer wait that Karl had expected--at least an hour. As he waited his stomach began to growl; he was getting really hungry but didn't dare leave his observation post until the men had left the island. Where had they gone, he wondered? Could they be circling around behind him? Just as he was thinking he should watch his back, the two appeared at the crest of the hill with a third man; Karl guessed he was a farmer who looked after the sheep.

From his vantage point it appeared the three were talking animatedly as periodically one or the other would point in this direction or that. Suddenly, the three turned and looked straight in his direction. He froze not daring to even breathe. Had they possibly seen him? So, what could they be talking about, then? A few minutes later Karl watched as they turned away and exchanged handshakes. The two agents began walking back to the pier while the farmer headed up the hill. Some search, Karl mused, with a huge sigh of relief. He couldn't help but think the Gestapo could teach the FBI a thing or two about conducting searches.

Hermann Wolfbauer had completed his mission and was looking forward to a speedy return trip to Lorient, when his radio operator handed him a message from Admiral Doenitz headquarters; it was marked Top Secret.

"This is insane," he exclaimed after reading the full message. "Truly insane. Doenitz has ordered us to pick up some Abwehr agent off the coast of Massachusetts. Didn't he think the mission he gave us was dangerous enough; now we have this foolishness. And, of course, we've just lost one of our air compressors, so we're going to have problems submerging for long periods. How could he possibly order us to do this? We don't even have a decent map of the bay we're supposed to enter. If I didn't know him better I'd suspect Doenitz was trying to get us all killed."

Wolfbauer's outburst didn't surprise the junior officers for he was well known for his sharp tongue. Yet, within the submarine service he commanded great respect. Not only was he one of the youngest holders of the Knight's Cross of the Iron Cross, he was, at the tender age of twenty-five, already well on his way to becoming an ace. His crew was absolutely devoted to him, to the extent that several members had painted a replica of his Knight's Cross on the U-boat's conning tower. There was also an unstated pride in the fact that Doenitz often gave his U-boat the riskier assignments. And, though his aggressive, though often unorthodox, style had gained him the reputation of being a "cowboy," even many of the more seasoned U-boat commanders accorded him a certain grudging respect.

Wolfbauer was in position to rescue Karl because he had just completed a mine-laying operation at the very mouth of New York harbor. The ship he commanded, U-232, was a type VIIC attack submarine, which under ordinary circumstances carried an arsenal of fourteen torpedoes. For the mining operation, however, ten of those torpedoes had been replaced by an equal number of TMA mines, which came with long chains and anchors attached. When these mines were launched from a torpedo tube, the anchor drifted to the bottom while the mine drifted up to a position just below the surface. Laying the mines was a relatively simple process, but doing so at the mouth of the America's busiest harbor made it difficult to avoid detection. Not content, however, with just laying the mines and slipping away, Wolfbauer had used two of his torpedoes to sink a 5,000-ton freighter. He had hoped to sink another on the return trip to France. And while publicly Wolfbauer had expressed annoyance at having to pick up the agent, secretly he saw it quite differently. Any mission, he decided, where ten mines are laid in the vicinity of New York harbor, perhaps two freighters are destroyed, and an Abwehr agent is picked off the American coast, is one deserving of some special commendation. Perhaps, he thought with a wry smile, he'd get Oak Leaves to go with his Knight's Cross.

Chapter Thirty-Two

Karl was up and about at the first faint light of dawn. Although he was stiff and sore from an uncomfortable night sleeping on the bare, uneven ground, he couldn't have cared less for today was the day. If everything worked out according to plan within a few hours he'd be aboard a U-boat on his way back to Berlin. As he did with greater frequency now he found himself thinking about the mission that had brought him here and wondered about its real purpose. There was something about it that was beginning to bother him. Was it possible that Canaris may have wanted the mission to fail, had in fact planned it that way? This notion was becoming increasingly difficult to dispel. After all, even if the mission had been remotely successful, how much damage could it have caused? Not enough certainly to have any significant impact on America's war effort.

On the other hand, having several German spies captured on American soil where they had been sent to commit sabotage against military facilities, now that could have at the least a significant psychological impact on the war. Roosevelt would be furious with Hitler and would use the subsequent trials to demonstrate just how monstrous his policies were. Thinking about it he could well imagine Canaris planning something like this to draw America more deeply into the war in Europe while making certain it didn't direct all its resources to the conflict with Japan.

Unfortunately, such speculation did little to raise Karl's spirits. If he were right about Canaris, there probably wouldn't be a U-boat on its way. He'd be more valuable as the chief villain of a sensational spy trial that would inevitably conclude with his execution in DC's now infamous electric chair. But, he had to stop thinking like this; it was driving him crazy. It would be far better if he focused instead on how he was get through the day without being detected.

After yesterday he wasn't sure what to expect from those looking for him. He'd been prepared for an exhaustive search of the beach and surrounding marshes so it came as a surprise to him when he saw how casually the whole thing was undertaken. Initially he decided they had just been reconnoitering the area in preparation for sending out larger search teams. This conclusion was reinforced later in the day when he spied a convoy of olive-green vehicles heading down Argilla Road in the direction of the beach. The convoy consisted of about a dozen large trucks, each pulling an artillery piece. As he watched they disappeared into the beach parking area.

Was all this for him, he had wondered? But, if so, why all the artillery pieces? Then, it dawned on him. They must have intercepted his message to Berlin and to have done this they had to have broken the codes Berlin was using. He would clearly have to warn Canaris about this when he got back to Abwehr headquarters. That's, of course, if he got back since it appeared now they were preparing a surprise party for the U-boat. He suspected it was too late to warn the U-boat away at this point, but there had to be something else he could do.

As he stood there, deciding whether he should take the chance of reaching the radio transmitter, he was startled to hear the sound of artillery fire. What could they be firing at? There would certainly be no U-boat out there at this time of day. Then it occurred to him they very possibly were establishing range since their maps would indicate exactly which route into the bay the U-boat would have to follow. They were not taking any chances; clearly they wanted to get this U-boat.

The firing continued throughout the morning hours effectively eliminating his range theory. Finally, around noon, it became more intermittent, then ceased entirely; it did not resume. Before Karl could come up with another explanation for the artillery barrage, he spotted the convoy leaving the way they had come. They had obviously come down for artillery practice, he sighed with relief.

Compared to the anxieties of the morning, his afternoon passed in relative calm. Try as he might, he could not detect any indication of search parties anywhere in the area. By mid-afternoon he even managed to fall asleep for an hour or so; he might have slept longer had not a stiff east wind begun to blow in off the ocean. Thick dark clouds now covered the sky and the temperature had dropped markedly; a storm was definitely in the making. He felt elated by it. The stormier the night, the easier it would be for a U-boat to slip into Ipswich Bay undetected. He was getting so anxious he would have liked to head for the beach at that very moment but accepted that it just wasn't a good idea.

At dusk he set out for what he could only hope would be a rendezvous with a submarine. He checked his flashlight, to be sure there was still life left in the batteries, then stuck it in a watertight bag. The flashlight would be his only means of communicating with the rescue party. He had already cleaned up his hideaway to eliminate any sign of his having been there; everything would be taken aboard the submarine in his duffel for later disposal.

The trip back to the beach was a little easier this time since he was by now following a familiar route. Even the water of the Castle Neck River seemed just a bit less cold. By nine-thirty he stood on the spot from which he would signal the U-boat; there was nothing left now but to hunker down and wait until midnight. He found a small grove of trees for cover since the last thing he needed was to run into a canine patrol as Thomas had. Other than the U-boat not showing, the patrols represented the only threat to his getting away safely at the moment.

As he waited in the trees he could hear the pounding of the surf; at least he wouldn't have to worry about anyone hearing him. The night was also pitch black. He had to turn on his flashlight to see his watch-
--it was eleven-fifteen. Suddenly, it seemed he could hear the ticking of the second hand and with every tick his anxiety level increased. Was there a U-boat out there waiting to rescue him? Or, had he just deluded himself into believing that Doenitz would ever order a submarine in here? He checked his watch again; it was ten minutes to midnight. Time to move. Cautiously he crawled to the top of the tallest dune. The conditions were perfect. Now, please, let there be a U-boat out there.

Twelve midnight. Well, this is it, he whispered grimly to himself. Staring out into the darkness, he flashed a SOS in Morse code with his flashlight. Then, waited for a reply. One minute, two minutes, three minutes, the time seemed to be racing by and no answering signal. Desperately, he flashed the signal again. Again there was a long agonizing wait. Then, suddenly, from out of the gloom came a faint flash of light. The U-boat had come; he couldn't believe it! He might just make it back to Germany after all.

He waited a few seconds, then slipped down the face of the dune and raced to the water's edge. Without hesitating he waded into the surf, trying to maintain as low a profile as possible. He was up to his chest when out of the blackness a rubber dinghy appeared to his right.

"*Hier, hier,*" he whispered hoarsely.

The raft swung up next to him and two men pulled him roughly from the freezing water.

"*Danke, danke,*" was all he could think to say. The men only nodded. Clearly their main concern was getting out of there as expeditiously as possible. Karl realized it was for him, too, at least judging by the pounding of his heart.

After what seemed like ages, though by his watch it was only about twenty minutes, a U-boat loomed up before them. Unlike the raft that was bobbing wildly, the heavier U-boat was relatively stable. Still, scrambling aboard was not the simplest task. It actually took Karl three attempts before he made it and even then it took two pairs of strong hands to haul him up. His efforts had not gone unnoticed as a voice shouted down, "Welcome to U-232; sorry we didn't have a red carpet to make your boarding easier."

Karl glanced up to see the grinning face of the captain looking back at him from the conning tower.

"You must be one important agent for Doenitz to risk losing a U-boat. You're also a very lucky one. Not many U-boat captains would have attempted to enter this bay without the proper charts. As for me, I can get in and out of anywhere," he proclaimed with a cocky nonchalance that made even a couple of the crewman chuckle. "Even so, we'd better get you below and get out of here. I've got myself one sexy French woman waiting for me in Lorient. And, who knows, if you play your cards right I'll make sure she has a friend for you. For whatever reason women seem to have this fascination about spies, though I've never understood why. I mean, be honest, compared to U-boat captains like me, your life is really quite boring."

Karl couldn't help smiling at the thought of his life being boring.

Just the same he felt such a sudden sense of relief and the captain's sense of humor only made him feel that much better; now if he could only get a beer.

He was quickly taken below where he was greeted by several of the crew, who were already making preparations for getting the U-boat underway. Never had the inside of a U-boat looked so good to him, which reminded him of his final comments to Captain Frisch; he owed him an apology. And, if it were possible, everything seemed even better when one of the ship's warrant officers invited him back to the captain's galley for a cup of coffee.

"No beer?" Karl asked.

"You've got to be kidding," one of the officers replied. "But the coffee is real. We were able to scrounge a few provisions from one of the Milk Cows working these waters. They knew we were heading back but they gave us a few things anyway. Our captain's amazing; he could probably talk Uncle Sam into giving him his top hat. I'll bet he has beer in his quarters."

The officer poured Karl his coffee. "Well, I've got to get back to my post; just make yourself comfortable. There's some heavy weather coming and the captain wants to take full advantage of it to get as far away from here as possible. The thick cloud cover should enable us to cruise on the surface, which means we'll get back to France that much more quickly. If there's anything you need, just let us know."

After the officer left, Karl sat back and slowly sipped his coffee. It tasted incredibly good especially after the little bit he'd had to eat in the past thirty hours. In fact, everything suddenly felt good. He couldn't believe it--that a U-boat had actually been sent and successfully picked him off the beach. For the moment, at least, Canaris had to be in everyone's good graces, or at least in Doenitz's. How long that would last, however, only time would tell. He couldn't help wondering what they might have heard about the fire at the shipyard. He was certain someone would have passed the word along. The real question was how much responsibility he should take for it? Though it was an accident that triggered the fire, it was the explosives he had hidden there that had caused the bulk of the damage. So why not take the credit?

And, anyway, he thought, at the rate the Abwehr's agents were being arrested by the FBI it might be the only successful act of sabotage conducted as a part of this operation. But that only brought him back to the question of the mission's purpose and, of course, why so many agents had been arrested. Had the whole thing simply been badly planned or had it somehow been compromised, he asked himself for the umpteenth time. That he had not been caught, at least until now, was just a fluke and probably aided by the fact that Thomas hadn't been with him. Working alone had unquestionably made it easier, initially at least, to avoid notice and blend into the local population. But clearly it had not been enough.

As the hours rolled by, however, Karl began to feel increasingly anxious about his return to Germany. One thing he now knew for certain, he could no longer support Hitler or his policies, if in fact he ever really had. He thought back to the only time he had attended one of Hitler's speeches. It was nearly ten years ago at a political rally in Wilhelmshaven. He had accompanied his stepfather, who was an outspoken supporter of Hitler and the National Socialists. His stepfather believed strongly in order and discipline and had concluded that only Hitler was capable of stopping the violence tearing German society apart, conveniently ignoring the fact that much of it was caused intentionally by Hitler's own supporters.

Arriving in Wilhelmshaven on the morning of the rally Karl and his stepfather were surprised to find the city completely decked out for Hitler's arrival; there was an almost circus atmosphere to the place. Everywhere larger-than-life pictures of Hitler were on display along with huge red banners with swastikas in the center. But there were also rows of burly storm troopers standing shoulder-to-shoulder whose presence was meant as a reminder that no protests of any kind would be tolerated.

As it turned out, the hall where Hitler was to speak proved far too small for the size of the crowd that had gathered to hear him. He and his stepfather were among those who had to stand in the street listening to Hitler's speech over loudspeakers set up for that purpose. The only glimpse he was therefore able to get of Hitler was as he alighted from his staff-car, but it was enough for him to think how unimposing Hitler looked in his plain brown uniform. He was even less impressed when moments later he heard Hitler's raspy, sometimes halting voice crackling out over the crowd. Was this the person all these people had come for, that his stepfather had been so eager to hear? It was difficult to believe. Hitler had proceeded to ramble on for nearly an hour before concluding with a guttural *Sieg Heil*; the crowd, delirious over Hitler's words, began chanting *Sieg Heil* over and over again.

Even now he could remember finding the experience both exciting as well as frightening, the latter when Hitler had begun speaking of creating a racially purified Germany. But he couldn't help agreeing with Hitler that Germany should never have been forced to agree to an unconditional surrender at the end of the war; that was England's doing. And, the massive reparations Germany was forced to pay bankrupted the country. Karl was even prepared to blame much of it on Germany's politicians, though he balked at blaming it all on the Jews. Unlike his stepfather that day, he came away wondering just how far Hitler would be willing to go to return Germany "to its rightful place as a leader of Europe."

Now, viewing Hitler's policies from the American side of the Atlantic, they appeared insane, especially his military policies. There was no way Germany could expect to win a two-front war. The Wehrmacht had already lost heavily on the Eastern Front and the real fighting in the West had hardly begun. If Germany were not to be overrun by the Red Army and reduced to rubble, the war would have to be brought to an immediate end and that would require removing Hitler, no easy task. Himmler's SS had infiltrated nearly every organization and they'd been ruthless in rooting out anti-Hitler elements. Oddly, as powerful and ruthless as the SS had become, it had not been effective in penetrating the Abwehr, thanks to Canaris. He made little secret of the fact he detested the Nazis, refusing even to become a party member. He had also made certain that those assuming positions of authority within the Abwehr were loyal to him rather than to the Nazi Party. Clearly, Canaris had to have friends in high places to survive until now, but how much longer he'd be able to depend on their support was another matter entirely.

Karl could remember hearing rumors even before he had left Germany that Canaris had come under the scrutiny of the SS. Though not confident enough to arrest him at that point, the SS had nevertheless arrested several officers under his command on suspicion of being involved in anti-Hitler plots. It seemed only a matter of time, then, before Canaris himself would fall victim. But, what did this all mean for him? Obviously, if he were caught here in America he'd be executed, but what awaited him back in Germany? Would the SS arrest him as soon as he stepped on German soil? Could it be that the SS was behind his being rescued?

Now he was becoming truly paranoid; he could feel his heart racing a mile a minute. Consciously, he turned his thoughts to Anne hoping this might calm him, though he doubted it. Did she despise him for everything that had happened? Somehow he'd have to find a way contact her when he got back to Germany. She was the first woman he had ever truly loved and he desperately needed to tell her that. He didn't want her to think he only used her as a convenient cover for his activities.

He was snapped out of his reverie by a sudden lurching movement. Almost immediately the U-boat began to dive at an angle that could only mean one thing—they were under attack. No more than a second or two later an alarm began to sound, followed by the command to "Battle stations." Everyone it seemed was in motion, squeezing past one another through passageways barely wide enough for a single man. As for Karl there was nothing for him to do but stay out of the way. He hated this feeling of helplessness. Even worse the incident was serving to remind him that in reality he also hated submarines. He could only hope was that it wouldn't be like this all the way back to France.

Anne meanwhile was feeling no less anxiety. The days following her "interrogation" were difficult ones. She was confined to her house without any idea what the FBI had in mind for her. After the shock of learning that Karl or Erich was a German agent, anything seemed possible. And, there was still the threat of arrest hanging over her head though that threat appeared to be gradually receding. Strange, she thought, feeling a momentary touch of self-pity, how much she had wanted to have a man in her life once again. Now suddenly there were too many of them and none with her best interest at heart. No, that was not entirely true. The police chief, there was something different about him. Unlike the others he had demonstrated genuine concern, even putting his life on the line for her.

None of her women friends had stopped by either. Clearly they had learned of Karl's being a German agent and as a result had probably been warned by their husbands to stay away from her. But, she was certain they wouldn't stay away for very long. If there were one thing they adored it was a delicious scandal, and this certainly qualified, though publicly they always felt the need to express shock about whatever behavior led to it. Well, the heck with them; if she had to she'd go it alone. And besides, now she had her dog to keep her company, and for the moment Honey seemed happy not to share her with anyone.

The following Sunday she was greatly surprised when Mack suddenly showed up at her door. He claimed he needed only a few minutes of her time though, in fact, he stayed for nearly two hours. When he had first arrived she could barely control her anger but by the time he left much of her anger had cooled. She even had to admit she had enjoyed his company something she didn't get much of these days. Over several cups of coffee he filled Anne in on what they had learned about Karl from his aunt in Chicago; she, of course, knew him by his real name, Erich. Though the aunt was frail and obviously in poor health, her mind had been sharp enough and she had been delighted to talk about her nephew. The agents who questioned her, Mack admitted, had not been entirely truthful with her and had chosen not to reveal the full extent of the charges against Erich in deference to her condition.

At any rate, according to her, Erich had been born on the very eve of World War I in the North German city of Bremen. Not long after his birth his father was called into the service and was subsequently killed during the Battle of the Somme; Erich was barely two years old at the time. Erich's mother, the aunt's sister, was left to raise the boy alone and as it turned out, it was simply too much for her. With the death of her husband, she found herself virtually penniless and soon began suffering from bouts of migraine. As they became more serious she took to her bed where she would remain for days at a time. If this weren't bad enough, Germany was plunged into chaos at war's end and cities like Bremen were engulfed in violence. Given these circumstances, then, it was no wonder that she wanted to get Erich away from there. So Erich was sent to live with his aunt in America until his mother could better care for him. He would not see his mother or Germany again for nearly five years.

Erich, the aunt had explained, was painfully shy when he first came to live with her and he had a great deal of difficulty at the German-

American school to which he was sent. Had it not been for his aunt's intervention, he most likely would not have been promoted. But, gradually he began to emerge from his protective shell and as he did so his classroom performance improved as well. By the end of his third year at the school he was ranked near the top of his class, his aunt had said with pride. And he was also one of the more popular boys.

Under gentle prodding from the FBI agents she admitted there had been one thing that had distressed her about Erich and in a way she blamed herself. When he wasn't in school Erich was often out playing on the streets and it was a tough neighborhood. Kids were always getting in fights and she worried that Erich might get hurt. On a number of occasions she had asked her husband if they could move to a better neighborhood but it always came down to money. Her husband just didn't make enough from his typesetter job and new jobs were hard to come by. So, she continued to worry until one day a neighbor reassured her that she had nothing to be concerned about. Erich she said could more than take care of himself. It was only then she learned that Erich had developed quite a reputation in the neighborhood as a scrappy fighter and was not in the least hesitant to go up against bigger and stronger opponents in defense of his friends. After hearing this, the aunt wasn't sure whether it made her feel better or worse.

Then one day, out of the blue, a letter arrived from Erich's mother begging him to come home. She had remarried, her health was fine, or so she claimed, and she wanted to have her only son back with her. By this time, however, Erich did not want to go back; America was his home now, and besides, he thought of his aunt as his mother now. Wasn't it his mother who had sent him away? It was at this point, the agents reported, that the aunt had begun to get very emotional. Apparently, the only reason Erich had returned to Germany and his mother was because his aunt had insisted on it. Of course, now she wished she had never done so. At this point she had become so emotional the agents had been forced to terminate the interview. At no time had the aunt displayed any sympathy whatsoever for her native Germany. As she had pointed out early in their questioning, she was an American citizen and very proud to be one.

By the time Mack had left that Sunday, Anne decided she couldn't be more confused. It was as if Karl and Erich were two totally different people. The picture Mack had originally painted of Karl was of a ruthless German agent who had beaten and possible even killed several people. She herself had witnessed what he had done to Eddie Sawaski as it seemed clear he had. But somehow this didn't quite jibe with either the Karl she had known or the one described by the aunt. Only the aunt's mention of his being a scrappy fighter, willing to take on much larger opponents, made her wonder. So, which was the real Karl or Erich?

In the days following Mack's visit that was all she could think about; it consumed her every waking hour. There were definitely two sides to Karl's personality she had become convinced of that. But she had become just as convinced that war and military training helped bring out the more violent side; it had to. Young men were being trained to kill. Her own son for God's sake would soon be doing the very same thing. How could she hate Karl for engaging in the same behavior as her son? If Karl, or Erich, had not been sent back by his aunt he'd probably be fighting on the American side against the Germans. So, what was the difference? One of these days the war would end and it wouldn't matter anyway. In the meantime she would continue to believe the only thing she could believe—that the love she shared with Karl was real and not just part of some Abwehr operation. What did the FBI know about love and passion and tenderness? The hell with them, she thought angrily, and the rest of the world as well.

She decided she'd better call her parents; she knew they'd be worrying. She also had a horse to groom and a garden to look after. There was no one else to do these things now. And, like a great number of women she'd better get accustomed to spending time alone. She was not the only woman to lose her man to the war, it was happening to more and more women every day. It was just something one had to deal with.

Chapter Thirty-Three

Navy Lieutenant Ralph Backstrom was at the controls of his twin-engine PBY Catalina, one of two assigned to fly anti-submarine patrol out of the Naval Air Station at Brunswick, Maine. To his right sat his co-pilot, 2nd Lieutenant Bill Baker, staring intently down at the frigid waters of the North Atlantic. Ordinarily, the two went out on patrol in the morning but on this day the airstrip had been socked in by heavy weather, which had effectively grounded all flights. It wasn't until early afternoon that the cloud cover began to show breaks and the order had come down for them "to get out there and find something."

As they sped out over the Atlantic, tiny patches of blue sky were already becoming visible and shafts of sunlight were flitting seductively across the choppy water. It was not going to be an easy patrol, however; a massive bank of dark clouds shrouded the sky to the east and as they continued in that direction they increasingly had to search for openings through which to scan the ocean below. For the moment, at least, the advantage still lay with the U-boats. They searched the area for nearly two hours, the Catalina pitching from one impenetrable cloudbank to another with only the intermittent breaks allowing for a view of the ocean below. Even then it was almost impossible to see clearly and they recognized how difficult it was going to be to detect an enemy submarine under these weather conditions.

"Well, what do you say, think it's time we headed back," Backstrom asked, the weariness audible in his voice. "We're beginning to get a little low on fuel and it will be dark in less than an hour."

"Yeah, I think your right," replied his co-pilot. "From the moment

I got up this morning and looked out the window I could tell it wasn't going to be a very productive day."

As he banked the aircraft to the north, Backstrom suddenly exclaimed, "Wait just a minute, what do we have here? I think I just spotted the wake of some kind of ship. Let's go down and take a look."

Slowly he brought the Catalina around in order to come in astern of the unknown vessel, slowly descending at the same time.

"Christ, is there no end to these clouds?" Baker muttered.

The two of them had been flying as a team for nearly two months and in all that time they had neither fired a shot nor dropped a depth charge except for practice. And if that in itself weren't bad enough, they had recently learned that Catalina crews stationed in Iceland had been credited with sinking two U-boats in the course of just the past three weeks.

Finally, they broke through the clouds but there was no sign of any vessel, only an endless expanse of wind-driven waves with their crests of white foam. Minutes passed and Backstrom began to wonder if he actually had seen something or whether it had just been his imagination.

"I'm going to circle around again and make one more pass. I'm positive I saw a ship's wake down there."

The aircraft was swallowed up by another bank of clouds though only for a moment and then they broke free into a patch of clear blue sky.

"There it is," said Backstrom with obvious relief. "And it's a submarine of some kind, I just can't tell from here whether it's one of ours or one of theirs.

"I got it," replied his co-pilot, directing his binoculars towards the vessel. "It's a German U-boat, one of their Type VIIC attack subs, I think, identification number---232. Seems to be heading out of town in a hurry. He could be heading for the North Atlantic convoy routes, or it could be that his mission is over and he's heading back home. Either way the U-boat's captain must have been using the clouds to escape detection but he's outsmarted himself this time. I don't even think he knows we're here yet."

"Good," replied Backstrom. "Let's see if we can't make his visit to these waters one he'll remember for the rest of his life, however short that may be."

No sooner had he uttered these words than the officers on the U-boat's conning tower suddenly began disappearing down the main hatch.

"They've seen us; they're going to crash dive," Baker yelled excitedly.

Backstrom brought the aircraft in as low as he dared.

"Prepare depth charges for release; shallow detonation, close pattern," he ordered.

"Depth charges ready for release," Baker replied.

The U-boat was almost entirely out of sight when the Catalina released its lethal load. Four depth charges came tumbling out of the sky, perfectly straddling the now submerged U-boat.

"Bingo," Baker shouted, as the ocean convulsed and a gigantic geyser of white foam rose into the air. For just a second a portion of the U-boat became visible, then quickly disappeared beneath the roiling waters.

"It looks like part of the conning tower was blown off the main structure. I think we got it."

After the depth charges had been released Backstrom had concentrated on getting the Catalina away as quickly as possible to avoid any flying debris. More than one aircraft had been brought down in this manner, typically when a direct hit had been scored. Now, he began to circle back to look for any evidence that the U-boat had been destroyed.

"See anything?" he asked Baker.

"Not yet. There should be an oil slick or, at least debris; I just don't see a thing. There's no way it could have survived our attack. I'm sure of that."

"I'll circle around one more time, then we've got to get out of here. We're really low on fuel and I have no desire to put down here at night."

They made another pass but could spot nothing.

"I know we got it," Baker repeated, the frustration apparent in his voice. "There's got to be something floating around down there. It couldn't have gone right to the bottom."

"Hey, it happens that way some time. It's just too bad it happened to us."

"So, what do we say when we get back?" Baker asked.

"We say we think we sank a German U-boat but were unable to confirm it. Nothing else we can do."

"So we don't get credited with a kill?"

"Afraid not, but we know we got him. And even if we didn't, we sure gave him a good scare," Backstrom replied with a weary smile.

The pilots were not the only ones cursing their bad luck; Mack was, too. Where could Stoner have gone? He couldn't possibly have slipped away without a single trace, but it was beginning to look like he had. Mack had received word of the radio intercept on the same day he read in the newspaper about a U-boat being attacked by a Navy Catalina off the coast of Maine, but there was nothing to link either of these incidents directly to Stoner. Mack discussed his predicament with Eddie whose condition had now improved enough that his doctors had begun to allow visitors. Other than confirming it was indeed Stoner who had shot him there was little he could add. Eddie was certain, however, that Stoner had escaped on foot and without help. So, it was possible that he was still in the area and the radio transmission may well have been his. He encouraged Mack to continue searching the local area, which he did without success. But gradually the trail became as cold as the New England weather and the incident became all but forgotten except by those who'd been directly touched by it.

Epilogue

November 1942

It was a bitterly cold day with the temperature hovering around the freezing mark. Gray clouds scudded across the sky propelled by a raw northeast wind that could slice through the thickest clothing. A few snowflakes flitted wildly in the air before alighting on the ground. According to the weather service, this was all a prelude to a massive winter storm that was moving up the Atlantic coast in the direction of New England. It would reach the Boston area by early morning and before it ended it was expected to dump anywhere from ten to fifteen inches of snow over the entire region.

Anne checked the back door a final time to be sure it was locked; she knew she would have to get underway soon if she were to reach Boston ahead of the storm. She walked slowly into the middle of the yard and stopped, gazing out at the broad expanse of marshland that had changed so dramatically. Only a few short weeks ago it had been a lush carpet of green rather than the dull, brown mat it had become as it waited for the first major snowfall of the season. And the trees, whose leafy crowns had provided such welcome shade during the heat of summer, now stood bare like silent sentinels. Only the majestic oaks seemed determined to defy the approach of winter though in time their lifeless leaves, too, would have little choice but to succumb to nature's fury.

She was going to miss this scene, even if she were only going to be away for a few months. She had decided to spend the winter with her parents who were both quite ill. Deep down Anne suspected the scandal over her relationship with Karl had been the cause of it and she couldn't escape the feeling of guilt that dwelt within her. Fortunately, they had never asked her any details of what had happened though she was fairly certain her father had asked his lawyer friends for information.

Involuntarily she glanced up at the empty apartment. A couple nights before she had had a dream about Karl, or at least she thought it was about him though she had never seen his face clearly. They were walking hand-in-hand along a beach when suddenly he had let go of her and began running along the waters' edge. She called out to him but he only ran faster until in time he disappeared from view. It had appeared all so real; it still did. But, what was she to make of it? Had Karl, if that's who it was, left her for good? Would she ever see him again? Or was it just that, a bad dream and nothing more.

She glanced up at the apartment one final time. Only Karl's ghost lived up there now, not that she really believed in ghosts. On the other hand, how else was she to explain the constant feeling she had that someone was watching her from up there. Admittedly, she had never actually seen anyone. Still, the feeling was so unnerving that once she even climbed the stairs and entered the apartment, just to make sure no one was there. But, that one visit was enough. Just glancing at the bed where she and Karl had first made love caused such pain she literally raced down the stairs slamming the door shut behind her. The worst part for her was the not knowing if he were even alive. It was as if he had just disappeared off the face of the earth.

It certainly felt that way to Mack McCarthy. In the weeks following Karl's disappearance, he had questioned Anne several more times but always at her house; to her relief she was never called to the police station again. And as time passed and it became more certain than ever that Karl had, indeed, managed to escape, the surveillance on her house came to an end. On one of his early visits Mack had informed her that the shipyard fire had probably started by accident, though the explosives ignited by the fire had done most of the damage. The FBI surmised that Karl had smuggled the explosives into the yard with the intention of destroying the shipyard at some later date but that Tom O'Malley had unintentionally done the job for him.

"This O'Malley guy was apparently an accident just waiting to happen," Mack had explained. "In fact, there's even a slight possibility that he may have committed suicide. Apparently he'd been very depressed since his wife's death. Anyway, it probably explains why Stoner was so stunned when you gave him the news about the fire. After all, he was the one who expected to start it."

On another occasion Mack told her that two more German spies had been caught, this time in Florida. She could see this news had only served to increase his sense of frustration. His entire demeanor had changed, she had noticed. His trademark grin had become more forced, while his face had developed a harder quality to it. Yet, in spite of the rough manner in which he had treated her earlier, she realized he was now trying to make up for it, and she couldn't help but appreciate it.

Anne was suddenly snapped out of her reverie by the barking of a dog; Honey had obviously flushed some kind of animal. As the barking became more excited Anne strolled down the slope into the woods that separated her property from the marsh. Honey was standing on her hind legs, her front ones planted firmly against the tree as if attempting to push it over. Above her, well out of harm's way, was the object of her attention---a very distressed gray squirrel.

"Come on, Honey, leave the poor thing alone; he's got enough problems just trying to get ready for the long, hard winter ahead."

Turning and starting back up the hill she noticed a pile of firewood all neatly stacked for aging. It was one of the last jobs Karl had done for her, the one when she had taken the photo of him. She still had the picture; Mack had graciously returned it to her unbeknownst to his superiors. Now, it remained the only tangible proof she possessed that Karl had ever truly existed. In the past few weeks it had become very easy to believe the entire episode had been nothing more than a figment of her imagination or perhaps a wonderful dream.

But, in fact, she knew very well it had all been real. The townspeople of Ipswich were not about to forget or forgive her for having an affair with a German spy. She had been warned that there were those referring to her as "that Nazi whore" and felt that she had been let off easily, that she should have gone to prison. Of course, these same people never much approved of the crowd who summered on Argilla Road anyway. They saw them as snobs what with their money and lavish parties and Ivy League degrees. In their minds that was exactly why she had been able to avoid prison time. Fortunately, a couple of her friends, who also lived on Argilla Road, had stopped by once or twice and they had agreed to look after her house while she was away; one had even agreed to take care of her horse.

Anne could tell they were still uncomfortable with the whole thing. Of course, they didn't say anything though she could tell they were curious. Anne wondered whether they were expecting her to apologize or something over the affair. Well, if that's what they were waiting for it was going to be a long wait, she had decided almost defiantly. To be honest, she had absolutely no desire to talk to them about it. For one thing, it was still too painful; perhaps, later, when time had done its part she might attempt to explain what really happened.

On the other hand, she might never say anything. She hadn't even discussed it with her son, Bob, who had spent a long, difficult Labor Day weekend with her. It was he, after all, who had first called her a "whore" for her relationship with Karl, and that was before anyone knew he was a German spy. She had neither apologized nor tried to explain what had happened between she and Karl. There was no point, she decided, since he'd never understand and there was too little time anyway. On that Tuesday he was leaving for San Diego where he would be boarding a destroyer bound for the Pacific. That had become the story of her life—men loving her, men leaving her.

Well, not all, for ironically she had recently bumped into Eddie Sawaski. It was the first time they had come face-to-face since she had found him lying right where she was standing now. He had lost a great deal of weight, but otherwise he had looked really good. She had felt terribly embarrassed at first seeing him. Eddie, however, had quickly put her at ease, in part because of his obvious delight in seeing her but even more so for the way he repeatedly thanked her for saving his life. So gracious was he that it made her feel guilty for the indifferent way she had always treated him. She remembered how in one of their conversations Mack had insinuated that Eddie had long had a crush on her and it had probably been his concern for her safety that had made him race off to her house without the proper backup. Anne could only imagine how painful it must have been for him to discover that she had been having an affair with Karl. On the other hand, if she had hurt him, he certainly hadn't shown it when they had met. She was amazed that he of all people seemed so willing to forgive her. She would like to make amends though she was uncertain if she'd ever be able to live in Ipswich again. She was suddenly overwhelmed with such a feeling of sadness she knew she would burst into tears if she remained there any longer.

Opening the door on the driver's side, Honey jumped in, then, clambered into the back. Anne took one last wistful look around before slipping behind the wheel. Starting the engine, she shifted the car into gear and slowly headed down the driveway.

It had certainly been no ordinary summer, she sighed, switching on the wipers. The snow was already beginning to accumulate on her windshield.

Postscript

No Ordinary Summer is a work of fiction; neither the characters nor the events described are real and any similarity with actual people and events is entirely unintended. That said, however, much of the context is grounded in historical fact including the sabotage operation directed against the United States. In June 1942, the Abwehr, Germany's military intelligence organization, did indeed initiate such an operation under the code name---Pastorius. As part of the operation eight German agents were landed on American soil by U-boat, four on Long Island and four in the vicinity of Jacksonville, Florida. The mission of these eight agents was to destroy power plants, port facilities, and factories contributing to the war effort with the intention of demonstrating America's vulnerability to Germany's military might. In fact, the operation was a complete failure. From the beginning Operation Pastorius had been infiltrated by the FBI and no sooner had the eight come ashore than they were arrested and jailed. Tried before a military tribunal in Washington, they were all found guilty. Six of the eight were put to death in the electric chair; the other two received life sentences. Hitler never again attempted such an ambitious operation on American soil.

As for Admiral Canaris, he remains one of WW II's most enigmatic individuals. A highly decorated submarine commander in the First World War he became head of the Abwehr in 1935. From the beginning he used this organization to undermine Hitler's plans, even going so far as to pass along strategic information to the Allies. While a strong supporter of the resistance there were times when he was forced to hunt them as conspirators to retain his control of the Abwehr. In the aftermath of the failed attempt to assassinate Hitler in July 1944, Canaris was arrested and the Abwehr was subsequently abolished. On April 9, 1945, after months of interrogation and torture, and only weeks before war's end, Canaris was hanged. He never gave up the single name of any member of the resistance.

About the Author

David Lindgren was born in Ipswich, Massachusetts, and educated at Boston University. For thirty-five years he served on the faculty of Dartmouth College in Hanover, New Hampshire, where he is now an emeritus professor. During his years at Dartmouth Professor Lindgren also acted as a consultant to a number of government agencies including the Department of Interior, NASA and the Central Intelligence Agency. He is the author of three books as well as numerous journal articles and book chapters. Professor Lindgren presently lives in Washington, DC.